A COMMUNITY
— with a —
SHARED FUTURE FOR HUMANITY

www.royalcollins.com

A COMMUNITY
—— with a ——
SHARED FUTURE FOR HUMANITY

Wang Fan & Ling Shengli

℞
—— *Books Beyond Boundaries* ——
ROYAL COLLINS

A Community with a Shared Future for Humanity

Wang Fan & Ling Shengli

First published in 2023 by Royal Collins Publishing Group Inc.
Groupe Publication Royal Collins Inc.
BKM Royalcollins Publishers Private Limited

Headquarters: 550-555 boul. René-Lévesque O Montréal (Québec) H2Z1B1 Canada
India office: 805 Hemkunt House, 8th Floor, Rajendra Place, New Delhi 110008

Original Edition © Hunan People's Publishing House

All rights reserved. Without limiting the rights under copyright reserved above, no part of this publication may be reproduced, stored in or introduced into a retrieval system, or transmitted in any form or by any means (electronic, mechanical, photocopying, recording or otherwise), without the prior written permission of both the copyright owner and the above publisher of this book.

ISBN: 978-1-4878-1127-3

To find out more about our publications, please visit www.royalcollins.com.

Contents

Preface ix

PART I A NEW GLOBAL VISION

Chapter 1 The Ideological Origins of a Community with a Shared Future for Humanity 3
  1 Ancient Chinese Culture 3
  2 China's Diplomatic Experience 11
  3 Interactions with Diverse Cultures 18

Chapter 2 The Features and Creation of a Community with a Shared Future for Humanity 23
  1 Main Features of the Community 23
  2 Fundamental Principles of Building the Community 30
  3 Main Approaches to Building the Community 34

Chapter 3 The Significance of a Community with a Shared Future for Humanity 41
  1 New Explorations of Chinese Diplomacy 41
  2 A New Theory of Social Development 46
  3 A New Stage for China's Interactions with the World 50

PART II NEW IDEAS AND INITIATIVES

Chapter 4 Upholding Justice While Pursuing Shared Interests — 59
  1 Main Features of the Approach — 60
  2 Putting the Approach into Practice in China — 62
  3 An Emblem of Chinese Diplomacy in the New Era — 67

Chapter 5 A New Asian Security Concept — 73
  1 Main Features of the Concept — 73
  2 An Inevitable Product of the Current Security Situation in Asia — 77
  3 A New Impetus for Building a Community with a Shared Future in Asia — 82

Chapter 6 The Belt and Road Initiative — 87
  1 BRI: From Abstract Ideas to Concrete Actions — 87
  2 BRI: Not an Overnight Success — 93
  3 BRI: Challenges That Cannot Be Ignored — 95
  4 BRI: Opportunities for China — 102

Chapter 7 The Asian Infrastructure Investment Bank — 107
  1 Forging Ahead — 107
  2 Fulfilling China's Duties as a Leading Economic Power — 110
  3 Winners and Losers in the Improvement of Infrastructure — 114
  4 Helping the Asian Community with a Shared Future — 117
  5 Encouraging the Building of a Community with a Shared Future for Developing Countries — 120
  6 Power Game or Institutional Innovation? — 123

PART III STRENGTHENING INTRAREGIONAL AND INTERNATIONAL CONNECTIVITY

Chapter 8 Building a Community with a Shared Future with Neighboring Countries — 129
  1 China's Regional Diplomacy since the 18th National Congress — 130
  2 The Main Approaches to Building the Community — 138
  3 The Main Challenges of Building the Community — 141

Chapter 9	**Endorsing the China-ASEAN Community with a Shared Future**	**145**
1	China-ASEAN Relations since the 18th National Congress	146
2	Main Approaches to Building the Community	150
3	Main Challenges of Building the Community	155
Chapter 10	**Facilitating the Development of a Sino-African Community with a Shared Future**	**161**
1	Sino-African Relations since the 18th National Congress	162
2	Main Path to Building a Sino-African Community with a Shared Future	169
3	Main Challenges of Building the Community	175
Chapter 11	**Forging a Sino-Latin American Community with a Shared Future**	**183**
1	China's Relationship with Latin America since the 18th National Congress	184
2	Main Approaches to Building the Community	187
3	Main Challenges of Building the Community	194
Chapter 12	**Managing Relations among Major Countries**	**199**
1	Relations among Major Countries since the 18th National Congress	200
2	Main Approaches to Improving Relations among Major Countries	209
3	Main Challenges of Improving Relations among Major Countries	218

PART IV   PARTICIPATING IN GLOBAL GOVERNANCE

Chapter 13	**Global Economic Governance**	**225**
1	The Existing Governance Structure and Its Main Issues	226
2	China's Involvement in Global Economic Governance: New Ideas and Measures	231
3	China's Involvement in Global Economic Governance: Strategic Demands and Policies	236
Chapter 14	**Maintaining Global Peace and Security**	**243**
1	The Existing Security Infrastructure and Its Main Issues	244
2	China's Involvement in Maintaining Global Security: New Ideas and Measures	248
3	China's Involvement in Maintaining Global Security – Strategic Demands and Policies	255

Chapter 15 Addressing Global Environmental Issues — **261**
   1 The Existing Governance Structure and Its Main Issues — 261
   2 China's Involvement in Resolving Global Environmental Issues:
      New Ideas and Measures — 266
   3 China's Involvement in Resolving Global Environmental Issues:
      Strategic Demands and Policies — 274

Chapter 16 Internet Governance — **281**
   1 A Tough Nut to Crack: Governing the World Wide Web — 282
   2 China's Involvement in Internet Governance: New Ideas and Measures — 286
   3 China's Involvement in Internet Governance: Strategic Demands
      and Policies — 296

Postscript — **301**

Preface

THE IMPLICATIONS OF GLOBAL TRENDS are immense and impressive. As economic globalization and informatization continue to develop, and as global challenges continue to arise across the world, each member of society becomes ever more dependent on others. With Xi Jinping at its helm, the Central Committee of the Communist Party of China moves closely with the times, and calls unequivocally for the development of 'a community with a shared future for humanity.' As interconnectedness and interdependency among countries grow on an unprecedented scale, the world has become a global village – a community with a shared future – where history and reality meet, and where national interests become increasingly intertwined. Thus, the Party has called for nations to come together to share rights and obligations, in order to boost the common interests of humanity.[1]

The notion of promoting 'a community with a shared future for humanity' was first introduced at the 18th National Congress of the Communist Party of China in November 2012. For the first time, this concept was placed on record, and subsequently enshrined as one of the core principles guiding Chinese diplomacy in the new era. President Xi Jinping has mentioned it well over a hundred times at various international and domestic conferences in the past five years, and has made sustained efforts to engage the international community on this front, pushing for the creation of such a community at bilateral, regional, and global levels.

Since the 18th National Congress, the Chinese government has put forward a series of new ideas, measures, and plans to encourage the building of a community with a shared future for humanity. The policy of upholding justice while pursuing shared

---

1. "What Xi Jinping Said to the World," People.cn, November 23, 2015, http://theory.people.com.cn/n/2015/1123/c40531-27843728-3.html.

interests, the New Asian Security Concept, the Asian Infrastructure Investment Bank, and the Belt and Road Initiative all reflect China's determination to forge ahead – a huge difference from its past strategy of concealing its strengths and biding its time. A community with a shared future connects the "Chinese Dream" with the goals of the rest of the world, and embraces many new ideas and measures. It has become a critical endeavor that will reshape the relationship between China and the world, and improve the fate of humanity.

The concept of a community with a shared future for humanity is a contemporary reflection of traditional Chinese culture, as well as a continuous sublimation of China's diplomatic experience. It embodies the desire of the Chinese people to conform to the current trend, and demonstrates the courage of a rising China, as it readies itself to share the responsibilities of the current era.

The concept of a community with a shared future for humanity is multifaceted, involving fields such as politics, security, the economy, and the environment. Politically, it advocates for partnerships in which countries treat each other as equals, engage in mutual consultation, and show mutual understanding. After the Cold War, political partnerships emerged as a new form of interaction among countries. They are neither confrontations nor alliances, but a new model of international relations that involves cooperation between countries. Such partnerships are essential for global development, and have been China's main strategy based on its reflection of the existing models of international relations. This is because countries can only work together to address the challenges of globalization when they are aligned. With regard to security, a community with a shared future encourages all countries to make sustained efforts for common security interests. In the world today, traditional and non-traditional security threats are interlinked, and the safety of a nation is closely related to that of the international community. No nation can maintain absolute security through its own efforts alone, so international cooperation on security threats is needed, now more than ever. A new security framework that endorses common, comprehensive, cooperative, and sustainable security in Asia can become an important guide for international cooperation on security issues, and can provide a secure foundation for a community with a shared future for humanity.

Economically, a community with a shared future encourages common development that benefits all. It regards innovation as a fundamental source of economic development, values the role of science and technology in increasing productivity, and places great emphasis on cooperation in scientific and technological development between countries. At the same time, economic development is highly dependent on international trade and economic cooperation. A balanced, equitable, and inclusive development model is needed to create an open, innovative, and mutually beneficial economic outlook. Culturally, a community with a shared future endorses mutual respect and inclusivity. The world is more colorful because of its diversity – every culture has its own heritage and characteristics, so we should treat each other with respect and not hostility, and enhance communication so as to draw inspiration from one another, drive the progress of humanity, and ensure peaceful development worldwide. Ecologically, a community with a shared future advocates for the co-existence of humanity and nature, and seeks to build an environmentally friendly society. To achieve cohesion between humanity and nature, we must continue our efforts in green, sustainable, and common development. This requires large, rich, and powerful countries to provide assistance to small, poor, and weak ones, so that a new approach to international assistance and cooperation can be established in order to push the United Nations (UN) 2030 Agenda for Sustainable Development.

A community with a shared future for humanity needs to be built over time, step by step, at bilateral, regional, and global levels. All countries in the world must work together to achieve the developmental goals of a community of shared interests, shared security concerns, and a shared destiny.

Building a community with a shared future for humanity requires an understanding of the four main attributes of contemporary international relations:

(1) Commonality. As countries in the world share common interests and face common threats, they should seek positive-sum solutions and not zero-sum ones;
(2) Interaction. It is difficult for any country to remain isolated from the international community. Countries should maintain a mutually beneficial relationship with one another, and come to see that they are systemically interrelated;
(3) Inclusivity. Diversity is the norm, so countries should respect each other's differences, and encourage harmony in diversity by being open-minded and inclusive;
(4) Coordination. The complexity of global affairs, the diversity of actors, and the overlap of interests call for the reinforcement of international cooperation. Coordination among major countries, institutions, and regions is needed to step up global governance and facilitate a peaceful transition of the international system.

Building a community with a shared future for humanity also involves the appropriate handling of four sets of relationships:

(1) The relationship between national sovereignty and community rights. A country and a community should never be pitted against each other. Instead, they should recognize one another and be tolerant of each other. The peaceful coexistence of countries is the basis for a community with a shared future for humanity;
(2) The relationship between national and international interests. It is not a zero-sum relationship, but a symbiotic one. A high degree of commonality and interaction between countries has resulted in an increasingly cooperative development of national and international interests. It conforms to the demands of the times, and is also consistent with the laws of nature;
(3) The relationship between partners and allies. Alliances are a conventional form of international security. They are highly targeted and exclusive, and run counter to the commonality and inclusivity for which a community with a shared future advocates. Partnerships, on the other hand, achieve security by means of coordination, so they are the best option for promoting cooperation between countries on political, economic, and security matters in the new era;
(4) Decolonization and new forms of international cooperation. Members of a community with a shared future need to protect and help each other to achieve common development. This is by no means a form of neo-colonialism, but a new form of international cooperation – one that is based on mutual benefit and respect rather than peremptory orders.

Furthermore, a pair of 'wings' and 'handholds' are needed to launch the community with a shared future for humanity successfully. The community plays an important role in China's current foreign policy. Therefore, the policy of protecting justice while pursuing shared interests and the New Asian Security Concept can be seen as its 'wings,' while the Asian Infrastructure Investment Bank (AIIB) and the Belt and Road Initiative (BRI) can be seen as its 'handholds.' Putting justice before its own interests demonstrates China's willingness to engage with the world and present a socially responsible image that a major country should possess. It serves as an important guide for China's diplomacy in the new era, as well as for the building of a community with a shared future for humanity. In addition to the New Security Concept and the Holistic Approach to Security, the New Asian Security Concept is inclusive and ahead of the times. It plays an integral role in the resolution of differences in security visions, systems, and threats between neighboring countries. At the same time, it sets an example for the rest of the world in terms of international cooperation on security matters, helping to create a security architecture that is imbued with a sense of justice, equity, and shared growth, which is needed in a community with a shared future for humanity. The community cannot be built overnight; it needs to go through three stages – a community of shared interests, a community of shared responsibilities, and a community of shared experiences. Therefore, down-to-earth, concerted, and step-by-step efforts are required. The AIIB and BRI serve as 'handholds' in the process of turning the above into a reality.

Furthermore, building a community with a shared future for humanity requires more strength at all levels:

(1) Building a community with a shared future with neighboring countries. It goes without saying that China views its neighbors as very important, so creating a more peaceful, stable, and prosperous geopolitical neighborhood has always been the objective of its diplomatic efforts.

(2) Building a China-ASEAN community with a shared future. After a 'golden decade' of development, China's cooperation with the Association of Southeast Asian Nations (ASEAN) is entering a new 'diamond decade.' A China-ASEAN community should reflect the common vision that China and ASEAN share. Their commitment to sharing both positives and negatives in an age of global interdependence can set an example for the building of a community with a shared future for humanity.

(3) Supporting the development of a community with a shared future with developing countries. China's relationship with developing countries has always been the foundation of its diplomacy. The development of a community with Africa, Latin America, and the Arab states is in the common interest of all parties, and can serve as a model for new forms of South-South cooperation, leading to the progress of humanity.

(4) Supporting the development of a community with a shared future for the whole of humanity. Maintaining good relations among major countries is vital to its creation. A new model of international relations based on win-win cooperation needs to be established so that mutual trust, international coordination, and global governance can be reinforced and sustained over time.

Finally, building a community with a shared future for humanity requires more effective global governance. There is an urgent need to reinforce global governance in the face of increasing global challenges. The international community has to work more closely in various fields to encourage global economic growth, reinforce physical and cyberspace security, and support environmental regulation. However, there are also many challenges to effective global governance, such as the varying severity of global issues, competition among major countries, systems, and ideologies, differences between relative and absolute returns, and the divergence of international and national interests. Countries should respond to these issues with the best interests of humanity in mind, and establish a sense of community with a shared future, so that global governance may continue to improve based on long-term perspectives and strategic priorities.

From the Chinese point of view, President Xi Jinping concludes that building a community with a shared future for humanity is the direction towards which we should work. He introduced this concept to the international community for the first time in March 2013, at the Moscow State Institute of International Relations. Since then, the Chinese government and its leaders have advocated for the building of a community with a shared future on a global scale through key international organizations, Chinese diplomatic events, and multilateral summits.

In September 2015, President Xi Jinping delivered a speech at the UN on working together to forge new partnerships based on win-win cooperation and to create a community with a shared future for humanity. For the first time, he elaborated on the political, security-related, economic, cultural, and ecological aspects of the community, and called upon the international community to make ongoing efforts in building such a community. In January 2017, President Xi Jinping delivered a speech on working together to build a community with a shared future for humanity at the headquarters of the UN in Geneva. He noted that the key to building such a community lies in collective action: The international community should step up its efforts in forming partnerships, responding to changing security landscapes, economic development, civil communication, and ecology.

Thanks to the significant efforts of the Chinese government and its leaders, the concept of a community with a shared future for humanity has earned increasing recognition and appreciation from the international community. Peter Thomson, President of the 71st session of the General Assembly of the United Nations, said: "I personally believe that building a community with a shared future for humanity is the only future for humanity on this planet." Philipp Charwath, Chair of the 55th session of the UN Commission for Social Development (CSocD55), commended China for its foresight in building a community with a shared future for humanity for the long-term interests of mankind, and said that all countries in the world and the UN would benefit from this idea in the long run. In February 2017, the CSocD55 called on the international community to take action "in the spirit of win-win cooperation, to create a shared future based on our common humanity." For the first time in history, the concept of building a community with a shared future for humanity was written into a resolution of the United Nations. At the 34th regular session of the Human Rights Council (HRC34) in March 2017, two resolutions were passed on "economic, social and cultural rights" and "the right to food," expressing the need to "build a community with a shared future for humanity." "Pakistan is willing to continue to reinforce the Sino-Pakistani community of shared destiny"; "African states should learn from Asian countries, and they should cooperate with each other to build a community with a shared future"; "The United Nations is willing to work with China to advance the cause of development and world peace, and realize the ideals of building a community with a shared future ..." People around the world have reached a broad consensus on the concept of a community with a shared future for humanity.

A single flower does not make spring, but a hundred flowers in full bloom bring spring to the garden. China is willing to work with other countries in the world to overcome the challenges of building a community with a shared future for humanity, such as power politics, the growing disparities between the rich and the poor, and cultural differences. It will take place in phases and in different sectors and regions, until a community with a shared future for humanity is established.

WANG FAN
Vice President and Professor of the China Foreign Affairs University,
Vice President of the China Institute of International Relations
August 2017

PART I

A New Global Vision

A community with a shared future for humanity is a global vision that transcends ethnicity, nationality, and ideology. By keeping the current trend of social development in mind, as well as its objective of maintaining world peace and development through mutually beneficial cooperation, the Chinese government has come up with a 'Chinese plan' for the future of humanity. The concept of a community with a shared future for humanity is a breakthrough in major-country diplomacy with distinctive Chinese features: it expresses the desire of the Chinese people to pursue peaceful and mutually beneficial development, as well as proposing new ideas for the development and progress of society, and reflecting China's efforts and sense of responsibility in resolving global challenges as a major nation.

Chapter 1

The Ideological Origins of a Community with a Shared Future for Humanity

The concept of a community with a shared future for humanity has its roots in ancient Chinese culture, and is a product of the diplomatic experience of the People's Republic of China and its interactions with the diverse cultures of the world today. It has inherited the essence of ancient Chinese philosophy as part of its cultural DNA, such as the worldview of Heaven and man as one (*tianren heyi*), the political vision of a world that belongs to its people (*tianxia wei gong*), and the social mindset of harmony in diversity (*he'er butong*). It is also based on the valuable experience that the People's Republic of China has gained over the past 70 years of diplomatic engagement. Drawing on the essence of global cultures with an open and inclusive attitude, the concept of a community with a shared future continues to guide China's diplomacy and encourage its people to work toward their vision of a better world.

1 Ancient Chinese Culture

The concept of a community with a shared future is rooted in ancient Chinese thinking. It can be traced back to the concept of harmony or cohesion, which lies at the core of the culture. The worldview of Heaven and man as one, the political vision of a world that belongs to its people, and the social mindset of harmony in diversity are just a few of the many important values that are found within the culture of harmony. When the concept of a community with a shared future was put forward, it breathed new meaning into these values, offering new insights into the world today. As the world becomes increasingly interconnected, Chinese diplomats see the pursuit of a community with a shared future as their guiding mission, and advocate for a new international outlook that endorses cohesive development and mutually beneficial interactions.

1.1 The unity of Heaven and man as a worldview

The global outlook of a community with a shared future for humanity originated from the ancient worldview of Heaven and man as one, and the political ideal of a world that belongs to its people. It is the contemporary manifestation of the 'Great Concord' (*datong*) – the traditional Chinese utopian vision of the world in which every state is at peace with one another (*xiehe wanbang*), and the concept of *tianxia* – the Confucian ideal of good governance.

The 'unity of Heaven and man' (*tianren heyi*) is a fundamental concept in Chinese philosophy and the essence of traditional Chinese thought. The main idea behind Chinese philosophy is the study of this relationship. During the Spring and Autumn and the Warring States periods, schools such as Daoism and Confucianism formed their own views on the relationship between humanity and nature. In the *Book of Changes*, it was written that:

> His [the ancient sage's] virtue is one with Heaven and Earth; his brightness is one with the sun and the moon; his order is one with the four seasons; his fortune is one with the gods and spirits. He may precede Heaven, and Heaven will not act in opposition to him; he may follow Heaven, and Heaven will help him to act at the most opportune moment.

The cohesive relationship between Heaven and man is highlighted in the paragraph above. However, it is the Confucian school of thought that makes up the bulk of this concept, as reflected in the *Doctrine of the Mean*:

> Only he who is possessed of the most complete sincerity can exist under Heaven and develop his nature to the fullest. Able to give full play to his own nature, he can do the same to the nature of other men. Able to give full play to the nature of other men, he can develop the nature of other beings to the fullest.

Able to give full play to the nature of other beings, he can help Heaven and Earth to cultivate life. Able to assist the cultivation of life by Heaven and Earth, he may form a ternion with Heaven and Earth.

Mencius wrote, "What happens without anyone causing it is owing to Heaven; what comes about without anyone accomplishing it is the mandate." According to Dong Zhongshu of the Han Dynasty, the interconnection between Heaven and man makes the two one and the same. In the Song Dynasty, Zhang Zai developed the theory further by proposing that humanity and nature are one and the same. He wrote:

> Confucian scholars achieve integrity through enlightenment and enlightenment through integrity; therefore, Heaven and human beings are united. If one achieves scholarship then one can become a sage; if one acquires Heaven then one cannot even begin to discard human beings.

At the same time, the brothers Cheng Hao and Cheng Yi expressed the Confucian idea of harmony between Heaven and man as a transcendental principle (*li*) that accounts for the existence of both humanity and nature. It was then developed into a school of thought for the study of *li*. Cheng Yi also believed that Heaven, Earth, and man are one because they are guided by the same principle – the Way (*dao*).

Renowned Chinese philosophical historian Zhang Dainian explained the two meanings embedded in the concept of unity between Heaven and man:

(1) It can mean that humanity and nature are one to begin with, or that there is a distinction between the two and they should be merged into one.
(2) There are two ways to explain why humanity and nature are one to begin with: the two are inherently interconnected, or they have similar forms. If we were to break down the inherent relationship between humanity and nature, it could be divided into two parts: humanity and nature are not distinct entities interacting with each other but a whole that is closely interlinked with no boundaries; human morality is derived from nature. The fundamental principles of nature apply to humans, because we are part of nature. Meanwhile, human nature often refers to the traits that make humans unique and different from non-human entities. In other words, the similarities that humans share with such entities are not part of human nature. From this point of view, even though human nature has a basis in

the principles of nature, it is essentially made up of the unique traits that developed after man was born of nature, and does not fall under the universal rule of the Way of Heaven. When we speak of the Way of Heaven and human nature as one and the same, it may seem like it is only natural for man to follow the Way of Heaven, but it also implies that human nature is the Way of Heaven, which means human morality is the rule of the universe. This is strongly anthropocentric and unacceptable. Humanity and nature having a similar form "also involves two aspects: the similar structure of the human body and the heavenly bodies, and the similar characteristics between Heaven and man. The former is a little too far-fetched, while the latter is similar to saying that human nature is the Way of Heaven."[1]

Therefore, the concept of the unity of Heaven and man reflects the interconnection between humanity and nature, and also refers to the peaceful coexistence of multiple opposing viewpoints, such as that between the individual and society, and that between the subjective and objective. These are the cornerstones of the community with a shared future for humanity:

(1) The interconnection between humanity and nature. In the study of Heaven and man, it was noted that humanity and nature were an organic whole with a high degree of interaction, interdependence, and interpenetration. Man is a part of nature and the two are inseparable. Heaven and man are also one to begin with, so they have to exist in harmony. This was noted in *Zhuangzi*: "Man exists because of Heaven, and Heaven, too, exists because of Heaven" and "Heaven and earth were born at the same time I was, and the ten thousand things are one with me."

(2) The peaceful coexistence of the individual and society. The link between Heaven and man is human nature – only through the cultivation of moral virtue can man achieve harmony with Heaven and realize the highest ideal of unity with it. From the Confucians' point of view, Heaven is the basis of all moral values and principles. Mencius believed that "all the ten thousand things are complete in me" and argued that man has an innate sense of morality. He wrote, "Therefore, to be sincere is the Way of Heaven, and to think about sincerity is the human Way." Furthermore, the *Book of Changes* suggested that "the superior person enriches his virtue to sustain all beings."

---

1. Zhang Dainian. *Key Concepts in Chinese Philosophy* (China Social Sciences Press, 1982), 181–182.

That is to say, human moral virtues give meaning and value to life in the universe, and the cultivation of such virtues endorses cohesion between individuals and their communities.

(3) The unity of the subjective and the objective. Man is inevitably subjective and self-justifying, while the opposite is the case for nature – it encompasses everything in the objective world and outside of one's mind, including the human body. When man is in cohesion with nature, it means that the subjective and objective worlds are merged, and the human body and mind are one. In other words, man is ideally with Heaven and Earth in terms of virtue; in brightness, with the sun and moon; in order, with the four seasons; in fortune, with the gods and spirits. According to *The Analects*, "a man can enlarge the principles which he follows, but those principles do not enlarge the man." Although nature is largely dependent on human activities, it is us who must adapt our subjective understanding to the ever-changing objective world.

The worldview of Heaven and man in unity is the essence of traditional Chinese thought, and also the fundamental viewpoint from which our observations of the world should be made. It guides us to examine the world from a holistic perspective, or as Laozi once said, "to see what is under Heaven from Heaven's perspective" – that is, to seek cohesion among differences and unite the world through the development of moral virtues. A community with a shared future for humanity is the exact manifestation of such holistic thinking. It holds that "humanity only has one planet, and all countries live in the same world." Therefore, an open and inclusive mindset, as well as harmony in diversity, are advocated among people of all races and nationalities.

1.2 'A world that belongs to its people' as a political vision

For thousands of years, the Chinese people have sought the political ideal of 'a world that belongs to its people' (*tianxia wei gong*) and relentlessly pursued a society of 'Great Concord' (*datong*). Building a community with a shared future for humanity is a means of achieving the aforementioned goals.

The political vision of a world that belonged to its people was pursued by the wise monarchs of Ancient China. According to the *Book of Rites*:

> When the Great Way prevailed, the world belonged to its people. The virtuous and competent were endorsed to office; honesty was valued and people lived in

cohesion. Therefore, they did not regard as parents only their own parents or as children only their own children. The aged found a fitting close to their lives, the robust their proper employment; the young were provided with an upbringing and the widow and widower, the orphans, and the sick, with proper care. Men had jobs and women had their hearths. They hated to see goods lying about in waste, yet they did not hoard them for themselves; they disliked the thought that their energies were not fully used, yet they did not use them for private ends. Therefore, all evil plotting, as well as cases of theft, rebellion and harm were prevented, so people could leave their outer gates unbolted. This was the Age of Great Concord.

Thus, in a world that belongs to its people, all power lies in their hands, and they have a say in electing people of competence and virtue as representatives to govern the country.

The political vision of a world that belongs to its people was an effective instrument that modern Chinese thinkers used to undermine feudalism. They propounded the idea of merit-based leadership, and were against monarchical rule. In the *Book of Great Concord*, Kang Youwei described his ideal society: "In the Age of Great Concord, the world belonged to its people: there was no social class distinction; everyone was equal." Liang Qichao then elevated this ideal into a moral imperative when he called on his countrymen to bear responsibility for the prosperity of society. This has inspired future generations of patriots to work towards the rejuvenation of the Chinese nation.

The political vision of a world that belongs to its people also guided Sun Yat-sen, the pioneer of China's democratic revolution, in his revolutionary career. Throughout his life, Sun worked hard to realize this vision, and reinforced the idea of it. He believed that the underlying principle of meritocracy was to stand up for the people's rights: "A meritocratic system (*gong tianxia*) is the opposite of a monarchical one (*jia tianxia*). In a world that belongs to its people, everyone will have equal rights." He strove to establish a meritocratic system through the implementation of the Three Principles of the People:

> The essence of the Three Principles is 'of the people, by the people, and for the people.' This means that the country belongs to all of its people, the government is jointly controlled by the people, and welfare benefits are shared among the people. In this way, the people have to share not only their assets but also all matters of power.

Although Sun Yat-sen's meritocratic system was not fully realized in his political career, his attempts and efforts have had a positive bearing on future generations.

The concept of a community with a shared future for humanity carries forward the inherent principles of a world that belongs to its people. These principles are reflected in the following aspects:

(1) Seeing the overall interests of society as more important than the personal interests of individuals, and promoting this as a public virtue. Ideally, when there is a conflict between public and personal benefit, the former should be prioritized to the extent that one forgets about his or her own interests. Confucius said, "The superior man holds justice to be of the highest importance." Mozi believed that "to be righteous is to benefit," and Mencius wrote, "I desire life, and I also desire justice. If I cannot have both of them, I will give up life and choose justice." Thus, emphasizing justice over benefit is consistent with the code of ethics and conduct put forward by Chinese society.

(2) Advocating for the prosperity of society as a personal responsibility, as is holding high regard for "being the first to worry about the affairs of the state (and the last to rejoice in its happiness)" and for "sharing responsibility for the rise and fall of the nation."

(3) Advocating for the unity and betterment of humanity as the essence of good governance and emphasizing the need for leaders who can enlighten their people with benevolence and justice, and at the same time win the favor of others by means of their virtue.

(4) Promoting the philosophy behind sayings such as "do unto others as you would have them do unto you" and "he who wishes to be established himself, seeks also to establish others; he who wishes to be enlarged himself, seeks also to enlarge others" as fundamental life principles.

1.3 'Harmony in diversity' as a social mindset

The character '*he*' in Chinese means cohesion or harmony, and is an important concept in traditional Chinese culture. Chinese people have long regarded musical harmony as an ideal, and its influence has extended far outside of music to encompass the concept of social cohesion and world peace. In *Zuo's Commentary on the Spring and Autumn Annals*, it is said that: "As with musical harmony, there is nothing that is not in accord." The idea is to achieve this state, like playing harmonious music with musical instruments. In this way, '*he*' emphasizes the concept of unity in diversity.

Harmony in diversity (*he'er butong*) is a phrase found in *The Analects*. Confucius wrote, "The gentleman acts in harmony with others but does not merely agree. The petty man agrees but is not in harmony with them." *The Commentary and Subcommentary on the Analects* explains further:

> Gentlemen share a harmonious relationship but may see things differently, so they 'do not merely agree' with one another. While ordinary men may share the same hobbies, they engage in rivalry for personal benefit, so they are 'not in harmony with one another'.

In other words, gentlemen may share the same values but behave differently. For instance, while they are all willing to dedicate their lives to serving society, some choose to be in a position of authority and others choose to be teachers. Despite not agreeing, these gentlemen can still build a cohesive society. However, ordinary men who share the same hobbies will inevitably get into conflicts as they fight for their own interests. Such similarities would instead result in social disharmony. Therefore, the pursuit of harmony in diversity is more of a quest for ideological cohesion than superficial similarities.

The concept of harmony in diversity is rich in ideas:

(1) It reflects the universal condition of unity in opposites. Harmony and diversity are a pair of opposites that are inherently connected. The former is abstract and intrinsic in nature, while the latter is concrete and extrinsic in nature. Harmony is built on the premise of diversity; diversity is a condition for achieving harmony. Thus, the two are interdependent and indispensable to the other.

(2) It embodies an open and inclusive attitude towards life. Harmony is unity in diversity, so acknowledging diversity in our society and developing tolerance and respect for differences is the key to achieving harmony and peaceful coexistence.

(3) It sheds light upon the principles of life. The criterion for distinguishing gentlemen from ordinary people is whether the person can "act in harmony with others but not merely agree."

Fei Xiaotong proposed that one must not only know how to appreciate the beauty of one's own creation, but also that of others. In this way, both types of beauty can co-exist, and the Great Concord can be achieved. This is said to be an excellent contemporary interpretation of the concept of harmony in diversity. Regarding the variety of cultures in the world today, General Secretary Xi Jinping has noted that cultural diversity is a fundamental characteristic of society. A community with a shared future for humanity can only be realized if the diversity and significance of each country and culture are recognized. There will be no distinction between good and bad; it is only differences in characteristics that are worth noting. To ensure peaceful co-existence and collective growth, the community has to respect the diversity of cultures and encourage multilateral exchange and dialogue.

In conclusion, the worldview of Heaven and man as one, the political vision of a world that belongs to its people, and the social mindset of harmony in diversity make up the cultural DNA of a community with a shared future for humanity – a concept advocated by China today. It adheres to the overall ideas and way of thinking propounded by the worldview of Heaven and man as one, which sees nature and society as an organic whole and argues that the peaceful development of each country is dependent on that of others. It also inherits the political vision of a world that belongs to its people, and the social mindset of harmony in diversity. At the same time, it advocates a policy of upholding justice while pursuing shared interests, ensuring holistic, symbiotic development in a community of mutual respect and equal opportunities.

2 China's Diplomatic Experience

The concept of a community with a shared future for humanity is deeply rooted in the People's Republic of China's diplomatic experience in the last 70 years, and has also proved to be a sublimation of it. Since the Qin and Han Dynasties, the Chinese people have formed their worldviews based on the social institutions of the 'Heavenly Empire.' However, the invasion by Western powers in modern times not only completely shattered their long-established concept of world order, but also caused them to experience the pain of humiliation and subjugation. Although the founding of the People's Republic of China in 1949 ended a century of humiliation in modern China, the unique circumstances of the Cold War led to China's estrangement from the Western-dominated international system, and resulted in a growing sense of isolation and distance between China and the rest of the world. It was not until the 1970s, when China returned to the United Nations and implemented its Reform and Opening-up policy, that it began to engage with the Western-dominated international system. As China expanded and intensified its relations with other countries, its understanding of the world began to change, as did its guiding principles and approaches to foreign affairs. There is no doubt that China's relationship with the world is undergoing profound changes. It has learnt important lessons from its extraordinary diplomatic experiences, such as being firmly committed to peaceful diplomacy, conforming to the global perspective of peaceful development as the current trend, and identifying its own international standing. These valuable experiences constitute a realistic basis for China's current proposal of a community with a shared future for humanity.

2.1 Commitment to peaceful diplomacy

Since the founding of the People's Republic of China, peace has been the core principle of its diplomatic philosophy. China has been pursuing a peaceful foreign policy under the guidance of peaceful diplomacy and continues to enrich and develop this concept according to changes in times and circumstances. The proposal of a community with a shared future for humanity expresses China's strong desire for peace. Putting the concept of peaceful diplomacy into practice has helped China create a favorable environment for peace and development and has also played an important role in maintaining world peace and stability.

At the beginning of the founding of the People's Republic of China, the first-generation party's leadership, with Comrade Mao Zedong at its core, firmly established an independent, peaceful foreign policy in a highly complex international environment, and joining proposed and advocated the Five Principles of Peaceful Coexistence with some developing countries. In April 1954, the Agreement on Trade and Intercourse Between Tibet Region of China and India first put forward the Five Principles of Peaceful Coexistence, namely mutual respect for sovereignty and territorial integrity, mutual non-aggression, non-interference in each other's internal affairs, equality and mutual benefit and peaceful coexistence. In June of the same year, the joint Statement of the Prime Ministers of China and India issued on June 28 and the Joint Statement of the Prime Ministers of China and Burma issued on June 29 both affirmed that the Five Principles of Peaceful Coexistence as the guiding principle of international relations. It was later accepted by many countries, and became a guiding principle for countries with different social systems to deal with each other, becoming a norm for international relations. The Five Principles of Peaceful Coexistence require that international disputes be settled by peaceful instead of military means. They oppose the indiscriminate use of force, encourage reasonable international competition, advance international cooperation, recognize and respect differences in political beliefs, values and religious beliefs among countries, recognize the choices made by countries for their social systems and development paths, as well as realize coexistence, development, and prosperity on the basis of respecting sovereign equality, mutually beneficial cooperation, and peaceful coexistence with all countries. At the 1955 Asian-African Conference (also known as Bandung Conference), Chinese Premier Zhou Enlai advocated the policy of "seeking common ground while putting differences aside" based on the Five Principles of Peaceful Coexistence to resolve the issues between Asian and African countries. The policy not only ensured a smooth meeting, but it also established a good reputation for the Chinese government. The Five Principles of Peaceful Coexistence and the policy of "seeking common ground while putting differences aside" provide peaceful policies and guidance for resolving all international conflicts and disputes, including countries with different social systems, and have become the principles generally accepted by the international community for maintaining international security.

The second-generation party leadership, with Deng Xiaoping at its core, continued adhering to the Five Principles of Peaceful Coexistence, and also expanded the scope of their application. Deng Xiaoping believed that "The Five Principles of Peaceful Coexistence are the best way to manage relationships between countries. Other methods, such as the 'big family,' 'group politics,' and 'sphere of influence,' will result in contradictions and intensify international situations. In summary, the Five Principles of Peaceful Coexistence are the most powerful policy for international relations." He went on, "The Principles of Peaceful Coexistence are effective at managing international relations as well as a country's internal affairs. It is under the guidance of these principles that China has peacefully resolved the Hong Kong and Macau issues, eased territorial sovereignty disputes with neighboring countries by 'shelving disputes,' and maintained its peaceful diplomatic environment, placing it in a favorable position to focus on opening up and modernizing."

The third-generation leaders, with Jiang Zemin at the core, put forward more specific requirements for peaceful diplomacy by proposing to establish a new security concept of "mutual trust, benefit, equality and cooperation," advocating the establishment of a new international political and economic order that is fair and reasonable, protecting the diversity of world cultures and democratizing international relations. In March 1999, Jiang Zemin narrated the new security concept for the first time in his speech at the Conference on Disarmament (CD) in Geneva, pointing out that the old security concept based on military alliances and the means of reinforcing armaments is not helpful to ensure international security, and is ineffective in creating long-lasting peace in the world. It is necessary to establish a new security concept that meets the needs of the times, and explore new ways to maintain peace and security.[2] On the basis of the Five Principles of Peaceful Coexistence, Jiang Zemin endorsed the establishment of a new international political and economic order and the democratization of international relations. He emphasized that the new order should guarantee the rights of all countries to enjoy sovereign equality and non-interference in internal affairs, and participate in international affairs on an equal footing, and guarantee the rights of all countries to develop, especially developing countries, as well as the collective development of all cultures.

The democratization of international relations means maintaining the diversity of cultures. At the Millennium Summit in 2000, Jiang Zemin emphasized, "Akin to the universe, which has not just one color, the world cannot have just one culture, one social system, one development model, and one value concept. All ethnic groups have contributed to the development of humanity. The diversity of different ethnic groups, religions, and cultures should be fully respected. The dynamism of global development depends on the coexistence of such diversity. In the spirit of equality and democracy, we encourage the mutual exchange among various cultures and learn from each other to seek common progress."[3]

On the basis of the new security concept, the central leadership with Hu Jintao as General Secretary proposed the concept of a "harmonious society." At the summit meeting on the 60th anniversary of the establishment of the United Nations in 2005, Hu Jintao delivered a speech entitled "Building Towards a Cohesive World of Lasting Peace and Common Prosperity," explaining the profound implication of a "harmonious society," and claiming that in the history of global development, the destinies of the people of all countries have never been so closely interdependent. "Common goals bind us together, and common challenges require us to be united. Let us work together to build a prosperous and cohesive world of lasting peace and common prosperity!"[4] The concept of a "harmonious society" is the inheritance,

---

2. "Speech by President Jiang Zemin at the Conference on Disarmament in Geneva (March 1999)," Xinhuanet, January 10, 2003, http://news.xinhuanet.com/misc/2003-01/10/content_685655.htm.

3. "Statement by President Jiang Zemin of the People's Republic of China at the Millennium Summit of the United Nations (Full Text)," CCTV.com, September 7, 2000, http://www.cctv.com/news/china/20000907/2.html.

4. "Towards a World of Lasting Peace and Common Prosperity (Full Text)," China Internet Information Center, September 16, 2005, http://www.china.com.cn/chinese/news/971778.htm.

development, and innovation of China's peaceful diplomacy concept, and is China's new concept and new paradigm for the international order. It reflects the new thinking that focuses on global security and the future of mankind.

The proposal of a community with a shared future for humanity is the inheritance and innovation of China's concept of peaceful diplomacy, indicating that the nation will continue to hold peace, development, cooperation, and win-win in high regard, and will work with the people of the world to encourage the building of a cohesive world of lasting peace and common prosperity.

2.2 Conforming to the global trend towards peaceful development

Confirming to the global trend is a starting point for China to formulate foreign strategic guidelines and policies. Since the founding of the People's Republic of China, the party and country have always emphasized understanding the characteristics of the times, striving to accurately assess the major and strategic issues related to the international situation, and constantly updating their outlook in response to changes, which guide them in the practice of Chinese diplomacy.

During the Mao Zedong era, China still followed Lenin's concept of "The New Era of War and Revolution." Mao advocated for the "Middle Zone" and "Three Worlds" theories to guide China's diplomacy. While discussing Mao's "Three Worlds" theory, Deng Xiaoping noted that the two superpower nations (the United States and the Soviet Union) were trying to dominate the world in different ways and bully developed countries that were less powerful. They were the origins of a new World War. The "Three Worlds" theory is significant in that it calls on the oppressed to unite against the hegemonic policy of aggression, establish an international united front against hegemony, and maintain world peace and security.

With the easing of the international situation and increasing public demand for peace and development in the 1980s, Deng Xiaoping strategically presented the scientific conclusion that "peace and development are the themes of our times." He said, "Currently, the real major world problems are global strategic issues involving peace, and economic or development challenges. Peace is an East-West issue, and development is a North-South issue. In summary, it involves everywhere, with North-South being the core issue." Deng believed that with peace and development, the competition among countries in the world had turned into one that involved integrating national strength, and China should concentrate its efforts to improve it. In this respect, the Chinese government continued to pursue an independent foreign policy that advocated for peace, opposed hegemonism, and maintained world peace, while enhancing strategic economic cooperation, in particular major Western nations, to achieve national prosperity.

After the Cold War ended, international political polarization and economic globalization intensified. Analyzing the characteristics of the international situation at the turn of the new and old centuries, Jiang Zemin reemphasized that "peace and development are themes of the world today." He noted, "The voices from countries for equal treatment and friendly coexistence are getting louder and louder. Peace, cooperation, and development are now mainstream." Taking guidance from this, Jiang proposed and implemented the "new concept of security" involving mutual trust, mutual benefit, equality, and cooperation," by walking the talk. China strives to resolve territorial and water disputes with its neighbors through peaceful negotiation, and regards the reinforcing of economic exchanges and cooperation as an important way to create long-lasting security for its neighbors by participating in varying regional economic cooperation efforts. China also worked hard to establish a regional security dialogue and cooperation mechanism.

Entering the 21st century, economic globalization and social informatization intensified, and China progressed at unprecedented speeds. Concurrently, a series of global challenges became increasingly prominent, alongside the emergence of regional hotspot issues. In response, Hu Jintao noted that seeking peace, development, and cooperation was the theme of the era. Thereafter, China advocated that all countries should work together to build a cohesive international society of lasting peace and common prosperity. After the 18th National Congress of the Chinese Communist Party, Xi Jinping remarked that "peace, development, and win-win cooperation have become the trend of our times," and advocated for the country to "establish a global vision, unify domestic development and opening up, and link China's development with the world, as well as the interests of the Chinese with people in all countries." The concept of a community with a shared future for humanity then emerged.

2.3 Identifying one's own international standing

International standing refers to a country's position in the international system, which is determined by its comprehensive strength and external environment. Identifying one's own international standing is a requirement for a country to successfully respond to changes in the global context and a prerequisite to formulating effective diplomatic strategies and policies. Although it is dynamic, there remains a basic posture within a certain period.

During the early days of the founding of the People's Republic of China, the new socialist country was united with the socialist camp by adopting a "one-sided" foreign policy, supporting the Soviet Union and other socialist countries, and fighting resolutely against capitalist nations. It also supported independence movements globally. However, following changes to the global situation and the breakdown of Sino-Soviet relations, China (which regarded itself as a Third World country) united with other Third World countries and opposed all forms of hegemony, which were the main goals of China's diplomacy.

Before and after China's Reform and Opening-up, it realized the importance of enhancing its comprehensive national strength and focusing its resources on developing itself, as it was still a developing nation that was poor and backward. Therefore, recognizing its international standing as an "underdeveloped country" resulted in China seeking to enhance its international status by restructuring and opening up, and developing economic relations with other countries globally, especially developed Western nations.

When the Cold War ended, China – the largest socialist country – significantly improved its comprehensive national strength. Conversely, various international forces reorganized, and the global situation transitioned to an alternation between the old and new. China's socialist system, Reform and Opening-up, and modernization, as well as its sovereignty and security, all faced unprecedented challenges. In response, Deng Xiaoping put forward a strategic foreign policy, namely to "hide your strengths, bide your time," which created a favorable external environment for China's Reform and Opening-up, and its economic development.

Today, a rising China has become a major power in the international system, and it has never been closer to the center of the world stage than it is today. This international standing also resulted in China shouldering the important responsibility of maintaining world peace and development like never before. The nature of a socialist country requires China to follow an independent foreign policy of peace, safeguard fairness and justice, speak up in the world, resolutely safeguard peace, and oppose war and all forms of hegemonism. China is still a large developing country, and it will still regard development as the top priority in governing and rejuvenating the country in the long run. Therefore, diplomatic work must ensure the creation of a moderately prosperous society. Also, China is a country with significant global influence. As a permanent member of the UN Security Council and a major nuclear power, China has inescapable responsibilities and obligations for world peace and stability. With this in mind, the Chinese government advocates for the concept of a community with a shared future for humanity.

3 Interactions with Diverse Cultures

Openness and inclusivity are the embodiment of "harmony" in traditional Chinese culture. During China's prosperous periods, it has always perceived and managed its relations with the world with an open and inclusive attitude. Today's China is also absorbing the essence of other cultures in the world. The concept of a community with a shared future for humanity also comes from China's absorption and reference to the essence of these cultures.

3.1 Cosmopolitanism

Cosmopolitanism is an ideology that transcends regions, borders, nations, and religions, and is human and world oriented. The concept of a community with a shared future for humanity regards the human race as a community, which is the core tradition of cosmopolitanism. Therefore, the concept of a community with a shared future for humanity is identical to cosmopolitanism and its contemporary reflection.

Cosmopolitanism connects the past and the present, and across the east and the west. The concept of cosmopolitanism in the West can be traced back to the ancient Greek period, when the Stoics advocated for the concept of "cosmopolitanism" and believed that everyone was born a "world citizen," firstly as a part of the Midgard, and it is only occasionally that they become a member of a particular nation, race, and class. The famous ancient Roman "philosopher king" Emperor Marcus Aurelius was lauded for his cosmopolitan thought by future generations. Immanuel Kant's notion of "perpetual peace" is a representation of modern Western cosmopolitanism. Kant linked cosmopolitanism with the concept of "public reason." He established a universal standard that transcended nationality and culture, and conceived a set of "world citizenship rights" for individuals to form and participate in the world union. He also advocated that the state should fulfill the rights of world citizens and states and other provisions to realize the "commonwealth of independent states" and "perpetual peace." Although Hegel, the main proponent of Western idealism, followed the viewpoint of nationalism, he also advocated a universal global ideological thought in his discussions of world history. He said, "The fate and deeds of nations in their relations are the dialectical development phenomenon of their ideological limitations. The universal spirit produced from this dialectic is the World Spirit." In contemporary globalization, various forms of cosmopolitanism prevail in the West, including "left-wing cosmopolitanism" espoused by Giddens, Herder, and Baker, who advocated for the integration of universalism and cultural pluralism to build a universal order. Conversely, "right-wing cosmopolitanism" endorses universalism and globalism that emulates the West's development model, especially the United States, as the world standard to establish a global integration dominated by superpowers. "Right-wing cosmopolitanism" has been criticized by Marxists as false cosmopolitanism – an embodiment of narrow nationalism.[5]

The globalist vision was embedded in Marx's thinking on human emancipation. He believed that modern society expanded on a global scale throughout history. "The self-sufficiency and seclusion of peoples in the past are replaced by inter-communication and interdependence among various groups. It is the same, both tangibly and in spirit. The spirituality of nations has become public property. One-sidedness and limitations by nations are increasingly impossible, resulting in the formation of world literature from national and local literature." Therefore, Marx's critique of capitalism was conducted from a global perspective of world history, where he proposed human emancipation beyond the nation-state communism. Apart from being a solution to capitalist modernity, communism itself is the historic liberation of the world and mankind.

In Eastern cultures, India and Islamic cultures reflect the cosmopolitanism spirit as well as China. Hinduism can be seen as an important part of Indian culture, with tolerance being its most prominent feature. Within the multi-religious fabric of Indian society, Hinduism adheres to the view that "all religions are the same, and all streams return to the sea," and holds that "just as different rivers come from different mountains and flow into creeks or directly into the sea, so do different sects. Hence, although views may differ, they will lead to you (God) eventually."[6] This religious view reflects the spirit of cosmopolitanism. A contemporary emerging world religion derived from Shiite Islam, Bahá'í advocates that "the Earth is but one country, and mankind its citizens" and strives to "establish a new world order that is inherently sacred" as well as "a road that unites everyone, regardless of country, religion and class," clearly expressing its cosmopolitan proposition.

The concept of a community with a shared future for humanity is a continuation and innovation of ancient and modern cosmopolitan ideas in China and abroad. It is a new systematic understanding of the development trend of humanity, and expresses China and the rest of the world's desire to breathe and share a common destiny.

---

5. Xi Ge, "Marx and Cosmopolitanism: Historical Investigation and Contemporary Revelation," *Social Sciences Abroad*, no. 1 (2012): 25–31.

6. Qiu Yonghui, "Tolerance and Transcendence in Hinduism." *South Asian Studies Quarterly*, no. 2 (2015): 69–75.

3.2 A shared future

More than 2,000 years ago, Aristotle said that "we are inherently social creatures." Marxism holds that "the human essence is no abstraction inherent in each separate individual. In its reality, it is the ensemble of the social relations." It is the social attributes possessed by human beings that resulted in the formation of blood-related communities such as family, clan, and race in the early phase. Following the expansion of social interactions, as well as survival and development needs, it gave rise to ethnic groups, countries, enterprises, social groups, governmental, and non-governmental organizations, forming independent communities. Hence, throughout human history, a community with a shared future for humanity has become one of the most universal notions. Civilization has also experienced various forms and stages in its development, including primitive, ancient, family, and ethnic communities, and national, class, life, national, regional, and global communities in modern times. For this reason, Marx stated that "the essence of man is the real community of man" in the process of creating historical materialism, and the goal of society is to establish a union of free beings.[7] In various communities, its members are closely related to the community they are in, and show solidarity with one another. Interactions between communities are wide ranging and operate on multiple levels, building communities of common destiny of a wider range and higher level, as well as communities of destiny with a wider range and a higher level, so that an individual's development must be attuned to societal development.

In world politics today, countries also look to the community model for cooperation and development, resulting in the establishment of various types of communities, such as the European Economic Community and European Union, the Community of Portuguese Language Countries, the East African Community, the Community of Latin American and Caribbean States, and the ASEAN community. The United States has successively proposed the establishment of the Atlantic Community and Pacific Community, while East Asian countries have vouched for an East Asian Community, and Australia for the Asia-Pacific Community. There is also the Global Community concept put forward by preeminent Professor of American History Akihito Irie. Although developed communities have varying degrees of development and forms, and differing implications and emphasis (with some focusing on common goals, interests, and institutionalized mechanism guarantees and others on subjective

---

7. Kang Yusheng and Hu Yinyin, "Towards a 'True Community': The Value of the Sinicization of Marxism," *Observations and Reflections*, no. 7 (2015): 12–17.

factors such as sharing, communication, participation, and identification) they reflected our need to seek cooperative development.

In summary, the concept of a community with a shared future for humanity is derived from the roots of traditional Chinese culture, and is also based on the diplomatic practices of the People's Republic of China over the past 70 years.

CHAPTER 2

The Features and Creation of a Community with a Shared Future for Humanity

A COMMUNITY WITH A SHARED FUTURE for humanity is very diverse, involving politics, security, development, culture, and ecology. Building a community with a shared future for humanity is a complex, long-term, and arduous task that requires a multi-pronged approach. China is striving to build a community with a shared future for humanity from the perspectives of its neighbors, new forms of international relations, a shared future for developing countries, and global governance.

1 Main Features of the Community

In September 2015, at the summits marking the 70th anniversary of the founding of the United Nations, President Xi Jinping proposed the "five-in-one" dimensions of a community with a shared future for humanity, which is to establish a partnership of equal treatment, mutual discussion and understanding; create a safe platform that is fair and impartial and endorses development and sharing; seek development prospects that are innovative, inclusive, and mutually beneficial; encourage exchanges that tolerate differences and are all-embracing; and build an eco-system that respects nature and green development.[1]

1.1 Establishing mutually respectful and equal partnerships in the spirit of mutual discussions and understanding

When the Cold War ended, partnerships became a new model for exchange between countries. A partnership was a form of international relations that was non-confrontational and non-aligned, based on coordination and cooperation. Unlike traditional alliances, partnership was neither bound by treaties nor obligations, nor was it directed against third countries. Rather, it involved consultation, dialogue, and cooperation on the basis of equality.

Establishing mutually respectful and equal partnerships in the spirit of mutual discussions and understanding is necessary for globalization. Economic globalization has intensified the interdependence of economies and interests of countries, and global challenges have led countries to express their solidarity with one another as their destinies are linked. Globalization has reduced the distance between countries, and has also fueled the power relations in the world. Every actor is an important member of the global community, and may have a significant impact on it. Therefore, in a globalized world, all countries – big or small, rich or poor, weak or strong – should treat each other as equals, and world affairs should be handled by all international actors with equal participation and through mutual discussions and understanding.

Establishing mutually respectful and equal partnerships in the spirit of mutual discussions and understanding is a strategic choice that China made after reflecting on traditional relationships between countries. Historically, in order to pursue a certain strategic goal, countries often formed alliances to forge close relations with other countries. Examples include multifarious vertical and horizontal alliances during China's Spring and Autumn Period, city-state alliances in the ancient Greek period, anti-hegemonic alliances based on the principle of power balance after a nation-state is established, first world alliances such as the famous "Triple Entente" and "Triple Alliance," Eastern and Western camps after World War II, and the current military alliance system led by the United States that still exists and is reinforced from time

---

1. Xi Jinping, "Working Together to Forge a New Partnership and Create a Community of Shared Future for Humanity – Speech at the General Debate of the 70th Session of the United Nations General Assembly," Xinhuanet, September 28, 2015, http://news.xinhuanet.com/politics/2015-09/29/c_1116703645.htm.

to time. Alliances are the norm. However, they bring about confrontations, which in turn lead to conflicts and wars, which undermine international security. In the 1950s and 1960s, India, Yugoslavia, and Egypt jointly proposed and established the Non-Aligned Movement, as a serious confrontation between two major military groups in the East and West during the Cold War posed a serious threat to the survival and development of the world, especially the vast number of small and medium-sized countries. Jointly proposed and established by India, Yugoslavia, and Egypt, the Non-Aligned Movement, whose purpose and principle were independence, self-determination, and non-grouping, was supported by many developing countries. China lent its support to the Non-Aligned Movement 1992, and pursued a non-aligned foreign policy.

Therefore, the requirements of the times and China's reflection on the traditional model of international relations have led it to advocate for and practice a new form of international relations, establishing mutually respectful and equal partnerships in the spirit of mutual discussions and understanding. Thus far, the Chinese government has established more than 70 partnerships of various forms and degrees with major countries, regions, and regional organizations globally. These partnerships differ from the traditional theories of international relations. Foreign Minister Wang Yi summed it up:

"The first thing is to seek peaceful cooperation. The sort of partnership advocated by China does not assume imaginary enemies or target any third party, and is committed to handling exchanges between countries through win-win cooperation rather than a zero-sum game, focusing on identifying the common interests of all countries, and exuding positive energy for the international community to reinforce dialogue and cooperation and avoid conflict and confrontation.

The second thing is to respect one another as equals. The sort of partnership advocated by China is based on the principle of equality of all countries by respecting their sovereignty, independence, and territorial integrity, their core interests and major concerns, as well as the social systems and development paths chosen by the citizens of all countries and promoting equal participation in international affairs and relations. Democratization and the rule of law have injected a new impetus.

The third thing is to advocate for openness and inclusivity. The sort of partnership advocated by China conforms to the general global trend of interdependence, and also conforms to the desire of all countries to live in harmony.

The fourth thing is to emphasize win-win and sharing. Selfishness and the winner-takes-it-all mentality are inappropriate and counterproductive. The sort of partnership advocated by China aims to share the fruits of success through cooperation to achieve common development and prosperity."[2]

Constructing a global partnership network has a political implication, and is an important way for China to build a community around a shared future for humanity. It is also an important manifestation of a specifically Chinese form of major-country diplomacy.

1.2 Creating a safe landscape of fairness and justice premised on co-creation and sharing

Throughout human history, the pursuit of security has been the unremitting pursuit and primary goal of policies in countries around the world. International relations have always revolved around seeking security, and avoiding conflict and war. Although we are now in the era of peace and development, where globalization is progressing quickly, security issues remain a matter of high concern to the international community.

Historically, countries have made attempts and efforts to manage their own security endeavors. They pursue national security by maximizing their strength or even establishing hegemony, forming a strategic balance of power, establishing international security organizations, formulating international security systems, and shaping values and awareness. While they have a favorable impact on the realization of national security to some extent, they do not fundamentally solve nations' security problems.

According to Xi Jinping, "In today's world, the implications and extensions of security are much richer, alongside a broader time and space and more complex factors. We share a common destiny and are interdependent."[3] Traditional security challenges remain serious, and security dilemmas still plague many countries. Territorial sovereignty disputes are complicated and intractable, and the regional security situation is constantly deteriorating. Military armed conflicts also occur from time to time, and the arms race is showing signs of intensifying in some regions. Meanwhile, global challenges are more prominent, and the interests of countries are increasingly converging. Global challenges such as economic crises, climate change, international terrorism, refugee issues, nuclear proliferation, and cybersecurity

---

2. "Wang Yi, "Partnerships Advocated by China Have Four Distinctive Characteristics," Ministry of Foreign Affairs website, March 20, 2017, http://www.fmprc.gov.cn/web/wjbzhd/t1447081.shtml.

3. Xi Jinping, "Towards a Community with a Shared Future and Creating a New Future for Asia – Keynote Speech at the Boao Forum for Asia Annual Conference 2015," *People's Daily*, March 29, 2015, 2.

are becoming increasingly prominent and severe. The international community is confronted with a complex security situation, where traditional and non-traditional security issues are intertwined.

In such a situation, security is shared. No country can seek absolute security on its own, and no country can gain stability from the turmoil of other nations. Therefore, it cannot be the case that one country is safe and others are not, or that some countries are safe while others are not, let alone the absolute security of one country at the expense of others. Security is comprehensive. Traditional security in political and military fields cannot be separated from security in non-traditional fields such as the economy, society, and ecology. Coordinated arrangements and advancements are required. Security can only be achieved through cooperation. The traditional means of seeking security with power as the core and confrontation as the feature will not help resolve security problems, but will aggravate security dilemmas instead. Safety also needs to be sustainable. When pursuing it, we should attach importance to development and build a solid foundation for safety through development. Therefore, the solutions for today's world are following the principles of fairness and justice, establishing new concepts of sharing, integration, cooperation, and sustainability within security, respecting and guaranteeing the security of every country, forming a security pattern of co-constructing and sharing, and building a universally secure world. The fundamental solution to the security challenges we face is also a necessity to build a community with a shared future for humanity.

1.3 Seeking development prospects that are open, innovative, inclusive, and mutually beneficial

Living a richer life is a simple human wish. Therefore, improving labor productivity and living standards is one of the top priorities of governments. With the rapid development of modern science and technology, social labor productivity has been greatly improved, and intensifying economic globalization has endorsed the continued improvement of the world's productivity levels and quality of life. However, while society's productivity is highly developed and continues to generate massive wealth, the development challenges facing the world are becoming increasingly complex. In recent years, global financial and economic turmoil had adversely impacted global economic and social stability. Severe natural disasters have resulted in loss of life and property, while climate change and the spread of deadly infectious diseases have threatened human development. In particular, the global economy was lackluster after 2008 financial crisis, with most countries facing the pressure of economic restructuring. It also adversely affected social development and political stability. In developed countries and regions such as Europe and the United States, trade protectionism was on the rise, anti-globalization forces were rising rapidly, populism and nationalism were surging, and xenophobia and isolationism brought huge challenges to economic globalization. It was not conducive to the development of the world economy.

Concurrently, the unbalanced development increased, the wealth gap widened, and the unsustainable development caused by scarcity of resources, persistent poverty, and environmental problems remained prominent, which exacerbated social unrest and brought about serious social and political security problems. It is difficult to achieve lasting peace and stability in the world without addressing the persistent underdevelopment of developing countries and creating conditions favorable for lower-income people to lift themselves out of poverty. Therefore, we should be committed to development as a whole, along with win-win cooperation and mutual sharing, and to gearing the global economy towards progress that is balanced and endorses common prosperity.

Economic globalization is an objective requirement for the development of societal productivity, and an inevitable result of scientific and technological progress. It is an objective historical process that is not dependent on our subjective will. The current anti-globalization ideological trends tell us that the problems do not lie only with economic globalization, but also with the design and solutions for managing it. Globalization is a double-edged sword that provides a strong impetus for development and also brings about some new situations and new challenges. It is only by adapting to and guiding economic globalization that we can mitigate its negative impact and make it better for every country and nation. To this end, President Xi Jinping advocated that China must first rely on innovation and create a dynamic growth model. Secondly, it must be committed to synergy and linkage to create an open and win-win cooperation model. Thirdly, it must commit to advancing with the times and creating a fair and reasonable governance model. Fourthly, it must uphold fairness and inclusivity, create a balanced and inclusive development model, and seek development prospects that are open, innovative, inclusive, and reciprocal.

1.4 Promoting cohesive and diverse cultural exchanges

The world is a diverse and colorful place. If everything were the same, progress and development would grind to a halt. In the context of economic globalization, all countries and ethnic groups are striving to protect their cultural identity, roots, sovereignty, and security. Respecting and protecting the cultures of all countries and ethnic groups is reasonable and just. Therefore, while cherishing and safeguarding their own cultures, they must also recognize and respect the cultures of others.

Exchange and mutual learning among cultures is a respect for cultural diversity and an important driving force for the progress of humanity and peaceful development of the world. The United Nations designated 2001 as the "UN Year of Dialogue among Civilizations," which advocated for equal exchanges, dialogue, and development among cultures. In 2005, the UN established the Alliance of Civilizations (UNAOC) to encourage mutual understanding and cooperation across countries, cultures, and religions. This reflected the fact that cultural exchanges and mutual learning are becoming mainstream, leading to revitalization across the board.

Equality and respect are the prerequisites for exchanges and mutual learning among cultures. All cultures are equal. Xi Jinping said that the culture of each country is rooted in its soil and has its own characteristics, strengths, and advantages. "Rich and colorful humanity has its value. It is necessary to handle the differences between one's culture and others rationally, and recognize that each culture is unique. We must insist on seeking common ground while reserving differences, learn from each other's strengths, and not attack or derogate others. Do not incur dislike when you see that another culture is different from yours. You must do all you can to transform and de-assimilate, and never try to replace it with your own. History has repeatedly proved that anyone who tries to use coercive methods to resolve differences between cultures will not succeed. To do so would be a disaster for the world." Therefore, we should uphold pluralism and the policy of seeking common ground while reserving differences. We should learn from each other and be all-embracing so that the world can be diverse and prosperous.

1.5 Building an ecosystem that respects nature and green development

Achieving the peaceful coexistence of man with nature is an important element of a community with a shared future for humanity. In today's world, green development and sustainable development are trending. The industrial era greatly improved social productivity, but it also resulted in increasingly severe environmental pollution. We have begun to face global ecological and environmental problems. In 1987, the World Commission on the Environment and Development released a report titled "Our Common Future," noting that ecological and environmental problems included the intensification of the greenhouse effect, the destruction of the ozone layer, the extinction of species, the erosion and degradation of soil, the expansion of deserts, the erosion of forests, and worsening air and water pollution. Environmental pollution directly threatens people's health and survival, and is a potential source of conflict and war. According to a 2014 report by the World Health Organization, air pollution caused seven million deaths worldwide in 2012. Conflicts and wars over water resources around the world, especially in the Middle East, have been raging. Although the international community has made notable achievements, many challenges remain, which illustrates that green development is necessary to meet modern needs.

Increasing the prominence of ecological protection reflects the "people-oriented" concept, which is the basis and value orientation of modern society. It emphasizes the fact that people are the underlying purpose and driving force of development, and advocates that everything revolves around and is dependent on themes. The ecological environment is the people's livelihood, and protecting it is an important project. Achieving green development guarantees the improvement of people's livelihood and well-being. To protect the ecological environment, we must rely on people. The key is to encourage a sense of responsibility for green and sustainable development, and firmly establish the concept of the peaceful coexistence of man with nature. Therefore, from an ecological perspective, it is necessary to build an ecological system that respects nature and green development.

2 Fundamental Principles of Building the Community

To build a community with a shared future for humanity, we must uphold several basic principles, such as sovereignty, win-win cooperation, openness and inclusivity, and peaceful coexistence.

2.1 The principle of sovereignty

Since the sovereign state system was formed in the mid-17th century, it has been the fundamental norm and cornerstone of the modern international system. The true essence of sovereignty is that all countries (big or small, strong or weak, rich or poor) are equal members of the international community and should be respected by it. They also have the right to choose their social systems and development paths, and have no right to interfere in the internal affairs of another country. In an anarchical society, sovereignty is the best line of defense – sometimes the only line of defense for many states. Today, although globalization and global interdependence are profoundly changing the Westphalian system with sovereign nation-states as its core actors, it is undeniable that the world operates under the system of sovereign states, with their interests being the highest criterion guiding their behavior, and sovereignty serving as the basic principle governing international relations.

A community with a shared future for humanity emphasizes the fact that the entire human community is the basic unit to maintain. The rights of this community are the core tasks and goals, and it advocates transcending some differences and conflicts between countries or between different cultures. However, building a community with a shared future for humanity is not about denying and abandoning the principle of sovereignty, but insisting that sovereignty is the most basic principle to follow. This is because in today's international society with sovereign nation-states as the core actors, we can build a peaceful, cooperative, and cohesive community with a shared future only by adhering to the Five Principles of Peaceful Coexistence with sovereignty as the core, insisting that all countries follow the purposes and principles set out in the UN Charter, and abiding by international laws and universally recognized norms of international relations.

In fact, national sovereignty and community rights are a symbiotic relationship. First of all, the relationship between individual countries and the community with a shared future for humanity is not a relationship of mutual opposition and exclusion, but one of mutual recognition and inclusion. The peaceful coexistence of individuals is the premise for the existence of the community. Therefore, national sovereignty and human community rights are not contradictory, but coexist in harmony.

Secondly, the rights of a community with a shared future for humanity are conferred by sovereign states and are maintained by sovereign states. Without national sovereignty, there are no community rights. Moreover, the community with a shared future for humanity is not a super-sovereign organization; it cannot issue orders to the state, and its influence on the state's behavior depends on the state's conscious behavior under the recognition of the community consciousness.

Finally, a community with a shared future for humanity provides a favorable environment for sovereign states to develop more fully. A community with a shared future for humanity is an ideal state of being for a country. Its existence ensures that national sovereignty can serve the domestic people better, thereby promoting national welfare. Therefore, in today's world of sovereign nation-state systems, sovereignty is still the basic principle that guides international relations, and the guiding principle for building a community with a shared future for humanity.

2.2 The principle of win-win cooperation

In a community with highly intertwined interests and shared destiny, win-win is a basic value. The prerequisite for a win-win situation is cooperation. Win-win cooperation has always been the key to China's handling of foreign relations.

It is also one of the basic principles of building a community with a shared future for humanity. The report of the 18th National Congress of the Communist Party of China noted: "Win-win cooperation means advocating the consciousness of a community with a shared future for humanity, taking into account the legitimate concerns of other countries when pursuing national interests, promoting the common development of all countries in the pursuit of national development, and establishing a new type of global development partner that is more equal and balanced. relationship, help each other, share rights and responsibilities, and encourage the common interests of mankind."

Globalization and global challenges have transformed the world into a community of destiny, joint interests, and interdependence. In it, the zero-sum is a thing of the past. The practicing of beggar-thy-neighbor policies, passing on the crisis, and harming others to benefit oneself is unethical, does not resolve the problem, and may worsen the situation. Win-win cooperation is the only option. "When facing global problems, it is impossible for any country to isolate itself and stand out on its own. It requires countries to work in solidarity ... to build a better home together," Xi Jinping noted.[4] In particular, when it comes to global issues such as climate change, it would be detrimental to others if you possess a utilitarian mindset, shirk your responsibilities, and take advantage of others.

Therefore, we must uphold the principle of win-win cooperation, "commit to helping one another," and oppose to prioritizing self-interests over others to build a community with a shared future for humanity.

2.3 The principles of openness and inclusivity

The diversity of cultures is a fundamental characteristic of our society. At present, there are over seven billion people in the world, 200 countries and regions, 2,500 ethnic groups, and 6,000 languages. Different ethnic groups have created their own unique cultures, and countries have their social systems and ideologies. We can

---

4. "Xi Jinping Emphasizes China as an Advocate and Practitioner of Win-Win Cooperation During a Symposium with Foreign Expert Representatives," *People's Daily*, December 6, 2012, 1.

build a peaceful, developing, and prosperous world, and a community with a shared future for humanity only by upholding the principles of openness and inclusivity, respecting the diversity of world cultures, promoting exchanges, dialogues, and peaceful coexistence among the world's diverse cultures, and absorbing the cultures of all countries and nations in the world.

China advocates for the principle of everyone thriving in parallel without hindering each other, and uses effective and inclusive mechanisms to obtain results, which is the essence of traditional Chinese culture. It is this open and inclusive mindset that shaped the history of Chinese culture stretching back more than 5,000 years. In today's world, with its diverse cultures, economic globalization and social informatization have brought countries and ethnic groups together, realizing a high degree of integration of interests and also achieving a shared destiny. Therefore, protectionism and xenophobia are not aligned with the interests of this open world and will undermine its development. Civilizations can coexist and thereby encourage the prosperity and development of the world only by expanding and intensifying the development strategy of opening up, upholding the principle of openness and inclusivity, and respecting the diversity of cultures.

The Chinese government is deeply aware that China's development benefits from economic and social factors that are intertwined with the rest of the world, and its future development is inseparable from it. In a globalized world, a single flower does not make spring, but a hundred flowers bring spring to the garden, as the saying goes. Therefore, President Xi Jinping pledged to the world that "China's opening to the outside world is not about a one-man show, but to welcome all parties to participate. It is not to seek spheres of influence, but to support the common development of all countries. It is not to create its own back garden but to build a garden of a hundred flowers shared by all countries."[5] Building a "garden of a hundred flowers" shared by all countries is also the goal of a community with a shared future for humanity.

2.4 The principle of peaceful coexistence

The concept of a community with a shared future for humanity is a contemporary manifestation of the traditional Chinese idea of the harmony of man and nature. It follows holistic thinking and holds that human society, the natural world, and

---

5. "Xi Jinping Attends Opening Ceremony of the G20 Business Summit and Delivers a Keynote Speech: Constructing an Innovative, Open, Interconnected, and Inclusive World Economy," *People's Daily (Overseas Edition)*, September 4, 2016, 1.

the relationship between man and nature should be unions and should complement each other in cohesive symbiosis. Therefore, peaceful coexistence is a basic principle for realizing global governance and building a community with a shared future for humanity.

As we are building this community, upholding the principle of peaceful coexistence necessitates two aspects. First, it requires multiple actors in the international community to participate equally in the governance of world affairs and realize the co-management and governance of public affairs. This requires coordinating the interests of all parties, which allows stakeholders to participate, share responsibilities, share interests, and synergize power, and also permits multiple actors to coexist in harmony and achieve social stability and order.

Secondly, it requires us to accurately understand and manage the relationship between national and community interests. In fact, it is not a relationship of exclusion nor a zero-sum game, but a relationship of cohesive co-existence. The community serves national interests. An important purpose for its existence is for the country to safeguard and expand its national interests. No individual in the world can exist in isolation. It is a community with social and relational attributes. Individuals in various relationships can only contribute to its development by creating a cohesive and friendly community, especially in today's world where global interdependence is entrenched. The community will provide them with a conducive external environment. Meanwhile, fulfilling the obligations of the international community is also the responsibility of each individual country. While a modern state is established from the empowerment of its own people, and serving its own people is its responsibility – a fundamental reason for its existence and the source of its legitimacy – it also exists in the international community and must assume international responsibilities. The maintaining of a conducive international social environment is an important national task. In any historical period, we can see the spirit of internationalism. Under the new conditions, a country should chart the lofty goal and make efforts to build a community with a shared future for humanity. This is a new international responsibility entrusted to the country in our time.

3 Main Approaches to Building the Community

The vision of a community with a shared future for humanity as an ideal society is not an empty slogan or a utopia, but a goal with a solid foundation, and it is the direction that the international community should strive towards. To inch towards this meaningful goal, we must reinforce our confidence and leverage our knowledge, and also be down-to-earth, working towards it in a targeted manner. At present, China's diplomacy is guided by the concept of a community with a shared future for humanity, which is based on building a community with a shared future for neighboring countries, a community with a shared future for developing countries, a new type of international relations, and a global governance structure featuring joint discussions and contributions, and mutual benefits.

3.1 Building a community with a shared future with neighbors as the first step

Neighborhood diplomacy – the foundation of China's development and prosperity – holds a principal position in China's diplomatic work.

Building a community with a shared future with neighbors is China's first step toward building a community with a shared future for humanity. China places great emphasis on this by building bilateral and regional communities of shared destiny with nations, regions, and cities such as Pakistan, Vietnam, Kazakhstan, South Korea, Kyrgyzstan, Cambodia, Myanmar, Indonesia, Bangladesh, Turkmenistan, Laos, ASEAN, Shanghai, Asia, and Asia-Pacific.

China's extremely complex geographical climate, coupled with prominent differences and diversity among countries, historical baggage, and converging interests of major powers, pose a severe challenge to building a community with a shared future surrounding it. However, China and its neighboring countries are connected by mountains and rivers, and are closely related to each other, bound by destiny. Also, neighborly friendships and mutually beneficial cooperation are the mainstays of its relations with neighboring countries. Building a community with a shared future around China is not just necessary but feasible. The CPC Central Committee, with Xi Jinping at its core, highlighted the principles of friendship, sincerity, mutual benefit, and inclusivity while upholding the fundamental policy of neighborliness and partnerships in terms of trust, security, and prosperity. The concept of neighborhood diplomacy endorses a common, comprehensive, cooperative, and sustainable new security concept in Asia. It enhances strategic trust, intensifies mutually beneficial cooperation, and reinforces people-to-people and cultural exchanges to build a community of values, development, and security, allowing the ideology to take root in neighboring countries. In particular, the implementation of a series of major strategic initiatives and measures, such as the "Belt and Road Initiative" and the establishment of the Asian Infrastructure Investment Bank, has also concretized the creation of a community with a shared future around China.

The relationship between China and its neighboring countries is complex and diverse, and the building of a community with a shared future for these countries must be specific, targeted, and diverse. For example, China has intensified its holistic cooperation with Pakistan, making the China-Pakistan community with a shared future into a model for neighboring countries. It has jointly built a closely linked community of shared destiny with Laos, and continues to be a good friend to Cambodia based on mutual trust, sincere partnership, and a community of shared destiny. With Kazakhstan it has reinforced cooperation in all areas, leveraging the advantages of political relations, geographical proximity, and economic complementarity, and transforming them into cooperation and sustainable growth, creating a community of mutual benefit and win-win cooperation. With Vietnam it has a relationship of mutual support and help, upholding the Party's leadership and the socialist path, and creating a community with a shared future of strategic significance. These proposals for a community with a shared future with specific intent demonstrate China's pragmatism in building a community with a shared future with its neighbors.

3.2 Building a community with a shared future for developing countries as a cornerstone

China is the largest developing country in the world, and developing countries are the foundation of its diplomacy. Africa is the continent with the largest concentration of developing countries and the largest number of least developed countries. The building of a China-Africa community with a shared future is of great significance in building a community with a shared future for developing countries. In this regard, Xi Jinping noted that "China-Africa relations did not develop in a day, nor were they bestowed by someone. We both stood through thick and thin, shared weal and woe, and walked step-by-step together." China and Africa "have always been a community with a shared future, and we are closely linked by common historical experiences, development tasks, and strategic interests."[6] China has rapidly grown into the world's second largest economy, but its international status and identity as a developing country have not changed. For most developing countries, including African nations, China follows the principle of pursuing the greater good and shared interests. It upholds the idea that a country benefits from justice, not interests, and advocates paying attention to justice rather than interests in international cooperation.

---

6. "Always Be a Reliable Friend and Sincere Partner - Xi Jinping's Speech at the Nyerere International Conference Center in Tanzania," *People's Daily*, March 26, 2013, 2.

Pursuing the greater good and shared interests is the essential requirement of a socialist country. "Justice" means that real happiness is common happiness, which is the basis of global development, especially the accelerated development of many developing countries. "Benefit" means to abide by the principle of mutual benefit and win-win, and not engage in a zero-sum game. In particular, when it comes to its relations with developing countries, China should prioritize justice over interests. In fact, "justice over benefit" and "sacrificing one's life for justice" are traditional virtues of Chinese society, and have been reflected in China's relations with other countries in various historical periods, in particular the People's Republic of China. According to Xi Jinping, "From 1950 to 2016, despite its low long-term development and low living standards, China has provided more than 400 billion yuan in foreign aid and implemented more than 5,000 foreign aid projects, including nearly 3,000 complete sets of projects. More than 11,000 training courses were held to train more than 260,000 people from developing countries in China."[7]

Guided by the proper concepts of justice and interests, China has built a comprehensive strategic partnership with African nations by upholding equality and mutual trust in politics, win-win cooperation in economic exchanges, mutual learning between cultures, mutual assistance in security, and solidarity and cooperation in international affairs to build a community with a shared future. By reinforcing dialogue among cultures and cultural exchanges, it enables the beauty of our own design, and makes the world complete, transforming the China-Latin America community with a shared future into a model for peaceful coexistence and mutual promotion of different cultures. Also, by treating each other with openness, replacing conflicts and confrontations with dialogues and exchanges, it creates a model of peaceful coexistence for China and Arab, which are countries with different social systems, beliefs, and cultural traditions. Alongside the vast number of developing countries, China is building a community with a shared future.

3.3 Creating a new type of international relations as the key

To create a new type of international relations with win-win cooperation at its core requires countries to "perceive a community with a shared future as the common goal to manage international relations, regard common interests as the important basis

---

7. Xi Jinping, "Sharing the Responsibilities of the Times and Promoting Global Development: Keynote Speech at the Opening Ceremony of the World Economic Forum Annual Meeting 2017," *People's Daily*, January 18, 2017,3

to manage international relations, view win-win as the basic principle to manage international relations, and see cooperation as the main way to manage international relations and establish a security pattern of equal treatment, mutual discussions, and understanding, seek developmental prospects that are open, innovative, inclusive and reciprocal, and encourage cohesive and inclusive cultural exchanges."[8]

Under the historical conditions of peace, development, cooperation, and win-win cooperation as the trend of the times, the latter is the greatest common factor in handling relations between countries. The key to the new type of international relations lies in the relationship between major powers. It is an important factor in determining the development tendencies of the international system and pattern. The Sino-US relationship occupies an extremely important position among the new major-country relationships, and is one of the most important bilateral partnerships in the world. Whether the rising China and the traditional great power of the United States can overcome the historical spell of the "Final War" and avoid the "Thucydides Trap" is not only related to China and the United States, but also to the future and destiny of mankind. In line with the current trend, China and the United States must abandon the Cold War mentality and zero-sum game and follow the new concept of building a fresh type of major-country relationship that is premised on non-conflict, non-confrontation, mutual respect, and win-win cooperation. As Dai Bingguo said, China and the United States "cooperate in almost every field, where their interests are intertwined and interdependent on one another. Our dialogue involves the sky and the ground, the air and the sea, electromagnetic space and even the 'Three-Body Problem,' and our cooperation has not only benefited China and the United States, but also changed the world, especially development and prosperity in the Asia-Pacific region over the past 30 years, which is related to the stable development of Sino-US relations."[9] As such, "major powers should respect each other's core interests and major concerns and manage conflicts and differences. As long as we continue to communicate and treat each other sincerely, the 'Thucydides Trap' can be avoided."[10]

---

8. Wang Yi, "Going on a New Voyage for the Development of China-Russia Relations – Commemorating the Fifteenth Anniversary of the Signature of the 'Sino-Russian Treaty of Neighborliness, Friendship and Cooperation,'" Ministry of Foreign Affairs website, July 18, 2016, http://www.fmprc.gov.cn/web/ziliao _674904/zyjh_674906/t1382248.shtml.

9. "Dai Bingguo's Speech at the Center for Strategic and International Studies in the United States," Ministry of Foreign Affairs website, July 5, 2016, http://www.fmprc.gov.cn/web/ziliao_674904/zyjh_674906 /t1377748.shtml.

10. Xi Jinping, "Building a Community with a Shared Future for Humanity Together – Speech at the United Nations Headquarters in Geneva," People's Daily, January 20, 2017, 2.

Concurrently, building a new model for the major-country relationship between China and the United States is the historical responsibility of the two major countries to maintain world peace and encourage common development.

As a representative of emerging major power relations, Sino-Russian relations have positive significance for relations between emerging countries. China and Russia are neighbors and former allies, but they also have historical grievances and differences in practical interests. Today, with major changes, major adjustments, and major developments, China and Russia are developing and intensifying their comprehensive strategic partnership of coordination, pursuing equality, trust, mutual support, common prosperity, and friendship from generation to generation, and striving to transform the advantages of high-level political relations into a better partnership. Their achievements in practical cooperation have pushed Sino-Russian relations to a higher level.

As the largest developing country and consortium of developed countries, China and the European Union are "two major forces" for maintaining world peace, "two major markets for promoting common development," and "two great cultures for promoting human progress."[11] Moreover, China and the EU are already each other's largest trading partners, and the interests of various countries are converging. Therefore, China and the EU should develop a partnership of peace, growth, restructuring, and culture based on the concepts of mutual respect, equal treatment, seeking common ground while reserving differences, win-win cooperation, and building a China-EU community with a shared future.

3.4 Establishing a global governance context of extensive consultations, joint contributions, and shared benefits as the stage

Today, with the ongoing progress of globalization and ever-increasing global challenges, reinforcing global governance is a common requirement of the international community. However, its fundamentals were formed in the early post-World War II period, and many institutional arrangements could no longer align with the profound changes in the international power structure and the great development of social informatization. In particular, since the financial crisis of 2008, the international community's calls for a restructuring of the economic

---

11. "Building Four Bridges of Peace, Growth, Reform, and Civilization – President Xi Jinping's Important Statement on China-EU Relations," *People's Daily*, October 16, 2015, 3.

governance system have never been louder. In this situation, China advocates for the establishment of a new global governance structure featuring extensive consultations, joint contributions, and shared benefits.

The establishment of a global governance structure featuring extensive consultations, joint contributions, and shared benefits is disregarding the past when a few countries monopolized the right to speak, managed global affairs, and exclusively enjoyed the results of global governance. It is about participating, brainstorming, and discussing. All participants leverage their strengths and unleash their potential, and continue to enhance them, allowing these efforts to benefit every participant fairly. Its purpose is to ensure that countries have equal opportunities and equal rights in global governance.

China advocates for the establishment of a global governance structure based on extensive consultations, joint contributions, and shared benefits. This does not mean that China should overthrow the original global governance structure, but rather restructure it to make it more adaptable to the current international environment and allow it to respond more effectively to global issues. Global issues have meant that every country and actor in the world has formed a community with a connected destiny. To manage global issues, it is necessary to reinforce global governance. Parties need to discuss this, and jointly build a global governance structure, eventually sharing the results.

In today's world where more than 200 countries and regions and a large number of international actors coexist, we need to build a better world by establishing a global governance pattern of extensive consultations, joint contributions, and shared benefits.

Undoubtedly, building a community with a shared future for humanity is a long-term and arduous task, but China has the confidence and capability to encourage this great historical process. As Xi Jinping noted, "Building a community with a shared future for humanity is a wonderful goal, which can only be achieved through a relay race from generation to generation. China is willing to work with member states, international organizations, and institutions to jointly encourage the great process of building a community with a shared future for humanity."[12]

---

12. Xi Jinping, "Building a Community with a Shared Future for Humanity: Speech at the United Nations Headquarters in Geneva," *People's Daily*, January 20, 2017, 2.

Chapter 3

The Significance of a Community with a Shared Future for Humanity

Proposing the concept of a community with a shared future for humanity is the result of the continuous exploration of contemporary Chinese diplomacy, and a new theory guiding the development of society amid new historical conditions. It is also an important reflection of the new stage of interactions between China and the rest of the world.

1 New Explorations of Chinese Diplomacy

China's diplomacy has always associated the preservation of sovereignty, security, and development interests with the promotion of world peace and development. While safeguarding national rights and interests, it is also a firm defender and builder of world peace, development, and cooperation. The concept of a community with a shared future for humanity reflects the strategic thinking of China's diplomacy to manage both domestic and international situations. It is a legacy and protection of China's diplomatic concepts, and an answer to the kind of world it aspires to build.

1.1 Inheriting and protecting Chinese diplomatic concepts

The values of peace, fairness, and inclusivity in the community with a shared future are the contemporary embodiment of traditional Chinese values, and the legacy and protection of contemporary Chinese diplomatic concepts.

(1) Peace

Peace is the core value of contemporary Chinese diplomacy. China is a peace-loving nation. Pre-Qin philosophers advocated for the idea that benevolence and good neighborliness are of great value to the country, which reflects the hope for peace that the Chinese people have held since ancient times, and their desire to have cordial relations with countries across the globe. In modern times, Chinese people – who have indelible memories of war sufferings – deeply appreciate how precious peace is, and pursue it tirelessly. As Xi Jinping said, "The Chinese fear turbulence, so what they seek is stability, and what they long for is peace in the world."[1] Since its founding, the People's Republic of China has consistently stayed true to a diplomatic concept centered on peace. It chose an independent foreign policy of peace from the start, and jointly proposed and advocated for the "Five Principles of Peaceful Coexistence" with other developing countries. In the wake of evolving domestic and international situations, China's concept of peaceful diplomacy has been continuously enriched and innovated in its legacy and continuation. It has experienced development from peaceful coexistence to a cohesive world and then to a community with a shared future for humanity. The latter reflects the Chinese people's deepest aspiration to achieve lasting peace in the world. Xi Jinping noted, "Peace, like air and sunshine, is hardly noticed when people are benefiting from it. But none of us can live without it. Without peace, development is out of the question."[2] To this end, "China will unswervingly follow the path of peaceful development" and "will never seek hegemony and expansion."

Although peace and development are the dominant themes of the times, the world today is not at peace. Traditional security threats remain severe, and non-

---

1. "Xi Jinping Emphasized in the Third Collective Study of the Politburo of the CPC Central Committee to Better Coordinate Domestic and International Situations and Lay a Solid Foundation for the Path of Peaceful Development," *People's Daily*, January 30, 2013, 1.

2. Xi Jinping, "Working Together Towards a Better Future for Asia and the World: Keynote Speech at the Boao Forum for Asia Annual Conference 2013," *People's Daily Online*, April 7, 2013, http://politics.people.com.cn/n/2013/0407/c1024-21046128.html.

traditional security problems increase day by day. Traditional and non-traditional security threats are intertwined and ever-evolving, making the world truly safe, yet dangerous. China's advocacy for a community with a shared future for humanity is a strong call for all of the countries in the world to jointly shoulder the responsibility of maintaining world peace.

(2) Fairness

Fairness is an inherent requirement of Chinese-style socialism. Upholding international fairness and justice is China's guiding principle within its foreign policy. Upholding fairness and justice also runs deep in China's diplomatic practice, against world hegemony and colonialism in the 1950s and 1960s and to any form of power politics today. China has always stood firmly on the side of developing countries, and has safeguarded their legitimate international rights and interests.

Fairness is the primary value proposition for building a world order. Since the formation of the state system, the anarchy of the international system has made self-preservation into the standard code of conduct for sovereign states. Many countries pursue power and interests unrestrictedly to protect themselves, resulting in power imbalances and power politics among countries, as well as constant conflicts, wars, and widespread exploitation and oppression. In today's world, in the face of the new "decentralization" of international power and coexistence of multiple cultures, the kind of value orientation used to build the world order is the primary problem that needs to be solved urgently. There is an old saying in China that "the wage of sin is death," which means that he who is unjust is doomed for destruction. Immanuel Kant noted that morality "is the totality of the unconditional law on which we should act," and that "real politics will not be able to move an inch without guaranteeing morality." Therefore, to build a world order, China must first comply with moral requirements, with fairness and justice as the foundation of morality.

The expression of international fairness and justice is sovereignty and justice, that is, respecting the political rights of all countries to participate in international affairs on an equal footing, and respecting the rights of countries to choose their own development paths. International fairness and justice are also reflected in the establishment of a fair and reasonable international political and economic order, which opposes the law of the winner-takes-it-all. International fairness and justice are also reflected in the inclusivity and mutual learning of different cultures, safeguarding the diversity of cultures, promoting exchanges and integration, and promoting mutual benefit and peaceful coexistence.

(3) Inclusivity

Chinese culture has multi-ethnic characteristics. It has illustrated its inclusivity through its interactions with the outside world. Therefore, traditional Chinese philosophy has always advocated for an inclusive attitude. Openness and tolerance have become core features of Chinese culture. In the early days of the founding of the People's Republic of China, Premier Zhou Enlai advocated for the policy of seeking common ground while reserving differences based on the "Five Principles of Peaceful Coexistence," which has been used to guide the peaceful settlement of all international conflicts and disputes, including among countries with different social systems, reflecting China's knowledge, openness, and inclusivity. Looking at the world, the history of human development is a history of multi-culture symbiosis.

In this diverse world, China must advocate for the spirit of openness and inclusivity, and build a multi-culture that grows together by learning from each other's strengths.

Inclusive development is also the aspiration of the international community. In 2005, the World Summit Outcome Document adopted by the United Nations General Assembly stated that heads of state and governments pledged to work to encourage well-being, freedom, and progress around the world, and to encourage tolerance, respect, dialogue, and cooperation. Openness and inclusivity are the prerequisites for dialogue and cooperation. It is through dialogues that misunderstandings and doubts are eliminated, and cooperation and development are endorsed.

1.2 China's exploration of a new world order

The world order refers to the rules of international behavior and the respective guaranteed mechanisms formed by the main actors in the international community, dealing with each other according to principles, norms, goals, and means of a certain world pattern. The world order is the bare minimum for the peaceful coexistence of members of the international community, and also society's yearning and pursuit of a better world. Throughout the history of human development, despite the constant conflicts and wars, our longing for a better world has never ceased, alongside the idea of a good world order.

In ancient China, the concepts of "world order," "world of great harmony" and "universal peace" embodied the pursuit of a better world order. In modern times, in the face of suffering within Chinese society, Kang Youwei imagined a utopian "world of great harmony" with no class, state, or private property – only equality and prosperity. Sun Yat-sen – the pioneer of China's democratic revolution – strove to realize this "world of great harmony" by establishing a Republic that was "owned, governed, and enjoyed by the people," thus placing the utopian "world of great harmony" into practice. However, Sun's bourgeois-democratic republic was short-lived.

After the People's Republic of China was founded, the "world of great harmony" remained an ideal, but it could only be a distant dream during the early days. The only realistic pursuit at that time was the realization of peaceful coexistence between countries.

Therefore, China's proposition to establish a new international political and economic order is based on the "Five Principles of Peaceful Coexistence." In 1974, Deng Xiaoping spoke about China's new international political and economic order for the first time at the sixth special session of the UN General Assembly. Firstly, China would establish political and economic relations between countries on the basis of the "Five Principles of Peaceful Coexistence." Secondly, the affairs of each country were to be managed by its citizens. Thirdly, no matter how big or small, rich or poor, all countries should be equal, and international economic affairs should be managed jointly by all of the countries in the world, not by one or two superpowers. Fourthly, world trade was to be based on equality, mutual benefit, and exchange of goods. Fifthly, economic aid to developing countries should not be attached to any political and military conditions; the sovereignty of recipient countries should be respected, and the international community should provide technical assistance to developing countries while respecting them. China's proposition for a new international political and economic order was aligned with the tide of time, and was widely supported by all of the countries in the world.

Reform and Opening-up profoundly changed China's relationship with the rest of the world. With continuous expansion on the integration of interests between China and the outside world, and with unprecedented exchanges, China's relations with the world have undergone historic changes. Increasingly, its future and destiny are becoming closely linked with the future and destiny of the world as a community with a shared future.

At the summit on the 60th anniversary of the establishment of the United Nations in September 2005, then Chinese President Hu Jintao formally proposed China's new concept for building a cohesive international order. He stated that China was willing to cooperate with other countries based on the new security concept of mutual trust and benefit, equality, and cooperation to achieve mutual security and development along with peaceful coexistence. After the 18th National Congress of the Communist Party of China, Xi Jinping led the CPC Central Committee to develop the strategic thinking of a cohesive world, and proposed the concept of a community with a shared future for humanity. This is China's new exploration of building a world order under the new historical conditions.

2 A New Theory of Social Development

A community with a shared future for humanity constitutes a new theory about the development of society. It is not just a new way of thinking that guides us to understand the world today, where globalization and the countries of the world are highly interdependent. It is necessary to adopt a holistic approach in understanding the world and solving the problems it faces. It is also a way to guide the development of all countries, and reflects the innovative development of the Marxist community theory under new historic conditions.

2.1 Holistic thinking within the new global outlook

Individualism is the core of the Western cultural value system. It is the basic Western way of thinking and value orientation, as well as the foundation of the Western theory of international relations, world outlook, and epistemology. Taking reference from the individual-based way of thinking and values, the starting point and destination of international relations are individuals, with national power and national interests being the decisive factors. For a long time, the dominant theory of international relations in the world came from the West, led by the United States. Therefore, the individual-based way of thinking and value orientation have profoundly affected the outlook of international society. However, the world we live in and the place where international relations unfold is not the result of separate and independent actors chasing their own interests, but rather a result of the connections and interactions by interrelated and interdependent actors. The world today is more holistic thanks to globalization. This is reflected in the mutual demands of countries and the coexistence of various actors in the international community, and also in the close connections in various fields such as politics, economy, society, and culture, and the overall unity of humanity and nature. The realistic development of the human world prompts us to look for values and ways of thinking that are different from individualism. This is holistic vision and thinking.

Holism is an ancient concept. It holds that things and processes in the world are not isolated and disordered natural accumulations, but rather a regular organic whole composed of various elements and interactions. Many international thinkers, both ancient and modern, have discussed the holistic nature of the world. The unity of man and nature advocated in ancient China, and the cosmopolitan thought common in both China and the West reflect people's cognition of the world as a whole. Hegel once said: "If a hand is cut off from the body, it can still be called a hand, but it is no longer a hand in essence." Therefore, we take reference from a holistic approach to knowing anything.

The world today is one where wins and losses are intertwined. Society faces problems such as uneven distribution of wealth, shortage of resources and energy, worsening of the ecological environment, terrorism, and increasing transnational crime, which are all linked, requiring people to understand the world based on overall interests rather than the state's, and use it as the starting point to build a new world order. A community with a shared future for humanity is a global outlook based on holistic thinking, and is a denial of the individual-based thinking that has long dominated the West. In state-to-state exchanges, the concept of a community with a shared future for humanity advocates for dialogue rather than confrontation, and partnerships instead of alliances. It advocates win-win cooperation and common development, and opposes self-serving and beggar-thy-neighbor policies. It emphasizes openness and inclusivity, exchanges, and mutual learning, and opposes isolation and exclusion. It focuses on the cohesion and unity of man with nature, and opposes binary opposition. It highlights a comprehensive, common, cooperative, and sustainable security concept.

2.2 Innovation of development concepts

For a long time, Western modernization theory has been a successful model for world development. It has successfully guided the practice of modernization since the dawn of modernity, and has been widely emulated by many developing countries. However, Western modernization theory – a guiding theory for the development of Western countries under specific historical conditions – has brought many problems and setbacks in the process of its promotion in other countries. Under such circumstances, development theories such as dependency and world systems emerged. Although pluralistic development theory has brought about diverse development paths in the world, there are still serious problems with holistic and inclusive global development. The reality of world development calls for a new concept.

With modern science and technology rapid progressing, the problems of unsustainable development caused by scarcity of resources, persistent poverty and environmental problems have become more prominent. In particular, the imbalance of world development has increased, and the wealth gap has grown, undermining world peace and development. According to Xi Jinping, "The richest 1% of the world's population owns more wealth than the rest of the 99% of the population combined, and the unequal income distribution and unbalanced development space are worrisome. More than 700 million people worldwide still live in extreme poverty. For many families, having a warm house, sufficient food, and a stable job are still luxuries. This is the biggest challenge facing the world today, and it is a major cause of social unrest in some countries."[3] Global development faces many challenges, and requires the emergence of a new concept that endorses balanced development and shared prosperity of the global economy.

While China – a developing country – has made great achievements in terms of economic growth rate and total scale in recent years, it still faces development problems. To this end, the idea of a community with a shared future for humanity perceives the development concepts of innovation, coordination, greenness, openness, and sharing as the core in managing the new challenges brought by globalization and adapting to the new world situation. Given this concept, China has established partnerships for common development with countries and regions around the world, created a balanced and inclusive growth model, and pursued a mutually beneficial and win-win cooperation and development path.

2.3 Contemporary innovations of the Marxist community theory

China's concept of a community with a shared future for humanity is the innovation and development of the Marxist community theory under contemporary conditions – a product of the combination of the basic principles of Marxism and China's specific practice, and an embodiment of the Sinicization of Marxism.

The community theory occupies a central position in Marxism, and has far-reaching implications. First of all, the social attributes of people are the prerequisites for the existence of the community. Marx opined, "But the human essence is no abstraction inherent in each single individual. In its reality it is the ensemble of social relations. It is only in a community that the individual has means of access to holistic development, which means that individual liberty is possible only in a community.

---

3. Xi Jinping, "Sharing the Responsibilities of the Times and Promoting Global Development: Keynote Speech at the Opening Ceremony of the World Economic Forum Annual Meeting 2017," *People's Daily*, January 18, 2017, 3.

In a real community, the individuals obtain their freedom in and through their association."[4]

Secondly, the community is an inevitable product of the development of productivity and relations of production. Marxism insists on historical materialism and believes that the emergence of the community is a historical necessity. Marx's "A Contribution to the Critique of Political Economy" and Engels's "The Origin of the Family, Private Property and the State" conducted in-depth studies on the forms of ownership in different stages of human historical development, as well as the emergence and formation of human social community and its development process, which revealed the historical inevitability of the emergence of the community. *The Communist Manifesto* states that "The bourgeoisie, though opening up the world market, has increased the production and consumption of all global countries. The local and national self-sufficiency and isolation of the past have been replaced by reciprocation and interdependence."[5] Therefore, the capitalist productive capability and mode of production allow the community to develop.

Thirdly, a communist society realizes that a union of free people is the real community. Although modern global history was formed after society entered the capitalist phase, this also reflects the possibility of forming a community. However, Marxism holds that a community dominated by the exploiting classes is "not only a completely illusory community, but also a new constraint for the ruling class," and therefore a "false community" in which "any expansion of exchanges destroys regional communism. Communism is empirically possible only as a sudden simultaneous action of dominant nations, which is based on the general development of productive forces and premised on the exchanges in the world associated with this."[6] Therefore, according to Marx's interpretation, the "real community" is the highest phase of the development of society, that is, the stage of the union of free people.

China's concept of a community with a shared future for humanity reflects the spirit of the times in the Marxist community theory. Although the communist society of the Marxist ideal is still merely a wonderful vision, the reality of global interdependence in today's world objectively requires that people establish a sense of openness, inclusivity, cooperation, and win-win guided by the common values of mankind, and collectively move towards the ideal goals of the "union of free people."

---

4. *The Collected Works of Marx and Engels*, vol. 1 (People's Publishing House, 2009), 501, 571.
5. *The Selected Works of Marx and Engels*, vol. 1 (People's Publishing House, 1995), 276.
6. *The Collected Works of Marx and Engels*, vol. 1 (People's Publishing House, 2009), 538–539.

3 A New Stage for China's Interactions with the World

In September 2014, Foreign Minister Wang Yi said in his speech at the opening ceremony of the China Foreign Affairs University: "At present, China's diplomacy has reached a new historical starting point. It has never been closer to the center of the world stage, and has never before so fully participated in various kinds of international affairs or shouldered such important responsibilities for safeguarding world peace and development like today."[7] The new starting point and status of China's diplomacy have also ushered in a new phase of interactions with the world, and the concept of a community with a shared future for humanity is its most prominent reflection.

3.1 The global significance of the "Chinese Dream"

The realization of the "Chinese Dream" of national rejuvenation is a major strategic concept proposed by Xi Jinping's CPC Central Committee, and it is also an important ideological achievement of Chinese leaders in coordinating domestic and international situations from a new historical starting point. Xi Jinping noted that realizing the great rejuvenation of the Chinese nation has been the greatest dream of its people since modern times. The basic implication of the "Chinese Dream" is to achieve national prosperity, rejuvenation, and happiness. There are "Two Centenary Goals": by 2021 – the 100th anniversary of the founding of the Communist Party of China – a moderately prosperous society will be built in all respects; by 2049 – the 100th anniversary of the founding of the People's Republic of China – a modern socialist country that is strong, democratic, civilized, and cohesive will have been built, to realize the great rejuvenation of the Chinese nation.

Realizing the "Chinese Dream" is a lofty ideal that has been continuously explored and pursued since modern times. It is only today that the dream has become a reality rather than an ideal and a goal. As Xi Jinping said, the Chinese people of yesterday found life "difficult," while the Chinese people of today have "experienced countless changes"; the Chinese people of tomorrow will "ride long winds and cleave

---

7. "Remarks by Minister Wang Yi at the Opening Ceremony of the China Foreign Affairs University," Ministry of Foreign Affairs website, September 2, 2014, http://www.fmprc.gov.cn/web/ziliao_674904/zyjh_674906/t1187515.shtml.

the waves." Now, the goal of the great rejuvenation of the Chinese nation is closer than at any time in history, and looks certain to be achieved.[8]

The "Chinese Dream" is the dream of the Chinese nation and its people. As repeatedly emphasized by Xi Jinping, "The people's yearning for a better life is our goal." Today, China has deeply integrated itself into the global system. While its rapid development benefits from the prosperity and development of the rest of the world, its development also provides unprecedented opportunities and broad space for common development for all countries. Therefore, it must establish a global vision, unify domestic development by opening to the outside world, link its development with global development, and combine the interests of its people with the common interests of the people of all countries, so that the "Chinese Dream" can be linked to global aspirations.

China is now a major global power, and it is getting close to the center of the world stage. New trends bring about new tasks. This means that China cannot be satisfied with developing alone, but must also offer benefits to the rest of the world. It must achieve its own goals through win-win cooperation with other countries. In this regard, Xi Jinping emphasized: "We will steadfastly follow the path of peaceful development and pursue a mutually beneficial and win-win strategy of opening up, which is committed to China's development and its responsibilities and contributions to the world, and benefits everyone. The realization of the 'Chinese Dream' brings peace to the world, not turmoil, and it is an opportunity, not a threat."[9] The "Chinese Dream" is not only China's goal of achieving national prosperity, rejuvenation, and happiness, but also a global dream of peace, development, cooperation, and win-win. Realizing a community with a shared future for humanity is also an important part of the "Chinese Dream."

3.2 China's plans for a new world order

Since the formation of the modern sovereign state system, the realization of international procedures under an anarchic system has been an important diplomatic

---

8. Xi Jinping, "Achieving the Great Rejuvenation of the Chinese Nation is the Greatest Dream of the Chinese Nation in Modern Times," China Communist Party News Network, July 17, 2015, http://cpc.people.com.cn/xuexi/n/2015/0717/c397563-27322292.html.

9. "President Xi Jinping's Joint Written Interview with the Media of the Three Latin American Countries," China Government Network, May 31, 2013, http://www.gov.cn/ldhd/2013-05/31/content_2416330.htm.

task for various countries. Western nations have generally formed four different worlds, namely hegemonic order, balance of power, legal order, and cultural order, centered on the power structure in the international system and the two basic rules, dimensions, institutions, norms, and identity within international society. The hegemonic order perspective is a view of power politics in which the establishment and maintenance of order require sufficient strength to ensure that a super-powerful country provides the world with stability, such as the 19th-century Pax Britannica and the 20th-century Pax Americana. The balance-of-power order concept also involves power politics, arguing that a stable international order can be maintained only when the power structure in the international system is in a state of relative equilibrium to allow states (especially major powers) to achieve mutual checks and balances. The legal order view holds that the rules and institutions in society, or the international legal and quasi-legal system, are the fundamental assurance of international order. The cultural order view focuses on culture, emphasizing order in the social sense, and holding that by constructing an identity for members of the international community, it helps to realize an international culture that is beneficial to others. By forming a certain cultural structure, it can establish true stability. The above concepts of world order are a response from Western countries to the real world, and a guide for development during different historical periods.

With a new series of accelerated changes in the world's configuration, and an intensification of global interdependence, the creation of a new world order has entered a period of activity. Major international forces have proposed their ideas and policies. For example, the United States – which occupies a dominant position in the international system – advocates for the establishment of a liberal international order based on democracy, freedom, and the rule of law under its leadership. The EU advocates for the establishment of an international system based on strong multilateral cooperation and good global governance. Russia advocates for a multipolar world order in which it can play an important role. Developing countries advocate for the establishment of an international order that facilitates their comprehensive and equal participation in international affairs. These world order concepts and propositions are not congruent with each other, profoundly affecting the direction of the world order.

However, the reshaping of the world order is fundamentally affected by changes in the global configuration. Since the beginning of the 21st century, these changes have accelerated. Within the international structure with sovereign states as its core, the speed of international power transfer is accelerating, with the East rising and the West declining. Meanwhile, the rise of multiple non-state actors has decentralized the traditional state-centered world order. Profound changes in the global power structure have brought serious challenges to the world order based on the original power structure. At the same time, economic globalization and social informatization have accelerated. A series of global problems have become increasingly severe, and interdependence has never been stronger. At the same time, no country or actor can deal with global challenges alone, and cooperation becomes inevitable.

Global development illustrates that there is only one Earth for mankind. All countries coexist, and we live in the same "global village." This requires us to build a new world order based on a macro perspective of a community with a shared future for humanity – a global outlook that transcends nation-states and ideologies, expresses China's desire to pursue peaceful development, and reflects its thinking about the future of humanity.[10]

3.3 China's role in a globalized world

Globalization is a growing trend in today's world. The large-scale development of social productive forces and the rapid advancement of science and technology have made economic globalization irreversible. Economic globalization endorses the flow of commodities, capital, personnel, and information technology, offering great convenience to productivity and lifestyles, and promoting exponential growth of global material wealth. However, it also leads to an inequitable distribution of social wealth, a further spread of global crises, deterioration of the ecological environment, and conflicts between cultures, which undermine world peace and development. In particular, after the international financial crisis in 2008, an anti-globalization trend emerged in Western developed countries and regions such as Europe and the United States, bringing a new historical turning point. Where is globalization heading? How will the globalized world be governed? These are key issues facing the world today.

Today, China is the world's second largest economy, largest trader of goods, and largest foreign exchange reserve holder. It is also a permanent member of the UN Security Council, and a nuclear power. Its status and roles are rising in global economic organizations, including the International Monetary Fund (IMF) and the World Bank, and it also occupies a pivotal position in emerging international institutions and international systems, including the Group of Twenty (hereinafter referred to as G20), Shanghai Cooperation Organization, and the BRICS. "Benefiting the world" is a concept of responsibility in traditional Chinese culture. Today, China

---

10. Guo Jiping, "Promising a Better Future for the World – Towards a Community of Shared future for humanity," *People's Daily*, May 18, 2015, 1.

is moving towards the center of the world stage, and has a responsibility to provide more public goods to the international community. Xi Jinping noted, "Let the torch of peace be passed on from generation to generation, let momentum for development continue, and let the light of culture continue shining. This is what the people of all countries expect, and it is also the responsibility of our generation of politicians."[11] Hence, the Chinese concepts of the tide of the times, building a community with a shared future for humanity, and achieving win-win and sharing are solutions to today's global problems, and reflect China's sense of responsibility as a major power.

With the ebb of globalization and the counterattack against anti-globalization, China has assumed the responsibility of a new type of global leader. The Chinese government believes that economic globalization is the historical trend, economic globalization is in the right direction, and the problems of unbalanced development, governance difficulties, digital divides, and fair deficits emerging today are issues arising from economic globalization. China must face the issue and try to solve it, instead of fearing it and not doing anything. These issues also require us to pursue a new kind of globalization. According to Xi Jinping, "The international financial crisis of 2008 reminded us of the need to reinforce coordination and improve governance, and encourage the creation of an open, inclusive, balanced, and win-win economic globalization to steer healthy development. It is even more important to divide the cake well and focus on resolving issues of fairness and justice."[12] As a major world economy, China should and can play a leading role. Xi also stated that "We must follow the road of open development, mutual benefit, and win-win results, and jointly make the world economy bigger" as well as "Support the multilateral trading system, observe the jointly established rules and, through consultation, seek all-win solutions to the common challenges we face."[13]

With the failure of global governance, China has proposed a plan to improve global governance. By building a community with a shared future for humanity, promoting the concept of global governance based on extensive consultations, joint contributions, and shared benefits, and updating the global governance mechanism, China will make the global governance system fairer, more reasonable, and more efficient. Specifically, in global economic governance, China endorses the restructuring

---

11. Xi Jinping, "Building a Community with a Shared Future for Humanity: Speech at the United Nations Headquarters in Geneva," *People's Daily*, January 20, 2017, 2.

12. Ibid.

13. Xi Jinping, "Promoting Openness and Inclusivity to Achieve Interconnected Growth: Statement on the State of the Global Economy at the G20 Hamburg Summit," *People's Daily*, July 8, 2017, 2.

of the share and voting rights of major international economic institutions such as the IMF and the World Bank to make them more illustrative and effective. For global Internet governance, China proposes a plan to build a community with a shared future in cyberspace, following the four principles of respecting cyber sovereignty, maintaining peace and security, promoting openness and cooperation, and building a positive order. For nuclear safety, China has put forward a systematic proposition to cultivate a community with a shared future in the field, building a fair, cooperative, and win-win nuclear safety system. For climate change, China's plan is to create a future of all-round hard work, cooperation for win-win results, upholding the rule of law, fairness and justice, inclusivity and mutual learning, and common development.

The key to building a community with a shared future for humanity lies in action. To create a new development path of win-win cooperation, China has creatively proposed and implemented the BRI. It has reinforced docking and interconnection with the development strategies of relevant countries and regions, realizing the complementary advantages of each country, and narrowing the regional development gap. It has catalyzed the process of regional integration, and has driven Eurasian countries and other relevant regions to achieve common development and prosperity. In the financial field, China has implemented the establishment of new multilateral financial institutions such as the Asian Infrastructure Investment Bank and the BRICS Development Bank. In implementing the United Nations Sustainable Development Agenda while promoting the 2030 Agenda for Sustainable Development, China has consistently increased its investment in South-South cooperation, and has shared its development experience and opportunities with other countries.

China's concept of a community with a shared future for humanity proposed is a new concept to guide its diplomacy, and also a new value proposition for global development – a distinctive feature of a specifically Chinese major-country diplomacy.

Building a community with a shared future for humanity is a long-term and arduous task. However, a journey of a hundred miles starts with a single step. All countries should take the world as their own responsibility and shoulder their domestic and international responsibilities. Through the joint and unremitting efforts of people across the globe, and a partnership based on equality, mutual consultations, and understanding, we will achieve a security pattern of fairness and justice with joint creation and sharing. It will create a development path that is innovative, inclusive, and reciprocal, as well as cultures that live in harmony thanks to healthy exchanges, respecting nature and green development as part of a community with a shared future for humanity.

PART II

New Ideas and Initiatives

A community with a shared future for humanity is one of China's major strategies in the new era, and is an expression of its call for a new world order. However, it does not stop at the level of discourse, but is endorsed through a series of new concepts, measures, and plans for Chinese diplomacy. From the perspective of the current new concepts and measures of Chinese diplomacy, upholding justice while pursuing shared interests and the new Asian security concept are the "wings" of a community with a shared future, while the BRI and the AIIB are the two major levers.

CHAPTER 4

Upholding Justice While Pursuing Shared Interests

IN A GLOBALIZED WORLD, COUNTRIES are increasingly interconnected and interdependent. As global challenges emerge, discussions about the direction of human development have intensified. As a rising power, China's answer to this is to build a community with a shared future for humanity. In the process of building it, how will China handle its relations with the outside world, especially with neighboring countries and developing countries, and what guiding ideology and values will Chinese diplomacy uphold? These issues are related to China's image and development, and whether the great goal of building a community with a shared future for humanity can be achieved. In this context, Xi Jinping has emphasized that in foreign exchanges, China must uphold justice while pursuing shared interests, treat and manage the relationship between "justice" and "interests" appropriately, and emphasize faith, friendship, justice, and morality.[1] Upholding justice while pursuing shared interests shows what kind of concept China will use to communicate with the outside world. It highlights China's image as a responsible major country, and provides important guiding principles for the creation of a community with a shared future for humanity.

---

1. "Xi Jinping Attends Central Conference on Foreign Affairs and Delivers Speech," Xinhuanet, November 29, 2014, http://news.xinhuanet.com/politics/2014-11/29/c_1113457723.htm.

1 Main Features of the Approach

In March 2013, Xi Jinping visited Africa for the first time. During the visit, he proposed the approach of upholding justice while pursuing shared interests, and stressed the need to reinforce cooperation with developing countries. Since then, he has discussed this approach many times on different occasions. "Upholding justice while pursuing shared interests" has since become a frequently used term in Chinese diplomacy, and its implications have been continuously enriched.

Xi Jinping noted that "Justice reflects one of our ideals for communists and communist society. In this world, some lead a good life, while others do not, which is not a positive development. Real happiness is when everyone is happy. We hope that the world will develop together, and particularly that developing countries will speed up their development. 'Interests' means abiding by the principles of mutual benefit and win-win. We are obliged to help poor countries as much as we can, and sometimes even pay more attention to justice than interests, sacrificing our interests for justice."[2] In July 2014, when giving a speech at Seoul National University in South Korea, Xi Jinping noted that "For a state, interests are not to be considered as a gain. Its gain will be found in justice." In international cooperation, China must focus on gains, but even more on justice.[3] When visiting Mongolia in August 2014, Xi stated that "China will cooperate with developing countries, and uphold justice while pursuing shared interests. It will not engage in 'a zero-sum game,' and will look after others' interests through specific projects."[4] At the Central Foreign Affairs Work Conference in November 2014, Xi emphasized the need to uphold justice while pursuing shared interests, manage justice and interests, offer foreign aid, and truly achieve justice and profit.[5]

What Xi Jinping said about justice and interests emphasizes common development and win-win cooperation, combines the two terms, and views the relationship between them from an independent, objective perspective, resolving the issues that separated them in the past. Upholding justice while pursuing shared interests means

---

2. Wang Yi, "Following the Correct View of Justice and Interests, and Playing the Role of a Responsible Power," *People's Daily*, September 10, 2013, 7.

3. "Xi Jinping's Speech at Seoul National University (Full Text)," Xinhuanet, July 4, 2014, http://news.xinhuanet.com/world/2014-07/04/c_1111468087.htm.

4. "Staying Together and Helping Each Other to Jointly Create a New Era of China-Mongolia Relations – Speech at the Great State Hural of Mongolia," *People's Daily Online*, August 23, 2014, http://cpc.people.com.cn/n/2014/0823/c64094-25523548-2.html.

5. "Xi Jinping Attends the Central Conference on Foreign Affairs and Delivers a Speech," Xinhuanet, November 29, 2014, http://news.xinhuanet.com/politics/2014-11/29/c_1113457723.htm.

that in foreign exchanges, China should not only pursue interests at the expense of morality, or undermine the interests of other countries and the common interests of the international community for its own interests. Instead, it should pay more attention to morality in dealing with developing countries to help them develop.

Upholding justice while pursuing shared interests is another achievement of China's diplomatic theoretical innovation in the new era, reflecting the distinctive characteristics of the times, and also carrying great practical significance.

The proposal of upholding justice while pursuing shared interests reflects the profound changes that have taken place in China and the rest of the world. Since the beginning of the 21st century, China's rise has accelerated significantly. The financial crisis in 2008 led Western countries into economic growth challenges, while China continued to maintain a stable development momentum. In 2010, China overtook Japan to become the world's second largest economy, and continues to narrow the gap with the United States. By hosting major events such as the Olympic Games and the World Expo, China's international influence has been continuously enhanced, and its rise has become an indisputable fact. As China rises, the international community gives it more attention, with both expectations and doubts about what role a strong China will play in the world. At the same time, it has also undergone another round of major adjustments and changes after the Cold War, and presents the following notable features. Firstly, the international balance of power has undergone significant changes. The collective rise of emerging market countries has changed the international balance of power. The dominance of Western countries in international affairs has been increasingly questioned and challenged, and the role of developing countries on the international stage has become increasingly prominent. In particular, the call of the international community to restructure the global governance system is getting louder.

Secondly, the power play between major nations and geopolitical competition has become more complicated. The Trump administration has pursued the "America First" policy, pursuing domestic restructuring and employment issues, and showing a certain inward-looking tendency, but it has not given up its dominance over global affairs. Europe's relationships with America and Russia have been strained since the Ukrainian crisis – a tit-for-tat move for the Syrian issue. In the Asia-Pacific region, the United States continued to maintain its alliance system in the region to cope with China's rise, and Sino-US relations still face many challenges.

Thirdly, a series of regional hotspot issues and non-traditional security problems have emerged, such as terrorism, climate change, and transnational crimes. The global economy is still reeling from the impact of the financial crisis, with populism and protectionism on the rise, and unbalanced development becoming increasingly prominent. In the face of these global challenges, no country can remain silent and deal with them alone. In this context, China proposes to uphold justice while pursuing shared interests in its diplomatic work, which shows what values it will uphold in its diplomacy in the new era, its attitude towards participation in international affairs, and the concepts it hopes the international community will use to manage relations among countries.

The proposal of upholding justice while pursuing shared interests is aligned with the demands of the times for the creation of a community with a shared future. Today, society is once again at a crossroads, and where the world is heading is an issue that must be faced. On issues concerning the future and destiny of humanity, China has proposed to build a community with a shared future, providing a Chinese solution for global development and human progress. It is a common cause for all mankind that requires the participation of all parties, and the way to manage the relationship between interests and justice is an unavoidable issue for every country. As a rising power, China's every move attracts attention. The proposal of upholding justice while pursuing shared interests clarifies the value orientation of Chinese diplomacy and shows the concepts it will undertake to participate in the creation of the community. The core value of this proposal is that apart from its own interests, each country should consider its responsibilities to the international community and other nations. During the process, each country should not just pursue its own development, but also consider the concerns of other countries, and contribute to the common development of mankind. It is only then that we can work together to tackle various global challenges and realize the historic goal of building a community with a shared future for humanity. Therefore, upholding justice while pursuing shared interests provides an action guide for Chinese diplomacy in the new era, and also spreads China's values to the world. It provides a new mentality for handling international relations, and injects new impetus into the building of a community with a shared future for humanity.

2 Putting the Approach into Practice in China

The core of following the concept of justice and interests is to properly manage the relationship between justice and interests and to maintain a good balance between them. For China, upholding justice while pursuing shared interests means combining its own interests with the common interests of mankind and its own development with the common development of human society, taking win-win cooperation and common development as the international goal, firmly safeguarding international fairness and justice, and promoting the development of the international order in a more just and reasonable direction. When handling relations with neighboring and developing countries, China must pay more attention to morality and responsibility, share its development opportunities with developing countries, help developing countries improve their development capabilities, and perceive achieving common development with developing countries as the ultimate goal.

2.1 Managing the relationship between justice and interests

The relationship between justice and interests has always been a hot topic in international relations. Justice in this case means morality. In today's world, each country's foreign policy is also governed by a balance between morality and interests. We often say that interests are the highest criterion in guiding a country's behavior, and there is no issue with that. Each country's foreign policy and diplomatic activities are ultimately for the interests of the country. However, regardless of morality and responsibility, countries pursue their own interests excessively, which will inevitably harm the interests of other countries, turning international relations into a zero-sum game with a winner and a loser. This undermines the stability of the international community and leads to conflicts and wars, which can be unbeneficial to the interests of their own countries.

The debate between justice and interests is a classic topic. Individuals and large countries alike will face the choice and trade-off between the two, and their choices reflect their values. For a long time, in the Western realist theory of international relations, national interest has been regarded as the supreme position, and it has become the fundamental law guiding the behavior of the state. In this case, the dispute between justice and interests ends with interests above all, and justice is dispensable. In modern times, Western countries have carried out barbaric colonization and plundering of countries in Asia, Africa, and Latin America, and they have frequently fought for hegemony driven by their interests. The struggle for power and profit has become the norm in international relations. Wars and conflicts have brought endless catastrophes to society. History has proved that the excessive and selfish pursuit of interests rather than justice does not conform to the trend of human historical development and will eventually give rise to hardship. Modern China suffered from colonialism and imperialist aggression, which made its own diplomacy more attuned to justice and interests. While pursuing its own national interests, it also paid attention to justice. Its socialist nature means that it has always supported developing countries while pursuing its own development, and has insisted on aiding Third World countries within its capacity even when it was not rich. Since Reform and Opening-up, the scale, quality, and effectiveness of China's aid to developing countries has been lifted to a new level with the enhancement of its comprehensive national power.[6] In traditional Chinese culture, the answer to the debate on justice and interests has been clear for a long time. People in ancient China emphasized that justice comes first, followed by interests, before the unity between the two.[7] The concept of upholding justice while pursuing shared interests reflects China's views of the history of Western colonialism and the concept of seeking profits, and also inherits and develops its mainstream concept of justice and interests alongside diplomatic traditions.

2.2 Maintaining world peace and stability and international fairness and justice

At present, the pursuit of peace and development is at an all-time high. However, the world is full of risks and challenges. Despite maintaining general peace and stability, local wars and regional conflicts occur from time to time. In the 21st century, some countries still embrace the Cold War mentality, believing in power politics, and continuing to provoke regional conflicts. Tensions have brought many uncertainties to the global situation. With China's rise, some countries have begun to advocate for the so-called "China threat theory," and use it as an excuse to make irresponsible remarks about China's modernized defense and protection of rights by accusing it of trying to challenge and subvert the current international order. Faced with such doubts from the outside world, China has repeatedly expressed its determination to pursue peaceful development to the outside world, emphasizing that it will never follow the old path of hegemony when it becomes strong. In the context of the return to calm in the South China Sea and the desire of regional countries for stability, countries such as the United States, Japan, and Australia continue to fan the flames by invoking South China Sea issue to contain China's energy and curb its further rise. In the face of this external interference, China insists upon the "dual-track approach" on the South China Sea issue, in which disputes should be properly resolved through consultation and negotiation by the countries directly concerned, and peace and stability in the South China Sea region should be jointly maintained by China and

---

6. Wang Yi, "Following the Correct View of Justice and Profits and Playing the Role of a Responsible Power," *People's Daily*, September 10, 2013, 7.

7. Qin Yaqing, "Upholding Justice While Pursuing Shared Interests: Concept Innovation and Practical Principles of Chinese Diplomacy in the New Era," *Seeking Truth*, no. 12 (2014): 55–57.

ASEAN countries.[8] On this issue, China did not bully the weak as a major power. Instead, it has sought solutions to the problem through negotiation and consultation, defending its own core interests and also maintaining regional peace and stability. For this, it has received widespread appreciation from the international community.

In addition, China has made important contributions to fostering global economic prosperity and promoting the restructuring of the international economic governance system. Since the global financial crisis in 2008, the world economy has been sluggish for a long time, and undercurrents of anti-globalization and populism are surging. Some countries have adopted trade protectionist measures to safeguard their economic interests. The free trade system, which once brought economic prosperity, has been challenged. When facing both new and existing challenges in the world economy, China has made important contributions to global economic growth through its development, insisting on following the right development direction of globalization, and opposing any trade protectionist measures. As an archetype of an emerging market country and developing nation, China has been calling for the restructuring of the current international economic governance system, enhancing the representation and voice of emerging market countries in the International Monetary Fund and the World Bank, and promoting the development of the international economic governance system in a fairer and more reasonable direction. This is part of its pursuit of justice. The aim is that the international governance system can be more democratic and open, and that developing countries can participate more fully in international affairs and benefit from it.

2.3 Continuing to improve the moral appeal and influence of Chinese diplomacy

After over 30 years of Reform and Opening-up, China has become the world's second largest economy, and its comprehensive national strength and international influence have been greatly improved. The rest of the world is worried that a strong China will no longer abide by international rules and do whatever it wants to pursue its own interests. It should be noted that many countries have such doubts, and most ideas such as the "China threat theory" that have emerged in recent years are related to this. Upholding justice while pursuing shared interests shows the principles that China will use to manage its foreign relations, the diplomatic concept that a strong China will pursue, and its response to the smearing and slandering of some Western

---

8. "China's First Proposed 'Dual-track Approach' to Managing the South China Sea issue Is of Great Significance, Phoenix.com, August 13, 2014, http://news.ifeng.com/a/20140813/41560447_0.shtml.

countries. Since the founding of the People's Republic of China, it has paid attention to safeguarding its national interests in its foreign exchanges, and has offered foreign aid and assumed corresponding international responsibilities. In the early days of the founding of the PRC, when it was still in a very challenging position, China provided a large amount of assistance to developing countries in Asia and Africa within its capacity, which reflects its early policy on foreign exchange and value orientation. With its increasing comprehensive national strength after the Reform and Opening-up, China has not forgotten its old friends and poor brothers, but has continued to support these developing countries. The scale and quality of China's foreign aid have greatly improved.

For example, shortly after the PRC was founded, it began to provide aid to African countries, supporting their national liberation movements, helping them build their states, and aiding in the creation of major projects including the Tanzania-Zambia Railway. At that time, political capacity took precedence over economic function, and economic benefits were not often considered. After China's Reform and Opening-up, the scale and quality of its aid to Africa significantly improved, and its aid policy stopped focusing on politics over economy, moving towards a balance between politics and economy, which was more pragmatic. Since the start of the 21st century, China's aid to Africa has increased significantly. Through the Forum on China-Africa Cooperation, a relatively complete working organization and mechanisms have been formed.[9] Since the 18th National Congress of the Communist Party of China, the new leaders have attached great importance to relations with African countries, and have reinforced assistance to Africa. In March 2013, President Xi Jinping made his first visit to Africa after taking office, and promised "sincerity, real results, friendship, and good faith." In December 2015, Xi visited Africa again, emphasizing that China and Africa have always been a community with a shared future and that China will reinforce the "Five Pillars" to ensure the smooth implementation of the "Ten Cooperation Plans" between China and Africa. Within Sino-African relations, the greatest "justice" is for China to leverage its development to boost Africa's, and to achieve mutual benefit and common development by upholding justice while pursuing shared interests.[10] Since 2000, China has helped Africa build more than 120 educational facilities, and nearly 40 farmland water conservancy projects. It has helped build and renovate more than 70 medical and health facilities, provided about 3,800 people with artemisinin-based

---

9. Shu Yunguo, "China's Aid to Africa: History, Theory and Characteristics," *Journal of Shanghai Normal University* (Philosophy and Social Sciences Edition), no. 5 (2010), 83–89.

10. "Ushering in a New Era of Win-Win Cooperation and Common Development between China and Africa," Xinhuanet, December 5, 2015, http://news.xinhuanet.com/world/2015-12/05/c_1117367109.htm.

anti-malarial drugs, and dispatched 7,000 medical personnel and 2,000 agricultural specialists. It has trained more than 80,000 personnel of various types in Beijing for more than 50 African countries and regional organizations, and has dispatched around 500 volunteers to 16 African countries.[11] Compared with Western countries that use human rights and democratization as additional conditions for aid, China does not attach political conditions to its aid to Africa. It aims only to help African countries improve their development capabilities so that they can achieve tangible benefits, which is widely appreciated.

3 An Emblem of Chinese Diplomacy in the New Era

Upholding justice while pursuing shared interests continues the fine tradition of Chinese diplomacy. It embodies the value pursuit of a socialist country, and has become a banner for Chinese diplomacy in the new era. It reflects the responsibility of Chinese diplomacy, portraying the image of China as a responsible major country to the outside world, and dispelling the rest of the world's doubts about what path China will take. Upholding justice while pursuing shared interests objectively analyzes the relationship between justice and interests in foreign exchanges, and reflects the new thinking of Chinese diplomacy in the new era. It also enriches and develops its own theoretical system of major-country diplomacy. Starting from the idea that mankind has become a community with a shared future, it emphasizes the importance of mutual benefit and the overall interests of mankind, and believes that this will lead the development of the international community by providing valuable guidance and moral support for building a community with a shared future for humanity.[12]

3.1 Providing guiding principles for handling relations with developing countries

Upholding justice while pursuing shared interests reflects the value pursuit of Chinese diplomacy, and provides a guiding principle for how to handle relations with developing countries. In China's diplomatic layout, it emphasizes developing countries as the fundamentals. Strengthening traditional friendships with developing countries is an important task within Chinese diplomacy. Against the background

---

11. "China Will Gradually Increase the Scale of Aid to Africa," Xinhuanet, July 26, 2016, http://news.xinhuanet.com/2016-07/26/c_129180437.htm.

12. Wang Zeying, "The Profound Implication, Value Function and Strategic Significance of the Accurate View of Justice and Interests," *Quest*, no. 11 (2014): 27.

of increasing national strength, how can China handle its relations with developing countries more effectively? When interests and justice are not congruent, how should China choose? Regarding these issues, President Xi Jinping proposed that diplomatic work involves upholding justice while pursuing shared interests in politics, achieving mutual benefit and common development in the economy, and avoiding costly "beggar-thy-neighbor" policies. A major socialist country, China does not have the hegemony in its DNA of a strong country that bullies the weak. It will continue to uphold international fairness and justice, and will safeguard the interests of developing countries. As a representative of developing countries, China will continue to work with them to oppose hegemonism and power politics. It will support the democratization of international relations, and help developing countries play a greater role in international affairs. As the world's second largest economy, China will continue to uphold the concept of mutual benefit and common development, promoting the restructuring of the global economic governance system, and making greater contributions to the sustainable and healthy development of the world economy. In managing foreign relations, it is necessary to properly handle the relationship between interests and justice so as to balance them, and help poor countries as much as possible.

Since the 18th National Congress of the Communist Party of China, China has embraced the ideals of "friendship, sincerity, mutual benefit, and inclusiveness" in its neighborhood diplomacy, and has proposed the BRI to integrate with its neighbors and jointly build a community with a shared future. In Africa, Xi Jinping noted that China and Africa have always been a community with a shared future, and common historical experiences and struggles have allowed the Chinese and African peoples to forge a profound friendship.[13] These actions and practices are the concrete results of China's practice of upholding justice while pursuing shared interests.

3.2 Exemplifying China's image as a responsible major country

Upholding justice while pursuing shared interests highlights the idea of justice, and portrays China as a responsible major country. Nearly 40 years of Reform and Opening-up have transformed China from a poor and weak country into the world's second largest economy. Faced with China's rise, Western countries (led by the United States) began accusing China of "free-riding," believing that it would

---

13. "Xi Jinping: China and Africa Have Long Forged a Community with a Shared Future," Xinhuanet, December 4, 2015, http://news.xinhuanet.com/world/2015-12/04/c_1117361280.htm.

only enjoy the benefits of Western public goods without taking the corresponding responsibilities. They believe that since China is already strong, it should fulfill more responsibilities and undertake more international obligations. On climate change, some countries ignore China's needs as a developing country, and blatantly ask it to take more responsibility, which is irresponsible behavior. On the North Korean nuclear issue, countries such as Japan and the US have exaggerated China's influence over North Korea, requiring China to exert greater pressure on it and play a bigger role in stopping its nuclear and missile development. In fact, China has been participating in both the climate change issue and the DPRK nuclear issue, seeking solutions to the problems with other countries. On global climate governance, China sticks to its commitments by supporting developing countries and emphasizing common but differentiated responsibilities, which in itself is the best interpretation of upholding justice while pursuing shared interests, and is a manifestation of China's fulfillment of international responsibilities. On the nuclear issue, as a permanent member of the United Nations, China has always strictly abided by and implemented the sanctions and resolutions of the UN Security Council, and took a series of actions to ease regional tensions, not only for its own interests, but also for regional peace and stability. As proven by the "China threat theory," "China free rider theory," and "China responsibility theory," Western countries have always viewed China from a narrow perspective by seeing it as a threat or asking it to do more. While the form is changing, the essence of how Western countries view China from a prejudiced viewpoint has not changed.

China has always been an active participant in global affairs, and has happily assumed its international responsibilities, fulfilling international obligations, and making important contributions to maintaining regional and global peace and stability, as well as economic prosperity and development. Hence, the talk of China being a "free rider" does not hold truth. In recent years, China has been the most important engine for world economic growth, making substantial contributions to the global economy in its recovery from crisis. China can be seen participating in UN peacekeeping efforts, working on the front line in the fight against the Ebola virus in Africa, and negotiating on Iranian nuclear and Afghan issues. Fulfilling its international responsibilities and providing public goods for the international community is China's best practice in upholding justice while pursuing shared interests, and reflects its image as a responsible major country. At the same time, it strongly refutes unreasonable accusations of irresponsibility and "free-riding" by Western countries.

3.3 Guiding the direction for the creation of a community with a shared future

As a value concept, the most important part of upholding justice while pursuing shared interests lies in its guiding actions. In the process of building a community with a shared future for humanity, if each country only pursues its own interests and abandons the pursuit of justice and responsibility, the world will remain in a cycle of wars and conflicts, and the goal of building a community with a shared future will never be achieved. A community with a shared future emphasizes the integrity of human interests and the relevance of the interests of all countries. It requires that all countries uphold justice while pursuing shared interests in their interactions, and properly handle the relationship between their own interests and the interests of other countries and mankind as a whole, being more conscious and undertaking greater responsibilities. As President Xi Jinping said, to uphold justice while pursuing shared interests, we must emphasize faith, empathy, justice, and morality.

To maintain honor, it is imperative to keep promises. As members of the international community, all countries should take actions and undertake their obligations while responding to global challenges. For example, although countries have different capabilities to combat climate change, they can contribute to energy conservation and emission reduction and fulfill their respective obligations instead of evading their responsibilities and abandoning their previous commitments. Emphasizing friendship means paying more attention to it when dealing with developing countries, and focusing on their demands and concerns. Unbalanced global development has become a problem that cannot be ignored. The wealth of the world's richest 1% exceeds the sum of the wealth of the remaining 99%. While developed countries have entered the post-industrial era, many developing countries are still in the initial stage of industrialization, and many challenges remain for funding and technology. Therefore, developed countries should extend a helping hand to support them. They must not care only about their own happiness and watch others live in poverty. Otherwise, the goal of a community with a shared future for humanity will never be realized. As a developing country itself, China provided foreign aid worth more than 400 billion yuan between 1950 and 2016, most of which was to developing countries, reflecting its emphasis on friendship. To encourage justice and establish shared interests is to safeguard international fairness and justice, and oppose hegemonism and power politics. At present, the most important thing is to oppose the monopoly of international affairs by major powers while ignoring the voices of small and medium-sized countries, opposing interference in the internal affairs of other countries, and promoting a fairer and more reasonable global governance mechanism.

Upholding justice while pursuing shared interests is an important achievement within China's innovations in diplomatic theory. It answers to the new changes in the international situation and the objective needs of China's new diplomatic tasks, and further enriches the core values of Chinese diplomacy. By doing so, it responds to the profound changes in the international pattern and the increasingly close ties between countries. For example, how does China perceive its relationship with the rest of the world? In what capacity will China participate in global affairs? What ideas and concepts will China adopt, and how will it conduct diplomatic activities? As an important part of the theoretical system of a major country with Chinese characteristics, the idea of justice and interests is deep and far-reaching. It reflects the new central leadership's strategic plan for China's future international status and role, and clears the doubts and accusations leveled against it. It also has important guiding significance for Chinese diplomacy in the new era, which will have a profound impact on human progress and development.

CHAPTER 5

A New Asian Security Concept

At the 4th Conference on Interaction and Confidence-Building Measures in Asia (CICA) in May 2014, President Xi Jinping proposed a new Asian security concept, namely "common, comprehensive, cooperation, and sustainable," which attracted a lot of attention from the international community. How do we understand the implication of the new Asian security concept? Why is China proposing such a thing right now? What would be its impact? Around the above-mentioned issues, heated discussions have been launched in China. The new Asian security concept is the nation's systematic view of Asian security issues in the new situation – a new concept and way of thinking designed to encourage security cooperation in Asia. Unlike the traditional security concept, it emphasizes security that is common, comprehensive, cooperative, and sustainable, which is of significance for promoting regional peace and stability, and building a community with a shared future for Asia and the whole of humanity.[1]

1 Main Features of the Concept

The new Asian security concept is comprehensive. Common, comprehensive, cooperative, and sustainable forms of security are interrelated and inseparable. At

---

1. "Xi Jinping's Speech at the 4th Conference on Interaction and Confidence-Building Measures in Asia (Full Text)," Xinhuanet, May 21, 2014, http://news.xinhuanet.com/world/2014-05/21/c_1110796357.htm.

the 4th CICA summit held in May 2014, President Xi Jinping described the main elements of the new Asian security concept, namely that it is common, i.e., respecting and ensuring the security of every country; comprehensive, i.e., coordinating and maintaining the security of traditional and non-traditional fields; cooperative, i.e., promoting national and regional security through dialogue and cooperation; and sustainable, i.e., paying equal attention to development and security to achieve lasting security.

1.1 Common security

There are many Asian countries, and they have huge internal differences, as well as complex and diverse security situations. Also, the security interests and demands of individual countries are diverse, and may even conflict with each other. In the context of globalization, countries are increasingly connected and interdependent. It is impossible for any country to deal with complex and diverse security situations alone, nor can it shut itself away. In frequent exchanges and interactions, countries are increasingly becoming a community with a shared future where interests, safety, and security are interlinked. Therefore, maintaining Asia's security and stability is in the interests of every country. This is the greatest common denominator of Asian countries, and it is also the basis for countries in the region to engage in cooperation regarding security.

For common security, we must first recognize the universality of security. We must drop the zero-sum mindset, and establish an awareness of a security community. At present, some Asian countries still embrace the Cold War mentality, upholding the zero-sum mentality, and disregarding the concerns of other countries to safeguard their own interests when it comes to security. The US and South Korea's insistence on deploying the THAAD anti-missile system is a concrete manifestation of this narrow security concept. The two nations used the North Korean threat as an excuse to forcefully deploy THAAD, undermining the regional strategic balance – a classic example of disregard for regional security and stability.

Common security means that security should be equal. The security and stability of Asia are related to the personal interests of every Asian country, and require their participation. All countries – big or small, rich or poor, strong or weak – have equal rights to participate in regional affairs. Gone are the days when small states were passively subordinated to regional security matters. Therefore, we must establish the concept of equal security cooperation, not allow a single voice to dominate or "power clubs" to flourish, and support the establishment of an open regional security cooperation structure, so that every country can have its own voice and express its security requirements.

Shared security also means that security should be inclusive. The diversity and differences among Asian countries are a reality that security cooperation must consider. We should not try to cover up diversity and differences, let alone give up security cooperation on this basis. Instead, we should work on reaching a broad consensus from all parties. The concept of inclusive security cooperation requires that we do not exclude any country, but that all nations in the region work together to achieve common security. The exclusive security pursued by military alliances and the "absolute security" pursued at the expense of other countries is a concrete illustration of the violation of the inclusive principle.

1.2 Comprehensive security

The security situation in Asia is extremely complex. In the traditional security field, the actions of major powers and geopolitical conflicts have always impacted regional stability. The ethnic and religious conflicts within the region are complicated, and there is always the risk of clashes, such as the North Korean nuclear crisis and the South China Sea dispute. Regional hotspot issues such as the conflict between India and Pakistan have added new uncertainties to regional security and stability. Traditional security issues with military security as the core are the top priorities of all countries and the focus of various security dialogues and cooperation mechanisms. At the same time, non-traditional security challenges such as terrorism, transnational crime, environmental security, network security, energy and resource security, and major natural disasters have become increasingly prominent, and the security pressure faced by countries has increased significantly. Faced with the challenges of non-traditional and traditional security, China has proposed the concept of comprehensive security, emphasizing the need to coordinate security in these areas. This highlights the fact that China's security concept works in the context of globalization, and pays attention to the diversity, transnationality, and linkage of security threats. It also emphasizes the importance of jointly responding to non-traditional security threats, and advocates comprehensive consideration of Asian security issues in social, cultural, religious, economic, and political aspects to comprehensively implement policies, devise overall plans, and coordinate the promotion of regional security governance.[2]

---

2. Cheng Guoping, "Asian Security Concept: Leading the New Direction of Asian Security Cooperation," *Qiushi*, no. 14 (2014): 57–59.

1.3 Cooperative security

There are only two ways to solve security problems. One is to seek security through force and war, and the other is to solve problems through dialogue and consultation and achieve security through win-win cooperation. War and peace or conflict and cooperation are two fundamental issues in international relations. Previously, resorting to war was a common way to solve security problems. However, history has repeatedly proved that war cannot solve security problems, and will instead create more security risks. Cooperative security requires people to look at security issues with an open and equitable mind, and not to monopolize regional security affairs, but to allow all members of the region to participate in the discussion around security affairs, brainstorm, and jointly deal with security challenges. It requires us to abandon the zero-sum game and Cold War mentality, avoid engaging in military confrontation and group security, and establish a new mindset of win-win cooperation, regarding dialogue and cooperation as the only way to solve problems, increasing mutual political trust through dialogue, and promoting problem resolution through cooperation.

1.4 Sustainable security

Development is the basis of security, and security issues do not exist in isolation. Many security issues are caused by a low level of development and a large wealth gap. At present, more than 700 million people in Asia live below the global poverty line. In some countries, livelihoods have not improved for a long time, and the wealth gap has been widening, resulting in intensified social conflicts and never-ending national turmoil, which in turn has provided breeding grounds for terrorism and extremism. Concurrently, the development levels of Asian countries are very unbalanced. Only through the promotion of common development can we eliminate weak links in regional security and effectively deal with the spill-over and proliferation of security threats. Non-traditional security issues in Asia are becoming increasingly prominent. Countries need to intensify regional cooperation and support, and assist relevant countries to solve development problems and improve the region's aggregate development and security levels. Therefore, many security issues in Asia can only be nipped in the bud through development.[3] Security is a criterion for development, and economic development is similarly inseparable from a secure and stable external

---

3. Zhong Sheng, "Development Is the 'Master Key,'" *People's Daily*, May 28, 2014, 3.

environment. The greater the economic development, the closer the economic ties between countries, and the higher the security requirements. For example, with the development of international trade, energy transportation and trade in goods will become increasingly dependent on sea lanes, and the safety of sea lanes will receive greater attention from all parties. The Chinese navy works with navies in Somalia on escort operations to make sure passing ships are not disturbed by pirates and to ensure the safety of sea lanes. Similarly, with the continuous advancement of the BRI (BRI), China must ensure the robustness of its security precautions because many countries along the BRI are facing the threat of terrorist activities. Hence, ensuring the safety of personnel, traffic routes, and normal economic activities are areas that China should consider.

2 An Inevitable Product of the Current Security Situation in Asia

The proposal of the new Asian security concept has a complex setting. When the Cold War ended, the overall security situation in Asia began to ease, and countries in the region started to make full use of the peaceful and stable external environment to develop their economies, creating a miraculous Asian economic rise. Today, Asia is the most dynamic and promising region in the world. Against the backdrop of economic globalization and regional integration, Asian countries have engaged in economic cooperation, established economic dialogue and cooperation mechanisms, and intensified ties with one another. However, while economic collaboration has advanced, cooperation in the security field has been lagging for a long time. There is still a long way to go to establish an inclusive and efficient structure for regional security cooperation. In reality, volatile factors affecting Asian security remain. Traditional and non-traditional security issues overlap, regional conflicts and hotspot issues are emerging, and security risks have become the greatest challenge to regional peace and development.

2.1 The security situation in Asia remains serious

Asia is a vast area with many countries, each with different geographical conditions, cultural traditions, social systems, and development methods. Territorial disputes and ethnic and religious conflicts within the region are highly complex, and foreign powers frequently interfere in Asian affairs to compete for influence within, which has adversely affected the peace and stability of the region. Overall, the security challenges in Asia consist of the following:

Firstly, the greatest impact on Asia's security situation has been the divisions caused by strategic competition among major powers. Asia's important position means that major powers want to participate in its security affairs to maintain their influence in the region. As part of the Obama administration's efforts to maintain its dominance in the Asia-Pacific region, the US shifted its strategic focus to the Asia-Pacific region by announcing that 60% of its military force would be invested in the region, consolidating and reinforcing its relations with regional allies such as Japan, South Korea, and Australia, and intensifying military cooperation with countries such as India, Vietnam, and Singapore, as well as seeking to multilateralize bilateral alliances and expand the influence of US military alliances. After Donald Trump took office, he changed his critical attitude towards allies such as Japan and South Korea during the campaign period, and successively dispatched key cabinet officials to appease Asian allies, reiterating their commitment to security. With the acquiescence and support of the United States, Japan's Abe government has consistently challenged the pacifist constitution, moving further down the road of militarization and Rightism, and severely damaging its mutual trust with China on the Diaoyu Islands and historical issues, resulting in continuing tension between the two countries. Needless to say, one important purpose of the United States increasing its attention and investment in the Asia-Pacific region is to contain China's rise and maintain its influence in the region. By doing so, it has seriously damaged its mutual political trust with China, resulting in Asia-Pacific countries having to choose sides, and negatively impacting regional security cooperation.

Secondly, as regional hotspot issues escalate, the risk of confrontation and conflict increases. Although the Cold War ended more than 30 years ago, the Korean Peninsula issue – one of its legacies – is still a key factor affecting peace in Northeast Asia. In recent years, North Korea has intensified its research and development of nuclear weapons and ballistic missiles. Since 2006, it has conducted several nuclear tests, significantly improving its nuclear strike capability. Frequent missile test launches have also made North Korea's ballistic missile technology more mature. In response, the United States has increased sanctions and military pressure on the DPRK. This tit-for-tat confrontation is likely to lead to mishaps. The DPRK nuclear issue has become one of the most pressing security risks in Asia.

Recently, the dispute between China and Japan over the Diaoyu Islands and the situation in the South China Sea have been relatively relaxed. However, with the lack of mutual political trust between China and Japan and the intensification of strategic competition, the Diaoyu Islands is still the biggest source of instability between the two countries, and the confrontation between them is likely to escalate.

After Duterte came to power, China and the Philippines reached a consensus on maintaining peace and stability in the South China Sea, cooling the dispute, dispelling the United States, and rejecting Japan's attempt to use the South China Sea issue to disrupt China. However, when disputes and differences persist, the South China Sea issue can easily become an excuse for other countries to provoke China. There is still a long way to go before peace and stability can truly be achieved in the South China Sea. In South Asia, India and Pakistan – two nuclear-armed countries – have been at odds for a long time, and conflicts have erupted from time to time over issues such as Kashmir. In the Middle East, the Israeli-Palestinian issue has never been resolved. The Syrian conflict and the Yemeni civil war have plunged the Middle East into a quagmire of conflict and war. In Central Asia, although the Afghan war has ended, stability in Afghanistan is still hard to come by, and reconciliation remains a distant dream. The security issues in Asia are more complex than on any other continent. No issue can be solved in a short time, and there is a possibility that it will intensify at any time.

Thirdly, non-traditional security issues such as terrorism, transnational crime, cyber security, maritime security, and natural disasters are becoming increasingly prominent. In Asia, these issues have also become an important element of security cooperation. Terrorism has long been a global nuisance, and Asian countries are no exception. Counter-terrorism and the maintenance of stability are issues of consensus for countries in the region. Southern and Western Asia are the hardest hit areas for terrorist activities. Concurrently, terrorist activities in Southeast Asia remain unabated, and the potential still exists in Central Asia.[4] The withdrawal of US troops from Iraq in 2011 and the Syrian civil war gave "Islamic State" – an extremist terrorist organization – the opportunity to develop and grow, resulting in a large number of casualties. In South Asia, India, Pakistan, and Afghanistan suffered the worst of the terrorist attacks, and terrorism has become the biggest security risk to regional stability and development. In Southeast Asia, the Abu Sayyaf insurgent group has become entrenched in the southern Philippines, and frequently conducts bombings and large-scale kidnappings. Countries such as Indonesia are also constantly plagued by terrorist activities instigated by "Islamic State." The anti-terrorism situation in Southeast Asia remains grim. In addition, issues such as transnational crime and network security are attracted more attention, and the diversification and complexity of security threats are becoming more apparent. Transnational crimes and drug

---

4. "Li Wei's Interpretation of the Development Status and Trends of International Terrorism," *China Review Network*, May 30, 2015, http://www.crntt.com/doc/1037/7/2/8/103772815.html.

smuggling mostly occur in border areas, making it difficult for a single country to deal with them alone. This also allows criminals to take advantage of the situation, which poses a great threat to the peace and stability of border areas. After the Snowden incident, countries began paying attention to network security. According to Xi Jinping, "The development of the Internet has raised new challenges to national sovereignty, security, and development interests"[5] and "Without cybersecurity, there can be no national security."[6] Jointly maintaining cybersecurity is also important – a new issue for Asian countries.

2.2 Asia lags behind in security cooperation

Asia has become one of the three major economic sectors alongside Europe and North America. The economic ties between countries are becoming closer, and the level of cooperation is improving. However, correspondingly, political and security cooperation in Asia has not kept pace with economic cooperation for a long time. Some intra-regional geopolitical conflicts and hotspot issues have not been effectively managed and controlled, and security cooperation has become a weak point in Asia. Since the Cold War, various security dialogues and cooperation mechanisms have been established by countries in the Asian region. At present, there are five main security mechanisms in the Asia-Pacific region. The first is the alliance system led by the United States and its bilateral and multilateral arrangements. The second is ASEAN-centered security dialogues and cooperation mechanisms such as the ASEAN Regional Forum and the ASEAN Defense Ministers' Meeting. The third is the Six-Party Talks and the Quartet on Afghanistan aimed at solving specific hotspot issues. The fourth is cross-regional security cooperation mechanisms such as the Shanghai Cooperation Organization and the CICA. The fifth is "Track 1.5" or "Track 2" security dialogue platforms represented by the Shangri-La Dialogue, Xiang Shan Forum, and Asia-Pacific Roundtable.[7]

The United States alliance system is characterized by exclusivity and military security orientation aimed at maintaining its dominance in the Asia-Pacific region

---

5. "Xi Jinping's Congratulatory Message to the First World Internet Conference," Xinhuanet, November 19, 2014, http://news.xinhuanet.com/world/2014-11/19/c_1113319278.htm.

6. "Xi Jinping: Building China from a Cyber Power to a Cyber Power," Xinhuanet, February 27, 2014, http://news.xinhuanet.com/politics/2014-02/27/c_119538788.htm.

7. Liu Zhenmin, "Practicing the Asian Security Concept and Creating a New Future of Asia-Pacific Security," Ministry of Foreign Affairs website, July 12, 2016, http://www.fmprc.gov.cn/web/wjb_673085/zygy_673101/liuzhenmin_673143/xgxw_673145/t1379368.shtml.

and the interests of its allies. The various security dialogues and cooperation mechanisms led by ASEAN are relatively loose, and the countries' focus on dialogue and exchanges makes it difficult to reach a binding agreement. Various "Track 1.5" and "Track 2" security dialogue platforms are facing the problem of decoupling from policy making, and their influence is still limited. The dilemma of Asian security cooperation is not the result of a lack of mechanisms and platforms, but rather the lack of an inclusive and efficient regional security cooperation structure.

2.3 The need to build a community with a shared future in Asia

Security cooperation is an important element of building a community with a shared future in Asia and the basis for other cooperations. Since the 18th National Congress of the Communist Party of China, President Xi Jinping has repeatedly emphasized the establishment of a sense of community with a shared future for humanity on a series of important bilateral and multilateral occasions, indicating that China is willing to work with other countries to encourage world peace, stability, prosperity, and progress. Thus, "building a community with a shared future for humanity" has become a frequently used term in Chinese diplomacy, and has also been listed as one of the main goals of major-country diplomacy with Chinese characteristics.[8] As an Asian country, China knows that its destiny is closely linked with that of other Asian countries. In the face of complex changes in the international situation, China is willing to work with other Asian countries to jointly maintain the overall prosperity and stability of the region and to build an Asian community with a shared future.[9] Currently, the economic ties between Asian countries are intensifying, alongside the level of economic cooperation. However, security cooperation in Asia has still been lagging behind for a prolonged period. The lag and inefficiency of security cooperation have led to an inability to effectively solve regional security issues, and have affected the process of regional integration. Economy and security are two important components of building a community with a shared future. Economic cooperation is not highly sensitive and has obvious mutual benefits. Also, since it is relatively easy for all parties to accept, it can be implemented quickly. However, due to its complexity and sensitivity, the cooperation of Asian countries in the security

---

8. Party Committee of the Ministry of Foreign Affairs, "The Theory and Practice of Major-power Diplomacy with Chinese Characteristics since the 18th National Congress of the Communist Party of China," *Seeking Truth*, no. 6 (2016): 20–22.

9. Liu Zhenmin, "Insist on Win-Win Cooperation and Join Hands to Build a Community with a Shared Future in Asia," *International Studies*, no. 2 (2014): 1–10.

field is relatively slow and lagging behind, which restricts the further advancement of economic cooperation. Security is the foundation of cooperation. Without a secure and stable environment, it is impossible to build an Asian community with a shared future. As Asia is still facing many security challenges, China advocates for a new Asian security concept that is common, comprehensive, cooperative, and sustainable, and has proposed new concepts and ideas for security cooperation in Asia. It is of great significance for Asian countries to jointly address various security challenges and strive to build a peaceful and stable Asia.

3 A New Impetus for Building a Community with a Shared Future in Asia

The new Asian security concept is proposed in the face of an increasingly complex security situation in the region. It is aligned with the push for peace, development, cooperation, and win-win in Asia. It transcends the traditional "micro" security thinking, which shows the world the type of security concept China will use to encourage security cooperation in Asia and enhances the outside world's awareness and understanding of its peaceful development path. The new Asian security concept has important significance for the construction of the Asian security community, and also adds new impetus to the construction of an Asian community with a shared future.

3.1 Conforming to the push for peace, development, cooperation, and win-win in Asia

Since the Cold War, Asia has maintained peace and stability without large-scale wars and conflicts, creating a favorable external environment for countries to develop their economies. Leveraging this situation, Asian countries have tapped into their potential for economic growth. They have participated in the process of economic globalization, created a miracle of Asian economic growth, and achieved sustained economic development and continuous improvement of living standards. At present, Asia accounts for one-third of the world's total economic output, and has become one of the most dynamic and promising regions in the world. Its voice and influence in world economic affairs have been significantly improved. Concurrently, in the context of economic globalization and regional integration, Asian countries are increasingly interconnected and interdependent. Various regional cooperation mechanisms have been established, and cooperation in important areas such as the creation of free trade zones and interconnections has continued to develop. The concept of a community with a shared future in Asia has been recognized by even more countries.[10] The push for peace, development, cooperation, and win-win is reflected in Asia. However, Asia's peaceful and stable development environment is constantly being undermined by emerging security challenges. The question of whether it can continue its momentum has become a talking point for the international community. In the face of an increasingly severe security situation, Asian countries must prioritize it, join hands to deal with it, and jointly safeguard the overall environment of peace and stability in Asia. China's new concept of common, comprehensive, cooperative, and sustainable security in Asia has opened up broad prospects for security cooperation in the Asia-Pacific region, which fulfill common aspirations of countries in the region to promote peace, stability and development, as well as the tide of time for peace, development, cooperation, and win-win results.

3.2 Providing new concepts and ideas for Asian security cooperation

At present, although there are various security dialogues and cooperation mechanisms in Asia, the security issue has not been effectively resolved. It is a case of many hands managing a single matter. The Asia-Pacific alliance system dominated by the United States is exclusive and targeted, with clear traces of the Cold War and a zero-sum mentality. It cannot effectively solve Asian security issues, and has become a tool for the United States to exert influence in the region, resulting in even more security issues. The various security dialogues and cooperation mechanisms led by ASEAN have become platforms for countries to declare their policies. Although mutual understanding has been enhanced, it is difficult to play a practical role in solving specific problems. On the Korean Peninsula issue, the Six-Party Talks have stalled, and it is hard to imagine a breakthrough in the North Korean nuclear crisis. While the Quartet mechanism on the Afghanistan issue has played an important role in promoting the reconciliation process there, its effectiveness at resolving the turbulence remains unknown. The SCO member states have achieved remarkable results in counter-terrorism cooperation and combating the "three evil forces," but their influence is limited to the sub-regional scope of Central Asia.

The reason for the problems above is that Asian countries have failed in terms of the security concept. It was agreed that although countries such as Japan and the US have entered the 21st century, their mindsets remain in the former era of Cold

---

10. Liu Zhenmin, "Asian Security and China's Responsibility," *International Studies*, no. 1 (2014): 24.

War mentality and zero-sum games. They are constantly stirring and creating trouble around China, seriously affecting the peace and tranquility of the region. Although the threat of the Soviet Union has disappeared since the Cold War, the United States has not retired its alliance system. Instead, it has consolidated and intensified it. The main reason is that the United States has not changed its thinking since the Cold War period, and still regards China as a potential threat to American dominance. Hence, it has built an encirclement against China to restrain its rise. This backward security concept has become the fundamental reason for the challenges faced in intensifying Asian security cooperation.

It is against this backdrop that China proposes a new security concept for Asia that is common, comprehensive, cooperative, and sustainable. It abandons confrontational thinking and the old security concept of "you lose and we win," and incorporates both traditional and non-traditional security challenges into the cooperation. It discusses security cooperation plans with all regional members through dialogue and consultation, and coordinates the two major issues of security and development, jointly maintaining regional peace and stability, and truly realizing common security and development.

3.3 Reflecting China's desire and determination to uphold peaceful development

Since Reform and Opening-up, China's economy has continued to develop rapidly, and its comprehensive national strength and influence in regional and international affairs have been consistently enhanced. Against the background of complex and diverse security challenges in Asia and the continuous reinforcement of the US military deployment in the Asia-Pacific region, the type of security policy China will adopt has become the focus of global attention. Some people believe that China will seek to establish a military alliance in the face of pressure from the United States, and Asia will return to the era of Cold War confrontation, while others believe that a strong China will no longer abide by the rules and do whatever it wants on regional security issues. Some countries in which China has territorial disputes are worried that it may resort to force in the future to solve problems. In the face of external doubts, China has repeatedly declared to the outside world that it will never seek regional hegemony and sphere of influence or exclude any country. Instead, a strong China will, as always, follow the path of peaceful development.[11]

---

11. "China's Peaceful Development," State Council Information Office website, September 6, 2011, http://www.scio.gov.cn/zfbps/ndhf/2011/Document/1000032/1000032.htm.

An important Asian nation, China has always been a constructive participant in regional security affairs, and has made important contributions to promoting regional peace and stability. For example, on the Iranian nuclear issue, China has participated in every negotiation. It has played an active role in highlighting the focus and difficulties of the negotiations, and even reached a final comprehensive agreement. Concurrently, China has also contributed to regional security cooperation, offering its knowledge to the building of a community with a shared future in Asia. At the CICA Conference in May 2014, President Xi Jinping proposed a new concept of common, comprehensive, cooperative, and sustainable security in Asia for the first time, and announced that China would embark on a road of joint contribution, shared benefits, and win-win, so as to achieve a win-win situation. "Joint contribution" emphasizes the fact that Asian countries jointly maintain the region's security and stability and participate in the creation of the Asian security community. "Shared benefits" means that every country can enjoy the fruits of security cooperation. "Win-win" is the ultimate goal of the Asian security concept; it is not about one country winning and the other losing. It also emphasizes that every country can benefit from cooperation. The proposal of the new Asian security concept reflects China's attitude of peace, equality, openness, and inclusivity, and demonstrates its desire and determination to adhere to peaceful development, displaying the security concept China will use to encourage security cooperation in Asia.

3.4 Adding new impetus to building a community with a shared future in Asia

Building a community with a shared future is a systematic project that requires Asian countries to make efforts in five aspects, namely partnership, security structure, economic development, cultural exchanges, and ecological construction.[12] Security is the foundation of development and the most fundament requirement for building a community with a shared future in Asia. Among the cooperations in various fields in Asia, security faces the greatest challenges and makes the slowest progress, and has become a shortcoming in the creation of the community. Whether Asian countries can achieve breakthroughs in security cooperation is directly related to whether the goal of an Asian community with a shared future can be achieved. As Xi Jinping has stated, "Towards a community with a shared future, we must adhere to the

---

12. "Xi Jinping's Speech at the General Debate of the 70th United Nations General Assembly (Full Text)," Xinhuanet, September 29, 2015, http://news.xinhuanet.com/world/2015-09/29/c_1116703645.htm.

realization of common, comprehensive, cooperative, and sustainable security."[13] In terms of cooperation, the new Asian security concept goes beyond traditional myopic thinking, emphasizing the integrity, comprehensiveness, collaboration, and sustainability of security. Security in Asia refers to the security of every country in Asia and not just the security of some countries and the insecurity of others. Therefore, we must establish a strong security community as well as a community with a shared future, and we must respect and protect the reasonable security concerns of every country. We must also consider security issues comprehensively, and coordinate the maintenance of security in traditional and non-traditional fields. We must also resolve differences with a cooperative mindset rather than force, pay equal attention to security and development, and encourage sustainable security through sustainable development.[14] The new Asian security concept will certainly enhance the vibrancy of security cooperation in the region, and will play a positive and constructive role in the building of a community with a shared future in Asia.

---

13. "Xi Jinping: Towards a Community with a Shared Future, Creating a New Future for Asia," Xinhuanet, March 28, 2015, http://news.xinhuanet.com/politics/2015-03/28/c_1114794507.htm.

14. Ibid.

CHAPTER 6

The Belt and Road Initiative

At present, the Belt and Road Initiative (BRI) is China's key foreign initiative, and involves five major areas, namely policy coordination, connectivity of facilities, unimpeded trade, financial integration, and people-to-people bonds, all of which have a significant economic, political, geopolitical, and cultural impact. It is crucial to the enhancement of China's strategic capabilities, and plays an important role in promoting the realization of a community with a shared future for humanity. However, the implementation of the BRI is not an easy task. It faces many challenges, such as power struggles among major powers and regional turbulence. There are four major risks, namely security, political, institutional, and economic. The implementation of the initiative is a challenging task. Executing is just as important as planning it. China must pay attention to the initiative's long-term, comprehensive, interactive, and uncertain nature, reinforce its strategic resilience and determination, maintain its strategic patience, carefully review the development of the initiative, and properly handle many aspects of its implementation. The mutual balance of elements must be consistently optimized and adjusted during the execution process.

1 BRI: From Abstract Ideas to Concrete Actions

If the community with a shared future for humanity represents a global dream, the BRI is an important starting point for connecting it to the "Chinese Dream."

1.1 Proposing the BRI

During President Xi Jinping's visit to Central Asia and Southeast Asian countries from September to October 2013, he proposed a series of major initiatives to jointly build the "Silk Road Economic Belt" and the "21st Century Maritime Silk Road," collectively referred to as the "Belt and Road Initiative."

Four years after the BRI was proposed, it has received positive responses and support from more than 100 countries and international organizations, and more than 40 countries and international organizations have signed cooperation agreements with China. Investment by Chinese enterprises in countries along the route has exceeded USD 50 billion, and a series of major projects have been implemented, which has driven the economic development of various countries and created a large number of employment opportunities. Through bilateral and multilateral cooperations such as the Asian Infrastructure Investment Bank (AIIB) and the Silk Road Fund, the BRI has formulated some detailed and feasible cooperation mechanisms, and has a relatively complete implementation system in place. This is of great significance to the transformation of China's power and the enhancement of its strategic capabilities.

The Chinese government sees the BRI as hugely important, and consistently endorses its planning and implementation. In November 2013, the "Decision of the Central Committee of the Communist Party of China on Several Major Issues Concerning Comprehensively Intensifying the Reform" adopted by the Third Plenary Session of the 18th Central Committee of the Communist Party of China stated: "We will accelerate the connectivity of facilities with neighboring countries and regions, encourage the Silk Road Economic Belt and Maritime Silk Road, and build a new pattern of all-round opening up." This marks the first time that the BRI was included in the planning sequence of major events in China. In December 2013, General Secretary Xi Jinping stated at the Central Economic Work Conference that China must "encourage the creation of the 'Silk Road Economic Belt,' promptly formulate strategic plans, and reinforce infrastructure connectivity."[1]

In November 2014, the 8th Meeting of the Central Leading Group of Financial and Economic Affairs discussed the "Silk Road Economic Belt" and the "21st Century Maritime Silk Road" plan, and initiated the establishment of the Asian Infrastructure Investment Bank and Silk Road Fund, which showed that great efforts were being made in strategic resource planning for the implementation of the BRI. However,

---

1. "Central Economic Work Conference Held in Beijing Proposes Six Tasks for Next Year's Economic Work," Xinhuanet, December 13, 2013, http://news.xinhuanet.com/fortune/2013-12/13/c_118553239.htm.

following the gradual implementation of the initiative, questions and accusations against it also increased, as some saw it as a Chinese version of the "Marshall Plan" – a grand strategy to challenge American hegemony, and a strategic plan to build a new international order.[2] The BRI is also suspected of interfering in the internal affairs of other countries. To avoid these adverse effects, the Chinese government has begun to deliberately downplay the strategic attributes of the BRI, and has increased the use of "initiatives" and "ideas."[3]

In March 2015, the Chinese government issued the "Vision and Actions for Promoting the Joint Creation of the Silk Road Economic Belt and the 21st Century Maritime Silk Road," which clarified the principles, framework ideas, priorities, and cooperation mechanisms of the BRI. This was the first time the Chinese government had made a comprehensive and systematic illustration of the BRI. In March 2016, the outline of the national "13th Five-Year Plan" was officially released, with the BRI as a special chapter, marking its inclusion in China's long-term strategic plan.[4] On August 17, 2016, General Secretary Xi Jinping attended a symposium on building the BRI in the Great Hall of the People, and delivered a speech emphasizing the need to summarize experience, reinforce confidence, and make solid progress by focusing on policy coordination, connectivity of facilities, unimpeded trade, financial integration, and people-to-people bonds. China will build a network of new mutually beneficial cooperation models and multiple cooperation platforms, focusing on jointly building a green, healthy, intelligent, and peaceful Silk Road. "We will encourage the spirit of perseverance by achieving the 'Belt and Road' step by step, so that it will benefit the people of all countries along the route."[5]

With the involvement of the Chinese government and leaders, the BRI has transformed from a Chinese initiative to an international consensus, and from a Chinese concept to an international cooperation, increasing day by day. According to Xi Jinping, "The BRI encourages all flowers to bloom. This road is not a private road for one party, but a sunny path for everyone to progress hand in hand." Today, more than 100 countries and international organizations have participated in the creation of the BRI. China has signed co-creation cooperation agreements with more

---

2. Jin Ling, "'One Belt, One Road': China's Marshall Plan?" *International Studies*, no. 1 (2015): 88–99.

3. Fenghuang.com Commentary Department, "'One Belt, One Road' Research Needs to Be Guarded Against Fakes," Phoenix.com, October 12, 2015, http://news.ifeng.com/opinion/fenghuanglun/fenghuanglun 062/1.shtml.

4. Zhao Yinping, "The BRI: Xi Jinping's Opening of "Dream Building," Xinhuanet, September 21, 2016, http://news.xinhuanet.com/politics/2016-09/21/c_1119594710.htm.

5. "Xi Jinping Attends the Symposium on Promoting the Creation of the BRI and Delivers a Speech," Xinhuanet, August 17, 2016, http://news.xinhuanet.com/photo/2016-08/17/c_129237311.htm.

than 40 countries or international organizations along the route, and has carried out international cooperation in production capacity with more than 20 countries, with dynamic participation from other international organizations, intensifying of financial cooperation represented by the AIIB and the Silk Road Fund, and a gradual implementation in several influential and iconic projects. The creation of the BRI from ground zero has made great progress, with results that have exceeded expectations. The BRI connects the Asia-Pacific economic circle in the east with the European economic circle in the west, and crosses mountains and deep seas, building the most impressive economic corridor in the world.[6]

1.2 Developing the BRI

The continuing development of the BRI by Chinese leaders is making solid progress. Since President Xi Jinping first proposed the initiative to the international community in September and October 2013, attracting a lot of attention from the international community, on subsequent visits or international occasions, he and other Chinese leaders have spared no effort to encourage the BRI. At the CICA Summit in May 2014, Xi stated that China would work with other countries to accelerate the creation of the "Silk Road Economic Belt" and the "21st Century Maritime Silk Road," establish the Asian Infrastructure Investment Bank as quickly as possible, and participate in depth. The process of regional cooperation endorses the mutual promotion of development and security in Asia.[7]

At the opening ceremony of the 6th Ministerial Meeting of the China-Arab States Cooperation Forum in June 2014, Xi Jinping stated that to achieve the common purpose and challenge of national rejuvenation, China needs to uphold the spirit of the Silk Road, encourage mutual learning between cultures, respect the choice of paths, insist on win-win cooperation, and advocate for dialogue and peace. The BRI is a road of mutual benefit and win-win results. China and Arab countries know each other because of the Silk Road, and are natural partners in the joint creation of the BRI. Both parties should follow the principles of extensive consultation, joint contribution, and shared benefits, and build a China-Arab community of interests

---

6. Zhao Yinping, "The BRI: Xi Jinping's Opening of 'Dream Building,'" Xinhuanet, September 21, 2016, http://news.xinhuanet.com/politics/2016-09/21/c_1119594710.htm.

7. "Xi Jinping's Speech at the Fourth Summit of the Conference on Interaction and Confidence Building Measures in Asia (Full Text)," Xinhuanet, May 21, 2014, http://news.xinhuanet.com/world/2014-05/21/c_1110796357.htm.

and a community with a shared future.[8] At the Boao Forum for Asia in March 2015, Xi Jinping stated that "the creation of the 'Belt and Road' follows the principles of consultation, co-creation, and sharing. It is not closed, but open and inclusive – a chorus for countries along the route."[9]

Thanks to China's advocacy, the BRI has also received positive responses from other regions. With the creation of Russia's Eurasian Economic Union, India's "Monsoon Plan," Mongolia's Prairie Silk Road Economic Belt, Kazakhstan's "Bright Road," and the EU's "Junker Plan," they are exploring the BRI with China. The BRI is a strategic connection to realize a common dream.

In 2016, the development of the BRI continued to make good progress. In January 2016, Xi Jinping's three-country trip to the Middle East created a "dream-building space" for the integration of the "Chinese Dream" and the Middle Eastern dream, from the promotion of the BRI Memorandum of Understanding to exchange and cooperation in five fields. At the end of March 2016, President Xi concluded a successful visit to the Czech Republic. In less than three months, he visited Poland and Serbia in Central and Eastern Europe again. The warming up of cooperation between China and Central and Eastern Europe is very much related to the creation of the BRI. President Xi held talks with Czech President Miloš Zeman, and the two sides agreed to reinforce the connection between the BRI and the Czech development strategy. In mid-October, President Xi started a trip to Asia to encourage the BRI. His visit had a compact and fulfilling schedule – state visits to Cambodia and Bangladesh, and bilateral meetings with leaders of Nepal, Sri Lanka, Myanmar, and Goa in India. In the meantime, the BRI has become a hot topic. In 2016, President Xi's diplomatic finale chose Latin America. In November, he attended the APEC (Asia-Pacific Economic Cooperation) Lima Summit and visited three Latin American countries. The BRI once again became a hot topic in Latin America. Seizing the opportunity of the APEC Lima Summit, President Xi once again introduced the BRI to the world, and welcomed all parties to participate in the cooperation, share opportunities, meet challenges, and seek common development.[10]

---

8. "Xi Jinping Attends the Opening Ceremony of the Sixth Ministerial Conference of the China-Arab States Cooperation Forum and Delivers an Important Speech," Xinhuanet, June 5, 2014, http://news.xinhuanet.com/politics/2014-06/05/c_1111002498.htm.

9. "Xi Jinping: Towards a Community with a Shared Future to Create a New Future for Asia," Xinhuanet, March 28, 2015, http://news.xinhuanet.com/politics/2015-03/28/c_1114794507.htm.

10. Zhang Minyan, "2016, Xi Jinping's 'Grand Narrative' of 'Belt and Road,'" Xinhuanet, January 3, 2017, http://www.xinhuanet.com/world/2017-01/03/c_129429761.htm.

In 2017, the BRI continued to move forward. At the World Economic Forum in Davos in January 2017, Xi Jinping announced to the world that it had achieved major achievements. From March 22 to 29, Li Keqiang paid an official visit to Australia and New Zealand, and the BRI extended to Oceania. During Premier Li's visit to New Zealand, the two countries signed nine cooperation agreements in the fields of economy and trade, agriculture, e-commerce, education, intellectual property protection, and environmental protection, including the "China-New Zealand Memorandum of Understanding on 'One Belt, One Road' Cooperation." New Zealand became the first developed Western country to sign such an agreement with China, creating a first for China-New Zealand relations. In mid-March, the UN Security Council unanimously passed Resolution 2344 on Afghanistan with 15 votes in favor. The resolution called on the international community to build a consensus on assisting Afghanistan, and reinforce regional economic cooperation through the creation of the BRI. It also urged all parties to provide a safe environment for its creation, reinforce the alignment of development policies and strategies, and encourage practical cooperation in connectivity. This was the first time that the BRI had been written into a UN resolution, and it also marked the fact that the BRI had been authoritatively recognized by the United Nations. When meeting with visiting Serbian President Nikolic at the end of March, Xi Jinping stated that it was necessary to encourage the BRI and Serbia's national strategy for re-industrialization, and steadily encourage major projects such as the Hungary-Serbia Railway. They would also explore the joint development of industrial parks, and realize infrastructure construction, production capacity cooperation, and industrial development, while reinforcing cooperation in agriculture, biomedicine, and renewable energy. Both sides agreed to expand tourism and cultural exchanges, and consistently enhance their friendship.[11] From May 14 to 15, the "Belt and Road Forum for International Cooperation" was held in Beijing. It was attended by heads of state and government of 29 countries, heads of three important international organizations (including the Secretary-General of the United Nations and the Chair of the International Committee of the Red Cross), and about 1,500 distinguished guests from more than 130 countries. Xi Jinping attended the opening ceremony of the summit forum, and delivered a keynote speech titled "Jointly Promoting the Development of the BRI." He also presided over the leaders' roundtable summit.

---

11. Xi Jinping, "Promoting the 'One Belt, One Road' Initiative and the Re-industrialization Strategy of Serbia Are Closely Linked," Shenzhen News Network, March 31, 2017, http://news.sznews.com/content/2017-03/31/content_15855999.htm.

Based on the actions of the Chinese government and the positive responses from the international community, the BRI has achieved good results. However, the initiative is a long-term undertaking. It is necessary to start from small details and focus on the difficulty and complexity of the implementation process.

2 BRI: Not an Overnight Success

When looking at the BRI from the perspective of process, we must focus on how long-term, comprehensive, interactive, and uncertain its implementation will be.

2.1 Long-term

The BRI is a systematic project, and its implementation is long-term, as Xi Jinping has emphasized. China must properly handle the overall planning and coordination, and manage the relationship between the government and the market. It must fully leverage the role of the market mechanism, and encourage the participation of both state-owned and private enterprises, while enabling the government to play its role at the same time.[12] The implementation of the BRI will not be achieved overnight, and requires a period of at least a decade. Some studies believe that in the long run, the BRI vision is not just within the "Two Centenary Goals." It is China's historical arrangement for its global strategies.[13] Although this statement may be somewhat exaggerated, the BRI is unlikely to bear fruit without a long period of practice. Its goal is to achieve policy coordination, connectivity of facilities, unimpeded trade, financial integration, and people-to-people bonds among countries along the route. It is not exclusive, and non-Belt and Road countries can participate too.[14] The creation of "connectivity" itself features large investments, a long cycle, and slow returns, and also requires China to maintain strategic patience in the implementation of the BRI, and to be prepared for various uncertainties. Also, creating "people-to-people bonds" is a long-term undertaking, which must be started from scratch to ensure smooth realization, which may require the consistent efforts of several generations to achieve.

---

12. "Xi Jinping Chairs the Eighth Meeting of the Central Finance and Economics Group of the Central Conference," People.cn, November 6, 2014, http://politics.people.com.cn/n/2014/1106/c70731-25989646.html.

13. The Central Party School Provincial and Ministerial Cadre Training Class (No. 57) The Second Task Group of the Research Topic on "Strategic Thinking and Leadership," "Research on the Risks, Challenges, and Countermeasures of the 'One Belt, One Road' Strategy," *Theoretical Perspectives*, no. 8 (2015): 59.

14. Ye Weiping, "The BRI and China's Economic Security," *Research on Socialism with Chinese Characteristics*, no. 5 (2015): 39.

2.2 Integration

The BRI involves many fields such as economics, politics, and humanities, and has relatively strong integration, broad strategic influence, and geographical significance. It goes beyond purely economic and cultural dimensions, and needs to establish a long-term comprehensive strategy.[15] The BRI focuses on economic development, but also focuses on politics, security, and people. Because of this, the research on policy formulation and implementation must be holistic and multilayered. Therefore, it is necessary to study the necessity, feasibility, general direction, and specific framework of the design and implementation of the initiative, and also to analyze the possible risks, difficulties, and challenges surrounding the implementation.[16] Therefore, the positioning of the BRI is comprehensive, as are its goals and ideas.

2.3 Interactive

The BRI is interactive. It is not a solo piece performed by China, but a chorus performed by all. Therefore, it is especially necessary to interact with all parties involved in the implementation process, and to understand its interactivity. Its implementation requires extensive consultation, co-creation, and sharing with countries along the route, meaning interaction with China during the implementation of the initiative. In addition, some major countries and non-participating countries will interact with China or other participating countries on the BRI issue, affecting the implementation of the BRI. Therefore, the initiative needs to pay special attention to the interaction between China and three types of countries, namely, major countries, other countries participating along the route, and non-participating countries.

2.4 Uncertainty

The BRI is an unprecedented major undertaking that faces many uncertainties. Its implementation is still in its infancy, and there are some uncertainties in elements such as the environment, goals, resources, and means, which need to be adjusted accordingly.

---

15. The Central Party School Provincial and Ministerial Cadres Advanced Course (No. 57) The Second Task Group of the Research Topic on "Strategic Thinking and Leadership," "Research on the Risks, Challenges, and Countermeasures of the 'One Belt, One Road' Strategy," *Theoretical Perspectives*, no. 8 (2015): 58–60.

16. Li Xiao, "India's Dilemma" in the Implementation of the 'One Belt, One Road' Strategy: The Dilemma and Countermeasures for Chinese Enterprises Investing in India," *International Economic Review*, no. 5 (2015): 19–20.

First, the countries and regions along the BRI are facing multiple geopolitical, political and economic risks. Many are still in transition, and the democratic rule of law needs to be improved, which brings uncertainty to the implementation of the BRI. Second, the goals of the initiative are ambitious, and the targets of the stages and fields are divided into varying priorities. For countries and regions along the route, the goals should also be focused and sequenced, requiring appropriate adjustments according to the environment. Third, resources are jointly provided by China, countries along the route, and even some non-participating countries. Apart from fluctuations in China's own resources, there are also uncertainties in the provision of resources by other countries, which may affect the development and consistent advancement of the initiative. Fourth, the means of the initiative are uncertain. Although they are diverse in terms of politics, economics, and culture, there are some uncertainties due to complex situations, such as the strategic environment, Sino-foreign relations, and the progress of the project.

3 BRI: Challenges That Cannot Be Ignored

Achieving a great cause always requires intensified efforts, and the success of the BRI cannot be achieved without difficulties and challenges.

3.1 Competition among major powers

The implementation of the BRI has caused major powers to pay attention to the areas surrounding China, and competition among them has intensified. The attitudes of the United States, Russia, Japan, and India are of the greatest significance.

The United States regards the BRI as a geopolitical challenge, and believes that China's attempt to control the heartland of Eurasia poses a challenge to American hegemony and is in conflict with the United States' "New Silk Road" and Asia-Pacific rebalancing strategies. The American hegemony regards the emergence of problematic countries or alliances in Eurasia as the primary challenge, and its strategic response is to make every effort to prevent the formation of hostile alliances and limit the development of hostile or potentially hostile countries. This also results in the United States intervening and seeking to expand its influence in the areas surrounding these countries. In the territories of South Asia and Central Asia where the initiative seeks key breakthroughs, the United States has also spared no effort in seeking to reinforce its geo-strategy. At the same time, the implementation of the United States' Asia-Pacific rebalancing strategy seeks to offset China's growing influence in the Asia-

Pacific region and maintain its dominance there. China's BRI is focused on land and sea, and it coincides with the two major strategies of the United States, which will undoubtedly intensify the geographical competition between the two countries. President Obama made it clear that the BRI and the creation of the AIIB would challenge the US's rule-making power and endanger its dominance in the Asia-Pacific region, which the US does not want to see.[17] Therefore, while implementing the BRI, China must firstly avoid direct confrontation and conflict with the United States, and secondly, guard against consistent disruptions by the United States due to Sino-American competition.

Russia is an important partner in the implementation of China's BRI. At present, its observation and attitude towards the initiative and the countries along it are relatively peaceful and pragmatic.[18] Although it welcomes the BRI, the method of reducing friction in specific areas of cooperation needs to be handled carefully. To synergize connectivity between China and Russia, it is essential to leverage their comparative advantages and seek cooperation points. It is also necessary to resolve the geographical competition between the two countries, and encourage economic mutual benefit and win-win results. Russia is a country deeply influenced by geopolitics, and it has always believed that its major status is dependent on its surrounding areas. In 2011, it proposed the "Eurasian Union," which evolved into the "Eurasian Economic Union," whose purpose is to strengthen Russia's relationship with its neighboring countries through economic cooperation, and enhance Russia's influence on the surrounding areas. Russia's "Eurasian Economic Union" and China's BRI have many overlaps. While it is conducive to the expansion of cooperation between China and Russia, it is also very likely to intensify the geopolitical competition between them, making it a taboo for China to enter its traditional geographical sphere of influence.[19] The layout of the BRI has intensified the "energy-capital" cooperation between China and Central Asian countries, raising Russia's doubts and concerns.[20] On the issue of Sino-Russian BRI cooperation, China needs to take a pragmatic attitude, and leverage its economic advantages. It must show consideration to Russia's traditional status, and

---

17. President Obama, "State of the Union," January 20, 2015, http://www.whitehouse.gov/sotu.

18. Wang Linggui, "Expectations, Welcome, and Anxiety: A View of the BRI by Foreign Think Tanks," Guangming.com, November 30, 2015, http://www.gmw.cn/sixiang/2015-11/30/content_17909772.htm.

19. "What Does Russian Media Perceive as the Two Major Strategies – BRI + 'Eurasian Economic Union'?" *Long Bao*, June 24, 2015, http://www.dragonnewsru.com/news/rc_news/20150624/15908.html.

20. Wang Yu, "Opportunities and Challenges of Energy and Resources Cooperation in the Context of the BRI, *People's Forum*, no. 7 (201): 83.

encourage the connection between China's BRI and Russia's "Eurasian Economic Union" to encourage mutual economic benefits and downplay the geographical competition.

The competition for regional influence between China and Japan will directly affect the implementation of the BRI. At present, the tensions in Sino-Japanese relations – a result of historical issues and dispute over the Diaoyu Islands intertwined with real interests and historical feelings – makes it unlikely for the relationship to improve in the short term. China's BRI is regarded as a strategic challenge towards Japan, which will further weaken its presence in Asia.[21] Japan is not resigned to this, and is gathering momentum in Southeast Asia, Central Asia, and other regions to compete with China. In Southeast Asia, Japan is carrying out geo-strategic operations based on geo-economics. Firstly, it is obtaining oil and gas resources through close energy cooperation with Southeast Asian countries. Second, it is maintaining close economic ties with Southeast Asian countries to maintain its economic advantages in Southeast Asia. Thirdly, it is promoting regional economic cooperation in East Asia to dominate the Southeast Asian economy. Fourthly, Japan is taking advantage of the South China Sea tensions by intensifying the Diaoyu Islands dispute and joining forces with countries such as the Philippines and Vietnam to exert joint pressure on China. In terms of geopolitics, Japan's main goal of geo-strategic planning in Southeast Asia is to seek control of the strategic maritime channel and political capital, and to plan for dominance in the East Asian region.[22] It has also intensified its geo-strategic focus on Central Asia due to increasing energy demands.

In August 2006, Japanese Prime Minister Koizumi visited Central Asia before leaving office, marking the intensifying of Japan's Central Asian diplomacy.[23] In Central Asia, Japan is implementing "Silk Road Diplomacy" to reinforce its influence in Central Asia through foreign aid and energy cooperation. China's BRI competes with Japan's regional strategy, especially in Southeast and Central Asia. It can be expected that the geopolitical competition between China and Japan in China's surrounding areas will become long-term and normalized. This will have an important impact on the implementation of the initiative.

---

21. Xu Yuanrong and Zheng Niya, "How Japan Views China's Belt and Road Initiative," Sohu.com, August 11, 2015, http://news.sohu.com/20150811/n418549544.shtml.

22. He Huoping, "Geo-strategic Reflections on Japan-Southeast Asia Cooperation after the Cold War," *Journal of Hubei Institute of Economics* (Humanities and Social Sciences Edition), no. 1 (2009): 82–83.

23. Xu Jianhua, "Japan's Central Asian Strategy," *Journal of Shenzhen University* (Humanities and Social Sciences Edition), no. 2 (2007): 67.

India is a rising power that cannot be avoided in the implementation of the BRI.[24] Relatively speaking, India views the implementation from a geopolitical perspective, seeing it as having the potential to affect the strategic alignment and implementation of the two countries. Some members of the Indian elite believe that the initiative will impact India's dominance in its sphere of influence in South Asia, and feel that the BCIM Economic Corridor will threaten the security of India's north-eastern region. The "21st Century Maritime Silk Road" is regarded as a maritime "string of pearls" to contain India, threatening its security and position in the Indian Ocean.[25] India has always regarded South Asia as a natural "sphere of influence." The BRI will undoubtedly help reinforce China's ties with South Asian countries, diluting India's influence in South Asia to some extent, and impacting its dominance in South Asia.[26] However, at the same time, the two countries have many opportunities for win-win cooperation as well. Therefore, finding ways to achieve positive interactions and avoid suffering a great loss for a small gain will become an important issue in the implementation of the BRI.

3.2 Internal risk spillovers from countries along the Belt and Road

Apart from intensified competition among major powers, attention should also be paid to the impact of internal risk spillovers from countries along the Belt and Road during the implementation of the initiative. As its implementation endorses closer geographical ties between neighboring countries and China, geographic risks and sensitivity among countries along the route will intensify. In these countries, the social system and economic structures are in their transition period. There are many uncertain factors in terms of politics, economics, and social development, and the legal and trade protection systems are imperfect, resulting in inevitable political, security, and economic risks.[27]

As for political risk, most of the countries along the BRI are developing or underdeveloped. Their economic and social development is lagging behind, and the

---

24. Li Xiao, "India's Dilemma in the Implementation of the 'Belt and Road' Strategy: Dilemma and Countermeasures of Chinese Enterprises Investing in India," *International Economic Review*, no. 5 (2015): 19.

25. Gan Junxian, " 'Belt and Road': Dragon and Elephant to Walk Alone or Dance Together?" *International Studies Research*, no. 4 (2015): 97.

26. Ibid.

27. Liu Hong, "Analysis on the Opportunities and Risks of the 'One Belt, One Road' Strategic Development," *People's Forum*, no. 10 (2015): 64.

political and social security situation is extremely complicated.[28] The geopolitics of these regions are complex. Local wars break out from time to time, and the political situation in many countries is also very unstable.[29] The political systems of the countries along the BRI vary greatly. A "gerontocracy" and "strongman politics" exist, and many countries are in political turmoil due to domestic power struggles. The BRI focuses on the creation of infrastructure such as transport, electricity, energy, and networks, and features of large investments, long cycles, and slow yields, depending on the political stability, policy continuity, and relations with China of the relevant partners.[30] In recent years, the "color revolution" has become an important influence on the political stability of neighboring countries, resulting in heightened political risks for some, which will also have an important impact on the creation of the BRI and increased uncertainty around its implementation.[31] China's overseas investment has suffered repeated serious losses due to changes in the political situations of the invested countries. In the context of China's observance to the diplomatic principle of non-interference in internal affairs, it faces new challenges and requires new ideas and countermeasures to safeguard its overseas interests more effectively.

As for the security risk, the complex ethnic and religious conflicts and prominent non-traditional security threats in the countries along the BRI constitute real or potential security risks. International terrorism, religious extremism, ethnic separatism, and transnational organized crime are rampant in regions such as the Middle East and Central Asia, resulting in long-term instability there. In the Middle East, the terrorist activities of the "Islamic State" have profoundly affected regional security. Among South Asian countries, India and Pakistan have the most frequent terrorist activities.[32] In addition, some countries experience wars due to religious conflicts and resource disputes. These security risks can easily affect the implementation of the BRI, making it more difficult to protect China's overseas interests. Its route connects the

---

28. Yang Siling, "Relationship Governance and Challenges between China and Countries Along the BRI," *South Asia Studies*, no. 2 (2015): 23–25.

29. Yang Liangmin and Wang Lin, "The BRI Has Entered a New Stage of Solid Advancement," *China Development Watch*, no. 9 (2015): 24.

30. Wu Zhicheng and Li Jintong, "Practicing China's Plan for Regional Cooperation and Global Negotiation and Co-governance: The BRI under the Leadership of the Central Government," *Contemporary World*, no. 5 (2015): 19.

31. Liu Rui, "From Three Steps to the BRI: Xi Jinping's National Economic Strategy Innovation," *Enterprise Economics*, no. 9 (2015): 5–11.

32. Yang Siling, "Governance and Challenges of Relations Between China and Countries Along the BRI," *South Asia Studies*, no. 2 (2015): 23–25.

Eurasian continent, where ethnic and religious cultures are very complex, covering various religions such as Buddhism, Hinduism, Islam, and Christianity. The political, social, and cultural systems derived from these religions vary greatly. What is even more fatal is that the exchanges and cooperation between countries are linked to multiple religious and ethnic conflicts,[33] and the security risks caused by this cannot be ignored. In the context of China's advocacy and implementation of the BRI, the "religious factor" should become one of the most important indicators in evaluating strategic risks.[34]

When it comes to economic risk, the BRI is guided by the government, while enterprises will become the main participants of the initiative. This means that China's "going global" strategy has entered a new stage. However, due to factors such as a lack of information, and cultural and legal differences, Chinese enterprises are facing many difficulties in "going global," of which co-existing peacefully with the locals and respecting local culture and related laws are the most pertinent issues. This is not only related to the smooth progress of the project, but also to the shaping of a positive international image for China. Chinese companies "going global" through the BRI face huge and complex economic risks, one of which is related to investment. Conversely, the investment environment of the countries along the BRI is not favorable. The Global Business Environment Report released in 2015 assessed the investment environment of 185 countries around the world, and most of the countries along the BRI were located outside 100, which means that they had higher investment risks.[35] Institutional risk is also an issue. When Chinese enterprises "go global," they also face the problem of aligning with international and domestic rules of the countries along the route. Many of these countries have imperfect and incomplete rules governing labor, land, financing, industrial policies, and law enforcement is arbitrary,[36] leading to greater institutional risks for Chinese companies. It is difficult for relevant interests to be fully guaranteed through the system. Another risk lies in engineering. The BRI focuses on the development of infrastructure projects. During the implementation of the project, the safety of engineering personnel and the prevention and control of natural disasters will affect the progress and quality of the project.

---

33. Yang Siling, "Governance and Challenges of Relations Between China and Countries Along the BRI," *South Asia Studies*, no. 2 (2015): 23–25.

34. Ma Lirong, "The 'Religious Factor' in the BRI and Asia-Africa Strategic Cooperation," *West Asia and Africa*, no. 4 (2015): 14–18.

35. Liu Huaqin, "The Prospects and Path Choices of Enterprises Going Global under the Background of the 'One Belt, One Road' Strategy," *Foreign Economic and Trade Practice*, no. 8 (2015): 7.

36. Jiang Heng, "Assessment and Management of Geopolitical Risks of the BRI," *International Trade*, no. 8 (2015): 21.

3.3 Uncertainty in China's relationships with countries along the route

In addition to strategic competition among major powers, the uncertainty of China's relations with countries along the BRI will also affect the implementation of the initiative.

Firstly, the countries along the BRI are complex, with diverse societies, frequent domestic challenges, and unstable policies towards China. Therefore, to implement the BRI successfully, China and participating countries need to establish paradigms and rules that will be recognized by all parties in the process of interaction. They must reinforce cooperation for common goals under a core identity to form collective feelings,[37] and China must enhance its capability to manage risks in its relations with countries along the route.

Secondly, China's relations with participating countries along the BRI vary. Due to competing interests, religious differences, and cultural diversity, some countries are skeptical of the BRI, with governments and people lacking trust in China.[38] Some countries even have a "China threat theory." This brings uncertainty to the strategic mobilization and support of the BRI. It is worth noting that China's participation in the creation of the BRI is dominated by state-owned enterprises, which are easily elevated to the level of transactions and competitions between countries overseas, and are also more likely to cause strategic confrontation, social dissatisfaction, countervailing, and anti-dumping in the host country, as well as other economic policy challenges.[39]

Thirdly, the BRI advocates for the principles of extensive consultation, co-creation, and sharing, which requires China to reinforce economic alliances with countries along the BRI. Many strategic plans are primarily based on national interests, which inevitably leads to differences between relative and absolute benefits. The impact of such differences on the Belt and Road international cooperation cannot be ignored. At the same time, policy communication and strategic docking will also have an impact on strategic interaction, resulting in uncertainty in strategy implementation due to differences in interests and changes in governments. For example, China-ASEAN

---

37. Yang Siling, "The Governance and Challenges of Relations Between China and Countries Along the BRI," *South Asia Studies*, no. 2 (2015): 16.

38. Yu Xiaofeng and Zhang Taiqi, "Harmony: The Value Paradigm of Constructing 'Inter-State Identity' – Taking the Countries along the BRI as an Example," *Journal of Northwest Normal University* (Social Science Edition), no. 6 (2015): 10.

39. Jiang Heng, "Assessment and Management of Geopolitical Risks of the BRI, *International Trade*, no. 8 (2015): 22.

cooperation faces structural problems such as lack of strategic mutual trust, weak national governance, and multicultural conflicts, which will result in a bottleneck in the creation of the BRI.[40]

In addition, the strategic competition among participating countries along the BRI in terms of project planning and capital allocation is also significant problem to be faced while implementing the initiative.

As globalization intensifies, the interactions and connections between countries around the world have become increasingly close. Although some countries are not currently participating in the BRI, their interactions with participating nations will still have an impact on the implementation of the initiative, and will increase the uncertainty of China's relations with countries along the route. This has created external risks in terms of security, politics, and economics for the BRI.

4 BRI: Opportunities for China

The BRI is China's major initiative in the new era, and it is also an important way for it to encourage consistent and positive interactions with the rest of the world. It will have a positive impact on China's surrounding environment and the promotion of a community of shared destiny.

4.1 Beneficial in enhancing China's surrounding geographical environment

Although the BRI is not entirely a geo-strategy, its geopolitical influence cannot be ignored, especially for the surrounding areas. It will play a role in reshaping the surrounding geopolitical environment.

Firstly, it will expand the surrounding geographical environment. Traditionally, China's surrounding areas primarily refer to the countries and regions that are geographically bordered and culturally similar to China. As China's power grows, alongside the expansion of foreign interests, the voice of its surroundings is amplifying. More importantly, China needs to reinforce its ties with large neighboring countries to truly achieve a geopolitical environment rather than simply a geographical surrounding, and the implementation of the BRI has become a key factor. Firstly, by implementing the initiative, China can greatly enhance its ties with regions such as

---

40. Zhou Fangye, "The Opportunities, Bottlenecks and Paths of China-ASEAN Cooperation from the 'Belt and Road' Perspective and Role of China-Thailand Strategic Cooperation Pathfinder, *Research on Nanyang Issues*, no. 3 (2015): 39.

the relatively distant Middle East, and Central and Eastern Europe, and implement a large periphery. Secondly, its implementation will encourage China's westward strategy by expanding the strategic space and reducing direct geopolitical competition with the United States. Thirdly, its implementation will encourage the connection between East Asia and Central Asia, Southeast Asia, South Asia, the Middle East, and Europe. It will realize the economic integration of the Eurasian continent, and expand China's geo-economics and political space.[41]

Secondly, the surrounding geopolitics, security, and economy will be integrated. The implementation of the BRI is conducive to defusing the economic and security pressures China faces. For a long time, the geo-economic cooperation between China and its neighboring countries has not brought about a corresponding improvement in geopolitics and geo-security. Integrating the three major geo-elements is an urgent problem to be solved in China's neighborhood diplomacy in the new era. Through the implementation of the BRI, China's production capacity and capital can be exported, and its geo-economic capabilities can be greatly exerted. More importantly, the BRI will share development dividends with neighboring countries and encourage the common development of neighboring countries. It will increase the closeness and recognition of its neighboring, which will help develop and integrate their geopolitics, security, and economies.

Third is the question of emotional geography. The BRI regards "people-to-people bonds" as an important goal. By inheriting and promoting the spirit of friendship and cooperation along the Silk Road, it has carried out extensive cultural, academic, and talent exchanges and cooperations, as well as media cooperation, youth and women exchanges, and volunteer services, laying a solid foundation for intensifying bilateral and multilateral ties. This is very conducive to creating a sense of emotional geography, enhancing China's appeal, affinity, and cohesion to neighboring countries, and becoming a strong gel for the initiative.

The fourth element is to reinforce surrounding geographical connections. The implementation of the BRI has resulted in China having geographical ties with neighboring countries. It is not a simple point-and-line layout. There are three land lines, two sea lines, and six economic corridors connecting various sub-regions, leveraging a large number of personnel, products, and capital circulation to achieve a network layout extending in all directions to reinforce China's geographical ties with neighboring countries.

---

41. Wang Zhimin, "Geo-economics and Political Analysis of the 'One Belt, One Road' Strategy, *Truth*, no. 4 (2015): 19.

The fifth element is to release geo-economic energy. The implementation of the BRI will greatly release the potential of China's geo-economics. It will transport excess production capacity, capital, and manpower to neighboring countries to achieve mutual benefit and win-win. The first step is to create a holistic opening-up for the Chinese economy, and jointly create an open, balanced, and inclusive regional economic cooperation structure. The second step is to create and cultivate new economic growth points on domestic, regional, and global scales, aimed at achieving the goal of rapid and sustainable economic development in China and the countries along the route. The third step is to develop the cooperative economic system in the surrounding regions and provide institutional guarantees for the surrounding geo-economic cooperation. The fourth step is to endorse the historical process of RMB internationalization, encourage financial cooperation in surrounding areas, and increase the proportion of the use of RMB in the region, which can prevent financial risks in the region, reduce transaction costs, and make a significant contribution to maintaining regional economic and financial stability and realizing the effect of currency geopolitics.

4.2 Beneficial in building a community with a shared future for humanity

The proposal of a community with a shared future for humanity is a major concept for China's new leadership. It is far-sighted, and adapts to changes in the international situation based on Chinese culture and diplomatic experience. However, the community with a shared future for humanity must not remain at the conceptual level. Its realization must be effected gradually. In this process, the BRI strategy has become an important starting point, and it can transform the community with a shared future for humanity from dream to reality. First, through cooperation in production capacity and strategic docking, the BRI can lay a solid foundation for a consensus of interests to build a bilateral community with a shared future. Second, through the consistent development of interconnectivity, neighboring countries can share more of China's development dividends, and perceive the warmth of a neighborhood community with a shared future. Third, through its consistent extension, China's cooperation with Arab, African, and Latin American countries will become more extensive and in-depth, building a community with a shared future. Fourth, through joint consultation, joint creation, and sharing within the BRI, China can strive to entice more developed countries to participate, and also garner their support. The interests of countries around the world will be closer, and the interests of a community with a shared future for humanity will be more solid, while the realization of a community with a shared future for humanity will be more likely.

For the implementation of the BRI, it is necessary to avoid strategic rashness, and focus on the difficulty and complexity of the strategic process, moving towards the consistent realization of the goals of the initiative. To this end, there are three points that need to be undertaken well in the strategic response. First is to maintain strategic restraint and avoid committing the mistake of strategic rashness due to success. The BRI involves many regions and countries, covering political, economic, and social fields. The required human, financial, and material resources are huge. It will be difficult for China to support it alone. Therefore, it must maintain strategic restraint and follow strategic reciprocity, adopting the progressive approaches of moving from a point to a line," and then from a line to an area. The development of key projects will help build strategic support, and their consolidation will drive development along the surrounding routes and realize a network aggregation effect.

Second is to reinforce strategic focus and ensure an unswerving strategic direction in an ever-changing strategic environment. The environment facing the BRI is extremely complex. There are differences in political systems, religious cultures, and laws among countries, and they face four major risks, namely security, political, institutional, and economic. This requires strategic focus to avoid panic, minor mistakes, and strategic loss. Strengthening strategic focus requires not only reinforcing the planning of top-level design, but also planning in advance and making proposals for possible challenges during the implementation.

Third is to maintain strategic patience. Since the goals of the BRI are long-term and comprehensive, and the difficulties and challenges faced in the implementation of the strategy are extremely complicated, hiccups are inevitable. To reinforce the practice of strategic patience, it is advisable to take a long-term view, and to place the initiative as part of China's long-term development to think, plan, and implement.

CHAPTER 7

The Asian Infrastructure Investment Bank

IN OCTOBER 2013, PRESIDENT XI Jinping held talks with Indonesian President Susilo in Jakarta, and mentioned the establishment of the Asian Infrastructure Investment Bank (AIIB) for the first time. "To stimulate the development of regional connectivity and economic integration, China proposes to establish the Asian Infrastructure Investment Bank and is willing to provide financial support for infrastructure projects in developing countries in the region, including ASEAN countries."[1] Today, the investment bank is officially in operation after much effort – a typical China-led supplier of regional public goods that provided an important support for the creation of a community with a shared future for neighboring and developing countries.

1 Forging Ahead

The AIIB is an inter-governmental Asian regional multilateral development agency led by the Chinese government, and its focus is on supporting the creation of infrastructure in Asian countries. It has been nearly four years since the idea was conceived. After taking shape as a prototype, it is now in the functional stage. Its

---

1. "China-Indonesia Relations Elevated to Comprehensive Strategic Partnership," *People's Daily*, October 3, 2013, 1.

development is consistent with a series of new concepts in Chinese diplomacy, of which it has become a representative. According to the AIIB's development plan, its headquarters are located in Beijing, where the legal capital is set at USD 100 billion, and the financing model adopts the PPP (Public-Private-Partnership) model for infrastructure creation. Looking back at the development of the AIIB, it was a new plan and mechanism created in response to the new neighborhood diplomacy concept, and it is helping to create an Asian community with a shared future.

As mentioned above, President Xi Jinping first proposed the establishment of the AIIB on October 2, 2013, during his visit to Indonesia. The new AIIB will cooperate with existing multilateral development banks in and outside the region to complement each other and jointly endorse the sustainable and stable development of the Asian economy. This can be regarded as the first presentation of the concept of the AIIB on the international stage, and it has also become an important new initiative in China's foreign policy. The reason why China chose to propose the AIIB concept in Asian countries shows its strategic consideration in regarding this region as an important platform for the bank.

Since the start of 2014, China has instigated communication with countries in and outside of the region, and many are interested in participating in the establishment of the AIIB. On October 24, 2014, after several rounds of consultations, the finance ministers and authorized representatives of China, India, Singapore, and 19 other prospective founding member countries gathered in Beijing, and decided to establish the AIIB, marking a new stage in its creation. From January 15 to 16, 2015, the second negotiation meeting for the establishment of the AIIB was held in Mumbai, India. At the meeting, it was decided that countries intending to be founding members had to submit a formal application before March 31, 2015. Since then, countries interested in the AIIB have reinforced their communication with China. In March 2015, European countries such as the UK, France, and Germany expressed their willingness to join the AIIB, which is major progress for countries outside the region. In April 2015, countries including Australia, South Korea, Russia, and Brazil expressed their intention to become founding members of the AIIB. As of April 15, 2015, 57 states inside and outside the region had expressed their interest in becoming founding members.

On June 29, 2015, representatives of the AIIB's 57 potential founding member countries attended the signing ceremony of the Agreement on the Asian Infrastructure Investment Bank (hereinafter referred to as the AIIB Agreement) in Beijing. Among them, the 50 countries that passed the domestic approval process formally signed the AIIB Agreement, and other prospective founding member states witnessed the signing ceremony prior to their approval. This marked the fact that its establishment had achieved phased results, and was irreversible. According to the provisions of the AIIB Agreement, it would come into effect six months later, and the AIIB would be officially established.

On January 16, 2016, the AIIB was officially opened after a period of 27 months – more than 800 days from the initial initiative to the final implementation. The first multilateral financial institution initiated by China, the AIIB would also provide new development opportunities for countries and regions in Asia and the rest of the world. In March 2017, the AIIB expanded its capacity for the first time, accepting the participation of 13 countries in the region including Afghanistan and Armenia, and eight countries outside the region including Belgium, Canada, and Ireland. The number of member countries reached 70, surpassing the Asia Development Bank for the first time. It was estimated that by the end of 2017, the AIIB member countries would exceed 90, accounting for nearly half of all countries in the world. Its influence would continue to expand.

The AIIB is an important attempt by China to implement its new diplomatic concepts and demonstrate its ability to create institutions. Although some countries are not happy with this, such as United States and Japan, and countries within and outside the region are also skeptical, China has forged ahead and pushed the AIIB to reach consensuses in many areas, achieving important developments, and realizing its establishment. As the saying goes, a just cause attracts much support, an unjust one finds little. The AIIB has attracted the participation of many countries, which reflects its popularity. Firstly, it is highly authoritative. Four of the five permanent members of the UN Security Council, namely China, Britain, France, and Russia (excluding the United States) are involved. Secondly, the AIIB has highly cohesive. It brings together important forces in world economic restructuring. Fifteen of the 20 G20 countries and five out of the G7 countries (the UK, France, Germany, Italy, and Canada) are members. It also reflects the solidarity of the BRICS countries, with all five participating. Thirdly, the AIIB has broad representation, particularly in terms of Asia's common interests. A total of 39 Asian countries have joined, the population and GDP of account for the vast majority of Asia. Fourthly, the AIIB is open and inclusive. Apart from the participation of Asian countries, 31 countries outside the region have joined, including 21 countries in Europe, two in Oceania, three in South America, four in Africa, and one in North America. This indicates that the influence of the AIIB has gone beyond Asia. As a multilateral financial development institution with broad representation, the AIIB will play a prominent role in the international financial order.

2 Fulfilling China's Duties as a Leading Economic Power

The AIIB is a China-led regional multilateral financial institution. Its main function is to provide capital services for the creation of infrastructure for countries in the Asian region to support investment in various industries including transport, energy, telecommunications, agriculture, and urban development. This is an important Chinese initiative to encourage neighborhood diplomacy in the new era, to cooperate with the BRI, and to practice the new diplomatic concepts of a community with a shared future for humanity, friendship, sincerity, mutual benefit, and inclusivity. The AIIB is not for China's sole benefit, but aims to aid the progress of developing countries.

2.1 Providing international public goods and shouldering the responsibility of a major country

When meeting the heads of delegations from various countries at the signing ceremony of the Agreement on the AIIB, Xi Jinping stated that its aims were to encourage infrastructure creation and connectivity in Asia, intensify regional cooperation, and achieve common development.[2] Since Reform and Opening-up, China's economic and social development has benefited from multilateral development banks such as the World Bank and the Asian Development Bank, and bilateral financial support from certain countries. China's development is inseparable from that of Asia and the rest of the world. With the consistent enhancement of its comprehensive national strength, China is also willing to make contributions to the cause of international development within its capacity.[3] As a permanent member of the Security Council, China has always been aware of the international responsibilities it shoulders. With the consistent enhancement of its comprehensive strength, it has also contributed to global development and paid it forward to the international community to the best of its ability. The establishment of the AIIB can be regarded as China's attempt to encourage the strong and the weak to help each other in the field of international institutions, and reflects its identity and responsibilities as a major power.

---

2. "Xi Jinping Meets with Heads of Delegations from Countries Attending AIIB Agreement Signing Ceremony," *People's Daily Online*, June 30, 2015, http://politics.people.com.cn/n/2015/0630/c70731-27227420.html.

3. Ibid.

2.2 Exploring the rational use of foreign exchange

Since Reform and Opening-up, China has undergone consistent development, and has accumulated large amounts of foreign exchange, far exceeding the amount it requires. Exploring the rational use of foreign exchange has become an important mission in China's economic diplomacy in the new era. Through the establishment of the AIIB, some foreign exchange can be invested into infrastructure in Asia, achieving win-win cooperation and common development – another important manifestation of China's new concept of justice and interests. American scholar C. Fred Bergsten has noted that the existing World Bank and Asian Development Bank cannot meet the needs of Asian countries for infrastructure investment, and their focus has already shifted to other places in recent years. Hence, the establishment of the AIIB is essential.[4] In Xi Jinping's speech at the AIIB's inaugural meeting, he said that "Asia's infrastructure financing needs are huge – a vast blue ocean. There is huge space for old and new institutions to complement each other, and various forms of cooperation can be carried out, such as co-financing, knowledge sharing, capacity building, and healthy competition. We can learn from each other's strengths and complement each other's weaknesses, improve together, and enhance the contribution of multilateral development institutions to Asia's infrastructure connectivity and sustainable economic development."[5] The establishment of the AIIB can address the infrastructure investment gap in Asia to some extent, and can play an important role in promoting Asia's development and prosperity.

2.3 Promoting RMB internationalization and reducing the potential risks arising from the dominance of the US dollar

Before the establishment of the AIIB, China had limited standing in the international financial system. Although it had advanced to become the world's second largest economy by 2015, the RMB had not gained a corresponding position in international settlements, accounting for only 1.47%, ranking seventh – lagging behind the US dollar, which had a proportion of 41.63%.[6] At the same time, the

---

4. Quoted from Liu Ying and Wei Lei, "AIIB from the Perspective of International Think Tank Scholars," *Southern Finance*, no. 6 (2015): 5–7.
5. Xi Jinping, "Speech at the Opening Ceremony of the Asian Infrastructure Investment Bank," *People's Daily*, January 17, 2016, 2.
6. Gao Lin, "The Significance of the Establishment of the AIIB from the 'One Belt, One Road' Strategy," *Chinese and Foreign Entrepreneurs*, no. 8 (2015): 1–2.

United States – which hindered the internationalization of the RMB – has greatly impacted China's interests. The US has long prevented the RMB from becoming a "basket" of currencies in the IMF, which significantly restricted China's international financial rights. Despite a long delay, the RMB was finally included in the Special Drawing Right (SDR), but it still is not proportionate to China's economy. As the saying goes, there is more than one way to skin a cat. Although the US and other Western countries are reluctant to internationalize the RMB prematurely, the trust in China's currency in its surrounding areas has increased. Internationalization has achieved initial results there, which is conducive to promoting the regional economy. Cooperation is important. The establishment of the AIIB is a follow-up, and can be implemented in conjunction with the BRI, which is highly beneficial in promoting the internationalization of the RMB and accumulating experience of managing it.

2.4 Enhancing China's status in the international financial system, and encouraging restructuring of the international financial system

After the global financial crisis of 2008, the status of emerging economies in the world economy steadily increased, and the international community began to call for amplifying the voice and influence of developing countries and emerging economies in the global economic governance structure. Some agreements have since been reached, such as the IMF and World Bank restructuring agreements, and the G20 was becoming an important coordination platform for global economic governance. However, these measures were sufficient to fundamentally change the international economic order, and were eventually shelved by the United States. Given the limited room for concessions by Western powers, the establishment of the AIIB can be regarded as an important attempt by China to encourage the restructuring and improvement of the global financial system, and it may be able to exert some force. Xi Jinping has said that the "Asian Infrastructure Investment Bank will complement the existing international financial development institutions. China is willing to work with all member states to make the AIIB into a new multilateral development bank that is professional, efficient, and clean, as well as jointly promote its development and contribute to the economic prosperity of Asia and the rest of the world."[7] As a regional multilateral development bank, the AIIB is a new member and

---

7. "Xi Jinping Meets with Heads of Delegations from Countries Attending the AIIB Agreement Signing Ceremony," *People's Daily Online*, June 30, 2015, http://politics.people.com.cn/n/2015/0630/c70731-27227420.html.

partner in the field of international development. Its appearance is China's attempt to restructure financial institutions, not to subvert the existing international financial order and replace multilateral financial institutions such as the World Bank and the Asian Development Bank. Instead, in a situation where financial capital prevails and the market economy dominates the world, it will use international rules to encourage win-win cooperation between China and other countries as the market economy dominates the world.

2.5 Endorsing regional cooperation and achieving common development

The establishment of the AIIB is an important attempt by China to provide regional public goods, help regional development, and render active support for the creation of a community with a shared future for neighboring countries, for Asia, and for developing countries. Xi Jinping has stated that "China's development cannot be separated from Asia and the rest of the world. We unswervingly pursue a mutually beneficial and win-win strategy of opening up. I propose to jointly build the Silk Road Economic Belt and the 21st Century Maritime Silk Road. The AIIB initiative is aimed at intensifying economic cooperation among Asian countries and achieving common development. We will strive to enable China's development to benefit countries in Asia and the rest of the world."[8]

Asia's development in the 21st century will occupy a greater position in global development. China's proposal of the BRI and the AIIB is based on the ideals of friendship, sincerity, mutual benefit, and inclusivity in neighborhood diplomacy, and is committed to working with Asian countries to solve practical problems faced by the region and achieve common development. The AIIB will complement the strengths of existing international development financial institutions, and its establishment is conducive in accelerating the promotion of infrastructure connectivity in the region, promoting regional economic cooperation, and injecting new impetus into Asian economic development. Xi Jinping emphasized that "When people work with one mind, they can work wonders." The AIIB should uphold open and inclusive regionalism, and welcome all interested countries to participate and achieve win-win cooperation. It should also pursue multilateralism, complement other countries with existing multilateral development institutions, reinforce cooperation, and jointly endorse the prosperity and development of Asia and the rest of the world.

---

8. "Xi Jinping Meets with Representatives from Countries Attending the Signing Ceremony of the Memorandum of Understanding on the Establishment of the AIIB," *People's Daily*, October 25, 2014, 1.

Assessing China's five motives to lead the establishment of the AIIB, it has no intention of challenging the Asia-Pacific order or world order, but instead is assuming more regional and global responsibilities within its capacity. The establishment of the AIIB is also a positive example of China promoting the building of a community with a shared future for humanity and putting it into practice.

3 Winners and Losers in the Improvement of Infrastructure

The establishment of the AIIB has not just attracted the participation of Asian countries, but also many countries in Africa, Oceania, and Europe. However, it has been resisted by other countries, such as Japan and the US. Its influence can be described as both far-reaching and complicated. At present, the AIIB has 70 member countries, and its scale is expected to continue expanding in future. In September 2015, current president Jin Liqun said that up to 20 more countries had approached the bank to join it. The doors of the AIIB are open to Japan and the United States, and it will continue negotiating with them.[9]

Regarding the AIIB's influence, there are two theories, namely to cause someone to fail with excessive praise, and to cause someone to fail by open attack. The former often places China and the United States in a confrontational position of equal strength, while the latter is usually a modulation of the "China Collapse Theory." Some believe that the establishment of the AIIB to resolve domestic economic difficulties is akin to trying to quench a thirst with poison. The "China market" expanded into a gimmick of the "Asian market," relying on market temptation to divert excess capacity, attract capital flows, and delay economic collapse.[10] However, in general, the reactions of countries around the world to the AIIB can be divided into three groups.

The first is the participation of Asian countries. Since the establishment of the AIIB, the inaugural batch of 21 intended founding members were primarily Asian countries, across Northeast, Southeast, South, and West Asia. Among the current founding members, a total of 39 countries in Asia have participated, including major nations such as India, Indonesia, and South Korea. More importantly, China's

---

9. "Jin Liqun: There are still 20 countries that want to join the AIIB, the door is open to Japan and the United States," Phoenix.com, September 21, 2015, http://finance.ifeng.com/a/20150921/13986397_0.shtml.

10. Xu Yanzhuo and Xue Li, "The Asian Dream Brought to Us by the AIIB," *Social Observatory*, no. 5 (2015): 47.

neighboring countries are involved, which is sufficient to show the AIIB's appeal. The fact that the AIIB can attract so many Asian countries to participate also reflects the fact that it benefits Asia, and has common Asian interests in mind.

The second group is the European countries that have followed the trend. The participation of more than 20 European countries also reflects the AIIB's strong appeal. European countries joined the AIIB after a strategic decision made after careful consideration, reflecting thinking and judgment on major issues such as world order, practical interests, and governance rules. Firstly, Europe's choice to embrace the AIIB is based on its strategic judgment of the evolution of the future world economic order, reflecting its efforts to maintain and consolidate its own position and influence. Secondly, it is a rational decision based on real economic interests. After the double blow of the financial and sovereign debt crisis, Europe's road to economic recovery has been fraught with challenges. Finding new economic growth points, and stimulating investment and demand has become the current priority of most European countries.[11] Finally, EU countries have strong geopolitical intentions in joining the AIIB – a product of their neo-engagement policy seeking to reinforce the EU's influence in Asia-Pacific affairs.[12] In any case, European countries are wise to follow the trend, regardless of their take.

The third group is made up of Japan and the US, which are stagnating, and boycotting the AIIB. Among the countries that have boycotted AIIB, Japan and the US are the most prominent. Japan's attitude to it has gone through a somewhat tangled process. Initially, the Japanese authorities did not show much concern, and the public was skeptical. The pace of the AIIB's development has surprised Japan to some extent. Japan claims that it refuses to join the AIIB for three reasons. First, it cannot guarantee that the AIIB is transparent and corruption-free. Secondly, the AIIB and the Asian Development Bank have overlapping functions, and the former is likely to replace the latter. Thirdly, it is difficult for Japanese companies participating in AIIB to win bids. However, these are all excuses. There are three substantive reasons: Firstly, Japan is worried that China will have financial dominance in the Asia-Pacific region, breaking the joint financial dominance of Japan and the US. Secondly, it is worried about weakening the "Arc of Freedom and Prosperity" value in its diplomacy, which will result in the weakening of its economic diplomacy in

---

11. Xu Gang, Si Wen, and Chen Lu, "An Analysis of the Reasons and Impacts of Europe's Joining the AIIB," *Modern International Relations*, no. 5 (2015): 9–11.

12. Zhao Ke, "The EU's Asia-Pacific Policy Pivoting to 'New Engagement'? – Understanding the Behavioral Logic of EU Countries Joining the AIIB," *European Studies*, no. 2 (2015): 28.

Southeast Asia. Thirdly, Japan needs to consolidate its existing strategic alliance with the United States, and must be consistent with it on this issue.[13]

The United States is also boycotting the AIIB. After China's announcement of its decision to establish the AIIB, the US government's attitude and policies were opposed to it. Not only did the United States refuse to participate, but it also tried to dissuade its allies, such as the United Kingdom, Australia, and South Korea. In essence, its concern is that the AIIB will help China improve its international image and influence, thereby eroding US influence in Asia.[14] The United States believes that China's creation of international financial institutions is a challenge to the dollar system, and endangers the financial system in the Asia-Pacific region that is currently dominated by Japan and the US.

In reality, the creation of the AIIB has exacerbated the divergence of interests between the United States and its allies. The current structural contradictions in Sino-US relations enable the easy magnification of problems between the two countries. The very different attitudes of the United States and its allies to the AIIB reflect the fact that they are not monolithic, but the effect of the AIIB on dividing the US alliance cannot be overemphasized. Since the Cold War, the United States and its allies have not coordinated on any issue. This is because their strategic goals and interests have diverged, resulting in increasing differences in their strategies and policies. According to Fu Mengzi, "Some international media outlets also believe that the UK's announcement that it was joining the AIIB marked the collapse of the United States' alliance system in Europe, while the entry of South Korea and Australia marked the collapse of its alliance system in Asia."[15] This sounds a little farfetched. Some scholars also believe that the EU's participation in the AIIB rather than following the United States in boycotting it does not mean a split between Europe and the United States. On the contrary, it is the result of coordination. Joining the AIIB is not only a pursuit of economic interests, but also a reflection of the EU's Asia-Pacific policy pivoting towards new engagement in recent years. Europe is trying to exert influence on China's BRI by joining the AIIB, which may lead to the emergence of new opportunities in the Asia-Pacific region. The EU wants

---

13. Wang Haibin, "Rejecting the AIIB, Showing Japan's Zero-Sum Thinking," *Social Watch*, no. 7 (2015): 46–48; Bi Shihong, "Japan: Whether to Join the AIIB or Not," *World Knowledge*, no. 8 (2015): 36.

14. Liu Ying and Wei Lei, "AIIB from the International Think Tank Scholars' Perspective," *Southern Finance*, no. 6 (2015): 4–5.

15. Fu Mengzi, "How Do You View the Influence of the AIIB?" *Modern International Relations*, no. 5 (2015): 1–3.

to be prepared for changes in advance.¹⁶ Meanwhile, the United States needs to reflect on how it failed to dissuade other allies from joining the AIIB. At the very least, from a moral perspective, China has rendered a lot of assistance, while the United States has done little. However, the joining of the AIIB by allies or partners of the United States is more of a pursuance of interests. They have also reinforced their relationship with the United States to counterbalance the policy impact of joining the AIIB, which is evident in their joining the Trans-Pacific Partnership (TPP).

4 Helping the Asian Community with a Shared Future

A close neighbor is better than a distant relative. Regardless of the geographical environment or mutual relationship, Asia is of exceptional strategic significance to China. It is the region where China's geopolitical, economic, and security interests are most closely related, and it is also the geographical support for the rise of China's great power. The new Chinese government sees the Asian region as greatly important. In October 2013, President Xi Jinping spoke at a symposium on diplomatic work with neighboring countries, saying that it is necessary to plan the general trend, focusing on strategy and operational planning to ensure success. A series of new initiatives, concepts, and measures in Asia's regional diplomacy, such as the community with a shared future, Asia's new security concept, the ideals of friendship, sincerity, mutual benefit, and inclusivity, and the "Belt and Road" have advanced China's regional diplomacy in Asia into a new stage, and continue to improve the destiny of the Asian community. It is crucial to build an Asian community with a shared future and encourage connectivity in the region. Through the implementation of interconnectivity, geographical ties in Asia can be intensified, and the integration of geo-economic, political, and security can be advanced. A geopolitical environment rather than a geographical surrounding can be truly realized.

In terms of concept implementation and action advancement, the establishment of the AIIB will contribute to the building of a community with a shared future in Asia. Conceptually, the AIIB is the true embodiment of the ideals of China's neighborhood diplomacy, namely friendship, sincerity, mutual benefit, and inclusivity; from an action perspective, the AIIB's operations are conducive to the advancement of the BRI, thereby promoting the realization of a community with a shared future in Asia.

---

16. Zhao Ke, "The EU's Asia-Pacific Policy Pivoting to 'New Engagement'? – Understanding the Behavioral Logic of EU countries joining the AIIB," *European Studies*, no. 2 (2015), 16.

For a long time, China's neighborhood diplomacy has upheld the principles of friendship and partnership with its neighbors, as well as the ideologies of good neighborliness, peace, and prosperity. The new government put forward the motto of friendship, sincerity, mutual benefit, and inclusivity, which is a clear declaration of China's following the path of peaceful development in light of the new situation. It is also an insightful summary of China's diplomatic practices and reflects innovative development of the new central leadership's collective diplomatic concepts. By implementing the ideals of friendship, sincerity, mutual benefit, and inclusivity in neighborhood diplomacy, pursuing good neighborliness and friendship, helping each other, and doing more good deeds, China can make neighboring countries closer, more friendly, more recognized, more supportive, and more able to rally and influence one another better. The establishment of the AIIB reflects the omnipresence of friendship, sincerity, mutual benefit, and inclusivity.

For the creation of a community with a shared future in Asia, the BRI is an important measure, and is conducive to reinforcing the connection and cooperation between China and Asian countries, forming an Asian partnership network, and thus promoting the gradual realization of the community with a shared future in Asia. The establishment of the AIIB has gone a long way to address the infrastructure investment gap of Asian countries, and helps the acceleration of neighboring interconnectivity projects. According to the Asian Development Bank's estimates, the investment needs of infrastructure creation in Asian countries from 2010 to 2020 is about USD 8 trillion, while the total annual investment into infrastructure creation by the World Bank in Asia is only about USD 30 billion – a huge funding gap. The AIIB initially identified capital of USD 100 billion, of which China deposited USD 50 billion, which can to some extent bridge the funding gap for infrastructure creation in its surrounding areas.

The AIIB primarily serves Asian countries, providing funds for their development, which is an important impetus for the common development and prosperity of Asia. The founding of the AIIB represents the vision of establishing a new regional or multilateral order with Asian countries and non-regional countries as the mainstay. It has finally become a reality, laying the foundation for the building of a community with a shared future in Asia.[17] Through the establishment of the AIIB, encouraging the development of infrastructure in Asia will greatly support resource complementarity

---

17. Fu Mengzi, "How Do You View the Influence of the AIIB?" *Modern International Relations*, no. 5 (2015): 1–3.

and development sharing in Asia, and will encourage Asian countries to become a community of interests, responsibilities, and destiny.

By endorsing the development of connectivity, the BRI will also achieve important breakthroughs and add wings to the "Asian dream." In terms of transport and communication, the connectivity will help reinforce the ties between China and Asian countries, and will encourage the building of a community of interests in Asia. More importantly, it can enhance Asian countries' recognition of China, so that the community with a shared future can take root in Asia. According to Xu Yanzhuo and Xue Li, "The establishment of the AIIB is not a unilateral alternative to confronting the existing financial structure and a new start, but a win-win decision based on a comprehensive consideration of domestic political and economic goals and international needs, which is beneficial to growing China's influence in the surrounding area and to enhancing the Asian countries' identification with China."[18] Highlighting China's affinity, appeal, and attractiveness through the AIIB can increase the positive views of Asian countries towards it, emphasizing interests and shared honor, and encouraging the building of a community with a shared future in Asia.

In summary, the establishment of the AIIB can significantly encourage the implementation of the BRI, and partly benefit Asian countries by using China's strong capital and production capacity. The AIIB has grasped the key issues in the development of Asian countries, and primarily focuses on infrastructure investment there, which can reinforce the interconnection among Asian countries, and also help encourage their sustainable economic development. This is of critical value in enhancing China's influence in the Asian region. The blueprint for connectivity is of great significance in solving the bottleneck problem in Asia-Pacific development, and we should continue to encourage it. The Asian Infrastructure Investment Bank is an important supporting platform for regional connectivity. Xi Jinping stated that "China will intensify mutually beneficial cooperation and interconnection with Asia-Pacific countries and maintain a peaceful and stable environment for development. China has proposed the 13th Five-Year Plan, and will encourage development that is innovative, coordinated, green, open, and shared. China has the determination, confidence, and ability to encourage sustainable and healthy economic development, create more opportunities, and reap more benefits for the Asia-Pacific region."[19]

---

18. Xu Yanzhuo and Xue Li, "The Asian Dream AIIB Brought to Us," *Social Observatory*, no. 5 (2015): 47–48.

19. "Xi Jinping Attends the 23rd APEC Economic Leaders' Meeting and Delivers an Important Speech," Xinhuanet, November 19, 2015, http://news.xinhuanet.com/world/2015-11/19/c_1117201003.htm.

The most critical element of China's current foreign strategy is identifying how to transform its strengths into corresponding international influence. This requires China to reinforce its capabilities in agenda setting and mechanism creation. The Asian region is a testing ground and a barometer for China to increase its influence. The establishment of the AIIB will help reinforce the bond of interest and emotional identity between China and Asian countries, and will contribute to the building of a community with a shared future in Asia.

5 Encouraging the Building of a Community with a Shared Future for Developing Countries

As the ancient Chinese adage goes, "be moral when you are poor, and share with others when you are rich." Currently, the AIIB's establishment is primarily aimed at building infrastructure in Asian countries. More precisely, it aims to help developing Asian countries strengthen the development of basic infrastructure. It is a sound policy to benefit poor countries and an important measure to practice China's new approach of upholding justice while pursuing shared interests. Some of the participating countries in Europe, Africa, and Latin America are still developing, and the AIIB is helping them too, promoting China-Africa, China-Latin America, and China-Arab relations, and partnering with other developing countries to build a community with a shared future. The Chinese government advocates for a new concept of justice and interests. President Xi Jinping stated that when forming relations with developing countries, China must use this concept. Politically, it must uphold justice and morality. Economically, it must endorse mutual benefit, win-win, and common development. Neighboring and developing countries that have enjoyed amicable relations with China for a long time, and have difficult development journeys, should take the interests of the other side into more consideration and pay more and take less during cooperation. This is to allow the vast number of developing countries to share China's development dividends and achieve common development.

One of the important reasons why China launched the AIIB is that it hopes to use its financial strength to encourage the common development of other countries, particularly developing countries. It is estimated that the moderate scale of China's foreign exchange reserves is between 1.495 trillion and 2.55 trillion US dollars. At present, China's foreign exchange reserves are close to 4 trillion US dollars, accounting for about one-third of the world's foreign exchange reserves, and its scale has exceeded a reasonable level. However, the main investment areas of China's high foreign exchange reserves are low-risk, low-yield assets such as US Treasury bonds.

Since 2010, they have been facing the problems of declining returns and a single investment portfolio and channel. The establishment of the AIIB can reinforce the effective use of China's foreign exchange, enrich the investment portfolio, and expand investment channels.[20] Although China is still a developing country, in terms of foreign exchange reserves, it has become rich. It is necessary to explore a new path for capital operation in order to make good use of the foreign exchange in hand, practice the justice and interests of China's new diplomatic concept, and create positive economic diplomacy. According to Zhang Wenmu, "The AIIB is both a historic opportunity and a challenge to China – an opportunity for us to learn how to manage international finance."[21]

The AIIB is an important manifestation of China's consistent commitment to regional and international responsibilities as its own capabilities increase. To a certain extent it can make up for the insufficient supply of regional and global financial products, which has far-reaching significance for endorsing the restructuring of the international financial system and pushing a more balanced and sustainable development of the global economy. The AIIB is also an important attempt by the countries that have become rich first to help other countries that have accumulated wealth later. Developing countries can unite and help each other, and developed and developing countries can also offer mutual aid. The AIIB will open up a new world for South-South cooperation, and will encourage justice and interests in Asia, working with the likes of the BRICS Bank, the Shanghai Cooperation Organization Bank, the China-Africa Development Bank, the Silk Road Fund, the China-Africa Fund, the China-Africa Forum, the China-Central Asian Nations Forum, the China-Arab Forum, the China-ASEAN Forum, the RCEP (Regional Comprehensive Economic Partnership) and other multilateral free trade and investment arrangements, as well as financial cooperation with neighboring countries, and currency swap agreements.[22]

As the largest developing country in the world today, China has always represented the interests and spoken up for the rights of developing countries. In the current international system, developing countries are at an overall disadvantage. One of the main reasons is that the largest international political and economic systems are dominated by developed countries. They are reluctant to implement restructuring

---

20. Gao Lin, "The Significance of the Establishment of AIIB from the 'One Belt and One Road' Strategy," *Chinese and Foreign Entrepreneurs*, no. 8 (2015): 1–2.
21. Zhang Wenmu, "The Political Significance of 'One Belt, One Road' and the AIIB, *Review of Political Economy*, no. 4 (2015): 204.
22. Wang Yuesheng, "The Deep Impact of the AIIB's 'New Circular Economy,'" *People's Tribune*, no. 4 (2015): 52–54.

for developing countries because of their vested interests. This is particularly evident in the international financial system. In international financial institutions such as the World Bank, the IMF, and the Asian Development Bank, the representation and voice of developing countries have not been amplified accordingly.

As China's participation in international financial institutions is relatively short, its position is not equal to its current economic strength, and its right to speak is relatively limited. In May 2014, China's attempt to expand the Asian Development Bank's share stalled. In a financial system dominated by Western countries, it is difficult for China to break the deadlock. Since it is difficult for China to request restructuring of the existing international financial system, it created the AIIB to encourage incremental restructurings and avoid intensifying zero-sum competition.

The establishment of the AIIB reflects China's philosophy of cohesion despite difference. Since the existing international financial institutions cannot meet the interests of emerging countries, China chose not to fight it, but to create new financial institutions instead. The existence of the AIIB does not mean that China wants to subvert the existing international financial system, but to supplement it. As AIIB president Jin Liqun said, "The AIIB . . . is a supplement to the World Bank and ADB, not a substitute. It is an improvement and advancement of the existing international financial order, not a subversion."[23]

Both for the World Bank and the Asian Development Bank, China's advocacy for the establishment of the AIIB is not a draw from the bottom line, but a useful supplement that can alleviate the huge gap in infrastructure investment in Asia. The AIIB fully expresses China's sincerity in terms of respecting the existing international order and the established powers, and embodies the characteristics of openness, freedom, and peaceful consultation. According to Wang Da, "The AIIB is conducive to complementing and improving the current international development financing system and promoting the integration and development of Asian economies. It is also of crucial significance for promoting the rebalancing of the global economy and the restructuring of the international financial order."[24]

During the launch of the AIIB, the main projects have been based on supporting the creation of infrastructure in developing countries, and recognizing the dominant position of developing countries in terms of voting rights and bank management positions. Therefore, the AIIB provides a financing platform for developing countries,

---

23. Xu Yanzhuo and Xue Li, "The Asian Dream Brought to Us by the AIIB," *Social Observatory*, no. 5 (2015): 47–48.

24. Wang Da, "China's Considerations and AIIB's Global Significance," *Northeast Asia Forum*, no. 3 (2015): 48.

adds impetus to the economic creation of developing countries, and also lays a foundation for building a community with a shared future for developing countries.

6 Power Game or Institutional Innovation?

China's attempt to provide international public goods via the AIIB has been met with skepticism from the international community. Some countries even believe that this is China's attempt to challenge the hegemony of the United States and seize world leadership. One of the keys to how to respond to the outside world's doubts about the AIIB is how China can explain to the international community that the AIIB is not an old-fashioned game of power, but rather an institutional restructuring that improves the global governance system. A major question from the international community is whether the AIIB is the beginning of China's subversion of the international financial system, or whether it is the product of a power game with Japan and the US.

One of the reasons why China launched the AIIB is that it was unable to utilize its positive energy within the existing international financial system. Countries such as Japan and the US stick to their traditional advantages, making it difficult for China to compete. However, its status in the financial system has now improved.

As far as the three major international financial institutions with the closest interests to China are concerned, its position among them is relatively limited. For the World Bank, China's voting rights have risen to third place after the latest round of adjustments, but the share transfer is not from Japan and the US. At the International Monetary Fund and the Asian Development Bank, the delaying tactics of Japan and the US make it difficult for China's position to improve in the near future. When countries view cooperation with each other based on relative benefits rather than absolute benefits, it is difficult for the international system to leverage its functions fully, and it may even become a tool for power games between countries. So, does the fact China spearheaded the establishment of the AIIB indicate that it is playing a financial game with Japan and the US? The answer is no. China's decision to create new institutions is not an attempt to subvert the existing international financial order, but to provide better regional financial public goods. At the same time, China is also open to Japan and the US joining the AIIB. Although AIIB and ADB overlap in some areas, the resources available to the two financial institutions are not sufficient to fill the gap in infrastructure investment in Asia, so there is no zero-sum competition between them. Instead, they can seek win-win cooperation.

Rather than a power game, the AIIB should be regarded as a form of institutional innovation. The theory of institutional change holds that an institution is a series of formulated rules, compliance procedures, and moral and ethical behavioral norms. Due to bounded rationality and a scarcity of resources, the supply of institutions is limited. With a change of the external environment or an improvement of rationality, people will continue to demand new institutions to realize the expected increase in benefits. When the supply and demand of the system are in balance, the system is stable; when the existing system cannot satisfy people's needs, changes to the system will occur. The ratio of the cost to the benefit of institutional change plays a key role in promoting or delaying institutional change. Only when the expected benefit is greater than the expected cost will the actor persist until the final realization of the institutional change, and vice versa. For the groups with a vested interest in the existing system, there is a strong "path dependence" phenomenon, which may become an obstacle to change. It also makes it difficult to realize top-down system change, which also makes bottom-up system change difficult. The restructuring of the system is a matter of course.

The current international financial system is facing a problem of institutional innovation. The existing international financial institutions such as the World Bank, the IMF, and the Asian Development Bank have many issues. The interests of emerging countries led by China have not been improved accordingly, and the representation of developing countries is very limited. For the restructuring of today's international financial institutions, the existing interest groups such as Japan and the US embody the phenomenon of "path dependence," which limits the restructuring of the existing international finance model. The establishment of the AIIB can be regarded as an institutional innovation to circumvent obstacles such as "path dependence." The AIIB is more innovative than other financial institutions in terms of institutional setup, organizational principles, and rules – an important reason why it can attract many countries from within and outside the region to participate.

Institutional innovation does not mean a power game, but a focus on how to reach consensus on rulemaking. Rules reshape power, and the main tendency in today's world is towards "rule politics" rather than "power politics." Rather than focusing on China leading the establishment of the AIIB, more attention should be paid to the formulation of its actual operating rules. The AIIB's rules are not completely opposed to the current Western-dominated financial institutions, but there are places for reference and improvement. Therefore, it is possible for China to reach a consensus on AIIB rulemaking with countries such as Japan and the US. The AIIB is an important force of innovation in the international financial system, but China should refrain from celebrating just yet. Looking ahead, the AIIB still faces a raft of challenges. The first is identifying how to achieve coexistence, cooperation, and complementarity with existing international financial institutions. The second is working out how to deal with internal governance issues and leverage the advantages of the AIIB's innovation. The third is deciding how to conduct business in a sound and methodical manner to achieve reasonable financial business. On these issues, China can cooperate with all countries willing to participate, as well as Japan and the US.

In short, the AIIB is an important attempt by China to implement its new diplomatic concept, which means that its future development will inevitably encounter difficulties, not only the vigilance of countries such as Japan and the US, but also in the operation of the institution. Through starting small and moving step by step, AIIB can be developed. This is of great significance in building a community with a shared future for humanity. In aiding the creation of infrastructure in Asian countries and improving the status of developing countries in the international financial system, the AIIB has become an important driving force for building a community with a shared future for humanity. Its development will also profoundly affect the community.

PART III

Strengthening Intraregional and International Connectivity

The realization of a community with a shared future for humanity must pass through bilateral, regional, and global stages of development, of which the regional phase is crucial. Efforts should be made to endorse the creation of a community with a shared future for neighboring countries, for China-ASEAN, and for developing countries, as well as the stable development of major-country relations.

CHAPTER 8

Building a Community with a Shared Future with Neighboring Countries

As part of China's overall diplomacy, its neighboring areas are an important support for peaceful development. In October 2013, the central government convened the first symposium on neighborhood diplomacy since the founding of the People's Republic of China, and made it a priority in China's diplomacy, highlighting its important position. At the meeting, President Xi Jinping stated that succeeding in neighborhood diplomacy requires achieving the "Two Centenary Goals" and the "Chinese Dream," which result in the great rejuvenation of the Chinese nation. A favorable surrounding environment enables China's development to benefit more neighboring countries and achieve common development.[1] In November 2014, the central government held a conference on foreign affairs, which further highlighted the importance of neighborhood diplomacy. To endorse its development, President Xi Jinping emphasized the importance of building a neighborhood community with a shared future, and upholding the ideals of friendship, sincerity, mutual benefit, and inclusivity, as well as following the principles of friendship and partnership with

---

1. "Xi Jinping Delivered a Speech at the Symposium on Diplomatic Work in Neighboring Countries, Highlighting the Need for a Conducive Surrounding Environment for China's Development and to Endorse China's Development to Benefit More Countries," *People's Daily*, October 26, 2013, 1.

neighbors, fostering neighborly ties, and intensifying mutually beneficial cooperation and connectivity with neighboring countries.[2] With its continuing development of neighborhood diplomacy, the creation of a community with a shared future for its surrounding areas has become an important goal for China.

1 China's Regional Diplomacy since the 18th National Congress

China is a vast country with many neighbors, which are diverse and in varying stages of development. While its relations with its neighbors are generally sound, territorial disputes and maritime rights clashes exist with some countries. Coupled with the intervention of major powers, the surrounding areas and countries suffer unrest from time to time. China's surrounding area is an important support for its foreign strategy, and is also a pilot area for China in its push to transform itself from a regional power to a world power. Since the 18th National Congress, China's diplomatic layout has been optimized, and the diplomatic status of neighboring countries has become more prominent. This is inseparable from the interests of China and neighboring countries and the situation in neighboring regions.

1.1 China's new neighborhood diplomacy since the 18th National Congress

Firstly, the economic ties between China and neighboring countries have become increasingly close. In recent years, they have consistently endorsed mutual benefit and win-win results, and the neighboring regions have become the primary areas of China's overseas interests. Neighboring countries account for about 40% of China's total foreign trade. Its investment in neighboring countries accounts for about 30% of its total foreign investment, exceeding the sum of its investment in other regions.[3] In terms of the distribution of laborers in the surrounding areas, the *China Statistical Yearbook* revealed that China's laborers in the surrounding areas account for more than 40% of its global labor force, be it engineering dispatch or labor dispatch. China's surrounding areas are also the main destinations for its citizens' outbound tourism. For example, in 2016, the number of outbound tourists who were Chinese citizens reached 122 million, of which the top 10 outbound destination countries were Thailand, Japan, South Korea, United States, Maldives, Indonesia, Singapore,

---

2. "Central Foreign Affairs Work Conference Held in Beijing," *People's Daily*, November 30, 2014, 1.
3. Mainland China's investment in Hong Kong accounts for 55% to 60% of Mainland China's outbound investment, after disregarding the Hong Kong factor.

Australia, Italy, and Malaysia, with neighboring countries accounting for eight of these destinations.[4] In addition, the interests of overseas Chinese are considered to be an important part of China's overseas interests. Since Reform and Opening-up, the distribution of overseas Chinese in the world has continued to increase. Its surrounding areas are the places with the largest distribution of overseas Chinese. This is not a minor test for China's overseas interests.[5] Therefore, developing good relations with neighboring countries is related to the maintenance of China's overseas interests, and must be highly valued in terms of strategy and policy.

Secondly, the status of China's neighboring regions in the global strategic landscape has been rising. At the beginning of the 21st century, one of the major changes in the international pattern was the improvement of the Asia-Pacific region's strategic position, which is included in China's surrounding areas. At present, the region has become the center of the global economy, and is the most dynamic zone in the global economy. According to Kong Xuanyou, "The Asia-Pacific region is the region with the highest concentration of emerging market countries, and it is also the region with the fastest economic development in the world. It plays a pivotal role in promoting the development and growth of the world economy."[6] Asia-Pacific economic development is full of potential. As Yin Zonghua notes, "The region accounts for 40% of the world's population, 57% of the total economic output, and 48% of the total trade volume. It is the region with the fastest economic development and the most active cooperation globally."[7] Its economic size and the vitality of its development are the reasons why many countries hope to hop on the "Asia-Pacific Economic Express," which will increase external factors and intensify competition in the Asia-Pacific region. The region has also become more visible in the international community. As such, China should pay more attention to its surrounding areas.

Thirdly, the surrounding area has become one of the most intensely competitive areas in the world. It contains major countries such as Japan, Russia, and India, as well as important medium-sized countries like South Korea, Australia, and Indonesia. With the improvement in strategic position of the surrounding regions, the major

---

4. "2016 Big Data on Chinese Outbound Tourists: 122 million Travelers Spend $109.8 Billion," Phoenix Finance, January 20, 2017, http://finance.ifeng.com/a/20170120/15159280_0.shtml.

5. Amy Chang, "Beijing and the Chinese Diaspora in Southeast Asia: To Serve the People," *The National Bureau of Asian Research*, June 2013, 2.

6. Kong Xuanyou, "Co-creating Asia-Pacific Peace, Security and Prosperity in the 21st Century," *Asia-Pacific Security and Maritime Studies*, no. 4 (2015): 1–3.

7. "Yin Zonghua: Accelerating Economic Integration in the Asia-Pacific Region, Strengthening the Vitality of the Free Trade Zone," *China News Network*, May 20, 2015, http://www.chinanews.com/cj/2015/05-20/7290252.shtml.

powers are paying closer attention to the Asia-Pacific region, which intensifies the competition among major powers there. Kong Xuanyou writes, "Apart from the remnants of World War II, Cold War grievances, territorial sovereignty disputes, and historical issues in the surrounding areas that brew from time to time, plus intertwined traditional and non-traditional security challenges, there is still room for zero-sum competition and Cold War thinking, and hot issues and local conflicts continue to emerge."[8] The existence of many problems and fierce competition between the major powers have exacerbated the security issues in the surrounding areas. It is particularly worth mentioning that, with the narrowing power gap between China and the United States, the competition between them in the surrounding areas has acquired the dual attributes of regional and global hegemonic competition, which undoubtedly intensifies the two nations' strategic competition in the surrounding areas. Apart from this competition, there is also a need to pay attention to the rivalry between China and India and China and Japan, which also has an extremely important impact on the situation and power structure of China's surrounding areas.

Fourthly, although there are many institutions in the surrounding areas, cooperation has been greatly restricted by their relatively low efficiency and the competition among them. Although there is a variety of cooperation systems in the surrounding areas, many of them have limited impact due to their lower execution ability. The competition among the various systems has resulted in an obvious "noodle bowl" effect, which makes it impossible to further the development of institutionalized cooperation in the surrounding areas. Some regional powers even regard institutions as a tool for competition, leading to increasing restrictions on institutional competition in the Asia-Pacific region. In politics, to maintain "10+3" or "10+6" there is competition between countries. In the economic field, there are differences between China and the United States and other major countries pertaining to the type of regional trade cooperation system to be adopted. For security, the coexistence of three security cooperation models in the Asia-Pacific alliance of the United States, the collective security of ASEAN, and the cooperative security of China has resulted in a division of Asia-Pacific security cooperation, making it difficult to achieve inclusivity. Although the competition between major powers in China's surrounding areas may not necessarily lead to military conflict, the current institutional competition has significantly intensified. All major powers want to play a leading role in the setting of rules and regulations. China, Japan, India, ASEAN

---

8. Kong Xuanyou, "Co-creating Asia-Pacific Peace, Security and Prosperity in the 21st Century," *Asia-Pacific Security and Maritime Studies*, no. 4 (2015): 1–3.

countries, and the United States have become important powers that affect China's creation of systems in surrounding regions.

In general, as the eastward shift of the global strategic focus has led to an improvement in the strategic position of the surrounding areas, it has resulted in increased strategic attention from major powers, intensified regional conflicts, and increased involvement of foreign forces, complicating the situation. In addition, China's rise makes the surrounding areas more complex. The region faces double superposition from global and regional power competition. As a result, the complexity of China's surrounding areas has increased, and the competition between mechanisms in the surrounding areas has intensified.

1.2 New horizons for China's neighborhood diplomacy

For China's strategic adjustment from a regional power to a world power, it is particularly critical to consolidate the strategic foundation of the surrounding areas. Therefore, China's diplomacy in these areas has consistently introduced new concepts and measures in the new era, revealing a fresh look and new horizons.

Since the 18th National Congress, the Xi Jinping's CPC Central Committee has made the surrounding areas the diplomatic priority. As China's diplomacy shifts from concealing its ability to working hard and making progress, neighborhood diplomacy has ushered in new opportunities. In this new context, neighborhood diplomacy has consistently introduced a series of new concepts and measures. The first new concept is to advocate for the ideals of friendship, sincerity, mutual benefit, and inclusivity, while the second is to launch a new Asian security concept. The first new measure is to launch the BRI, followed by preparing for the AIIB's establishment, working towards Lancang-Mekong cooperation, and reinforcing the "two-wheel drive" of the Shanghai Cooperation Organization.

The ideals of friendship, sincerity, mutual benefit, and inclusivity in neighborhood diplomacy are a clear declaration of China's following the path of peaceful development under the new situation and an innovative development of the new diplomatic concepts.

"Friendship" refers to emotionally enhancing the sense of closeness and identity between China and neighboring countries. The soundness of state-to-state relations lies in friendship between people. Frequent political interactions have also led to personnel exchanges between China and neighboring countries in education and tourism. This has increased people-to-people exchanges, enhanced neighborliness and friendship, solidified the foundation of China's exchanges with neighboring countries, and endorsed neighborly friendships that can be passed down from generation to generation.

"Sincerity" refers to getting along with people in a sincere and trustworthy manner. China's sharing of its opportunities with neighboring countries is not empty talk. The BRI and the AIIB are a demonstration of its sincerity. Even if there are disputes with some neighboring countries, China will negotiate with them on an equal footing with sincerity, and will strive to handle them properly, rather than bullying the weak and making them submit by force. China also handles hotspot issues in its surrounding areas impartially, and plays an active role as a major country in upholding justice and maintaining order in the region.

"Mutual benefit" refers to benefiting the surrounding areas and win-win cooperation. Neighboring areas are an important support for China's development. It should continue sharing its development opportunities, dividends, and experience with neighboring countries, so that its development can benefit its neighbors, intensify the ties of the neighborhood community of interests, and consolidate the foundation of the neighborhood community with a shared future.

"Inclusivity" refers to China demonstrating itself as a major country that is open and inclusive, seeking common ground while reserving differences, and being cohesive in diversity. China fully respects and adapts to the various needs of countries in the region for development, as well as their diversity. China's inclusive mentality is clearly reflected in its cooperation with neighboring regions. In both the economic field and security field, China seeks commonality, i.e., common participation, development, and benefits.

The new Asian security concept is a major element of China's neighborhood diplomacy. It is the legacy and development of the new security concept and the overall security concept, and is an important part of a specifically Chinese form of major-country diplomacy. As Shi Yuanhua notes, it emphasizes the fact that "the peaceful development of Asia is closely related to the future and destiny of humanity. Asia's stability contributes to world peace, and its rejuvenation contributes to global development. Peace, development, cooperation, and win-win have always been the mainstream in Asia."[9] The new Asian security concept is systematic, and "the ideals of commonality, comprehensiveness, cooperation, and sustainability contain a new understanding of Asian security, as well as the thinking behind the

---

9. Shi Yuanhua, "The Historic New Development of China's Neighborhood Diplomacy since the 18th National Congress of the Communist Party of China," *Journal of China's Neighborhood Diplomacy*, no. 1 (2016): 25.

purpose, means, and method of realizing Asian security,"[10] as Han Aiyong notes. The specific implication of the new Asian security concept includes four aspects, namely commonality, comprehensiveness, cooperation, and sustainability. Common security is the goal, comprehensive security is the substance, cooperative security is the means, and sustainable security is the goal. In short, if the security of China's surrounding areas is unstable, it will be difficult to build a community with a shared future. To solve the complex security problems in the surrounding areas, there must be a consensus of ideas. The new Asian security concept is conducive to bridging the many security differences in the Asian region and promoting coordinated actions and consensus actions for security cooperation.

In terms of development history, the major BRI was primarily aimed at China's surrounding areas initially, and was proposed during President Xi Jinping's visit to neighboring countries. As it is viewed as a matter of high importance by the central government, the entire country (including central ministries, local provinces and cities, as well as state-owned enterprises and private enterprises) are participating in the initiative. It is of great value in promoting China's neighborhood diplomacy. Firstly, it is conducive to enhancing the integration of interests between China and neighboring countries. Although China currently has close economic ties with neighboring countries, there is still great potential to be tapped into. With connectivity enhancements brought about by the BRI, the cooperation between China and neighboring countries will be more convenient, frequent, and sufficient. Secondly, it is conducive to the integration of the political, economic, and security elements of China's neighborhood diplomacy. For a long time, the limitation of China's neighborhood diplomacy has lain in the separation of politics, economy, and security, which has resulted in the formation of a "dual pattern" in the surrounding areas. Although the BRI is dominated by economic cooperation, it also plays a positive role in enhancing political relations between China and neighboring countries, promoting security cooperation, and advancing the overall coordination of China's neighborhood diplomacy. Thirdly, the BRI can add value to the realization of a community with a shared future in the surrounding areas. Its realization must start from small steps, with the promotion of interests, responsibilities, and emotions. The eagle needs to spread its wings, and the BRI is undoubtedly the most powerful pair of wings at present.

---

10. Han Aiyong, "The Security Dilemma in East Asia and the Enlightenment of the New Asian Security Concept," *International Studies*, no. 5 (2015): 58–59.

(1) Leading the establishment of the AIIB

The AIIB's primary investment targets are Asian countries, and the main member countries are from Asia, which makes it a major initiative to benefit China's surrounding areas. It has addressed the main factor that restricts cooperation in the surrounding regions: backward connectivity. Through the AIIB's large capital investment, connectivity in the Asian region will develop rapidly, which will reinforce the connection between neighboring countries, consolidating the foundation of the neighboring community of interests, enhancing the sense of intimacy and recognition of neighboring countries, and promoting neighboring countries. All of this is beneficial to realizing a community with a shared future.

(2) Creating a new mechanism for Lancang-Mekong cooperation

China and the five countries on the Mekong River are connected by mountains and rivers, and a tradition of friendship has been passed down from generation to generation. They are natural cooperative partners and close friendly neighbors. At present, China has established a comprehensive strategic partnership of cooperation with the five Mekong countries, with closely intertwined interests and a solid foundation for cooperation. The establishment of the Lancang-Mekong cooperation mechanism can be described as a natural course of development that is conducive to stimulating the inherent development potential of all countries, and will also inject new vitality into the development of surrounding areas. The five Mekong countries are important members of ASEAN, and China firmly supports ASEAN integration and community building. The cooperation mechanism is a useful supplement to the China-ASEAN cooperation framework, and will help to build an upgraded version of all-round China-ASEAN cooperation. It is also a new form of south-south cooperation that demonstrates China's firm determination to join hands with the five Mekong countries to implement the United Nations' 2030 Agenda for Sustainable Development with practical actions.

Chinese Premier Li Keqiang stated that reinforcing the Lancang-Mekong cooperation and enabling the Lancang-Mekong countries to be friendlier and closer is the common aspiration of the countries and peoples of the region. The aim is to make things happen, seek cooperation, focus on promoting development, and join hands to build a Lancang-Mekong community with a shared future that offers mutual assistance, equal consultation, mutual benefit, and win-win cooperation.

In March 2016, the first Lancang-Mekong Cooperation Leaders' Meeting was held in Hainan. Prime Ministers of the six countries gathered in Sanya for a discussion, which centered around mutual political trust, connectivity, production capacity, and people-to-people exchanges. These countries have reached a series of consensuses that are expected to encourage Lancang-Mekong cooperation to achieve practical results and add new highlights to neighborhood diplomacy.[11]

(3) Strengthening the "two-wheel drive" of the Shanghai Cooperation Organization (SCO)

China's peaceful development is inseparable from the support of neighboring regions, and the SCO is a model of China's neighborhood cooperation. After its establishment in 2001, the SCO developed rapidly in all aspects over ten years, realizing an increase in member states, an expansion of cooperation fields, an improved mechanism, and enhanced international influence, making it a model for regional cooperation. Today, the SCO is at a critical stage. The future trends in its development will be capitalizing on its geo-economic advantages by pursuing energy cooperation, connecting with the Silk Road Economic Belt, catalyzing pragmatic cooperation, and realizing the "two-wheel drive" of its security and economic cooperations.

Security cooperation is the cornerstone of the SCO, and it is in the common interests of China, Russia, and Central Asian countries to jointly combat the "three evil forces." It is precisely because of this common geo-security interest that security cooperation has become its driving force. In addition, it is imperative to speed up the SCO's pragmatic cooperation premised on security cooperation. It is only through win-win economic cooperation that it can truly uphold mutual trust, mutual benefit, equality, consultation, respect for diverse cultures, and the pursuit of common development advocated by the "Shanghai Spirit." Also, only through the development of pragmatic cooperation can the SCO be built into a community of interests and shared future for the member states, offering a reliable guarantee and strategic support for the member states to seek common stability and common development.

Since 2013, the SCO has fully implemented the Treaty on Long-term Neighborliness, Friendship, and Cooperation, signed the Agreement on Cooperation between SCO Member States, and approved a series of resolutions such as the Development Strategy of the SCO until 2025. The goal is to realize the "two-wheel drive" of security and economy for the SCO's development, so that the interests of

---

11. "Li Keqiang: Join Hands to Build a Lancang-Mekong Community with a Shared Future," Xinhuanet, March 23, 2016, http://www.xinhuanet.com/politics/2016-03/23/c_1118421512.htm.

the SCO member states will be closer. This will be more conducive to the realization of the neighborhood community with a shared future.[12]

2 The Main Approaches to Building the Community

Building a community with a shared future is China's long-term design for neighborhood diplomacy, but it must be implemented gradually if it is to achieve concrete results.[13] Wang Fan writes, "In advancing the building of a community with a shared future, the key points are to observe changes, capitalize on the situation, highlight cooperation, emphasize alliances, and focus on building. We must work well and be moral, and we must formulate rules and shape the situation."[14] Former Deputy Foreign Minister Liu Zhenmin stated that "China is an important force in building a community with a shared future in Asia, and it can do so with five major measures. Firstly, it can endorse neighborliness and friendship through high-level exchanges. Secondly, it can endorse the common development of Asia through its own development. Thirdly, it can encourage the building of a community with a shared future through regional cooperation. Fourthly, it can endorse security cooperation to maintain peace and stability in Asia. Fifthly, it can enrich the implication of a community with a shared future through people-to-people and cultural exchanges."[15]

Although the scope of the community with a shared future in Asia is different from that of its neighbors, the ideas and stages are generally the same. Zhou Fangyin writes, "The community with a shared future has many profound meanings. The first step in its creation is probably to build a relatively in-depth and complete economic community by improving the level of regional economic integration, followed by building a security community on this basis, and then a mature neighborhood community with a shared future that contains political, economic, security, social, cultural and other implications."[16] Some scholars also believe that to endorse the creation of a community with a shared future, three aspects should be borne in mind.

---

12. Ling Shengli, "Security and Economic 'Two-Wheel Drive' SCO Development," *Overseas Network*, September 15, 2014, http://opinion.haiwainet.cn/n/2014/0915/c353596-21078223.html.

13. Zhou Fangyin, "Strategic Choice of China's Neighboring Environment and Neighborhood Diplomacy," *Contemporary World*, no. 10 (2016): 13.

14. Wang Fan, "The Theoretical Significance and Promotion of a Community with a Shared Future," *Contemporary World*, no. 6 (2016): 4.

15. Liu Zhenmin, "nsist on Win-Win Cooperation and Join Hands to Build a Community with a Shared Future in Asia," *International Studies*, no. 2 (2014): 7–10.

16. Zhou Fangyin, "Community with a Shared Future: Important Elements of the National Security Concept," *People's Forum*, no. 16 (2014): 33.

Firstly, to endorse the community with a shared future and when implementing it between states, it is necessary to highlight commonality, interaction, inclusivity, and coordination in the relationship. Second, it is necessary to solve the key points of non-interference in internal affairs and exert constructive influence, non-alignment, cooperative partnerships, decolonization, and new types of regional cooperation. Thirdly, it is necessary to go through three stages, namely a combination of in-depth interdependence, compatible systems between countries, and a community with a shared future.[17] In summary, the creation of a neighborhood community with a shared future divided into three phases.

2.1 Phase 1: Building a community of peripheral interests

A continued intensifying of the integration of interests is the foundation for the creation of a neighborhood community with a shared future. Through economic, trade, and investment cooperation, China can continue endorsing the gradual intensification of its interests with neighboring countries, as well as expanding and enhancing common interests. For the creation of a community of interests, apart from increasing common interests between countries, it is also essential to reinforce the institutionalization of mutual cooperation. This involves pushing forward the creation of surrounding free trade zones, reinforcing the formulation of investment rules in surrounding areas, and consolidating and intensifying the achievements of surrounding economic and trade cooperation through a series of regional cooperation systems, as well as contributing to the lasting maintenance and development of mutual interests. At present, the improvement of the neighborhood interconnection strategy brought about by the implementation of the BRI is conducive to promoting the integration of interests among neighboring countries, and is of great help in the realization of a community of interests. However, the implementation of the BRI also faces various risks – some of them political and economic – which must be properly dealt with and gradually endorsed.

2.2 Phase 2: Building a community for neighborhood security

The creation of a community for neighborhood security is a key part of the creation of a neighborhood community with a shared future. One cannot be realized without

---

17. Wang Fan, "The Theoretical Significance and Practical Promotion of a Community with a Shared Future," *Contemporary World*, no. 6 (2016): 6–7.

the other. However, it faces many obstacles. Firstly, there are differences in security concepts. The proposal of the new Asian security concept will help to resolve these differences of opinion. As Han Aiyong writes, "The realization of common, cooperative, comprehensive, and sustainable security advocated by the new Asian security concept will completely break the dual pattern of separation of the regional economy and security, and will help to establish a new architecture for security cooperation that is development oriented, endogenous, cooperative, and innovative."[18]

The second challenge in the creation of a community for neighborhood security is how to absorb the US Asia-Pacific alliance. This also makes it very important to reconcile the two goals of building a neighborhood with a shared future and building a new type of major-country relationship between China and the United States.[19] The Asia-Pacific alliance with the United States is a legacy of the Cold War, and despite its current limitations, it will not be withdrawn any time soon. For the creation of China's peripheral security community, the first challenge is how to integrate the US Asia-Pacific alliance with an inclusive peripheral security cooperation.

The third challenge is to endorse the creation of a community for neighborhood security in multiple stages. Neighborhood security issues are extremely complex. Historical issues and current disputes are intertwined, making it difficult to resolve them. To realize the creation of a community for neighborhood security, China must adopt a step-by-step approach:

(1) Enhance the existing security dialogue mechanism and problem-solving mechanism;
(2) Establish a dispute dialogue mechanism in various fields;
(3) Establish a dispute settlement mechanism in various security fields;
(4) Establish a comprehensive dialogue mechanism in various security fields;
(5) Establish comprehensive security problem-solving mechanisms in various security fields and
(6) Build neighborhood security communities premised on mechanism coordination.[20]

---

18. Han Aiyong, "The Security Dilemma in East Asia and the Enlightenment of the New Asian Security Concept," *International Studies,* no. 5 (2015): 51.

19. Wang Jisi, "Security Architecture in the Asia-Pacific Region: Goals, Conditions and Vision," *International Security Studies,* no. 1 (2016): 4.

20. Liu Shengxiang and Zhang Nan, "Overall National Security Concept and China's Southeast China Multilateral Security Mechanism," Central China Normal University, *Journal of the Chinese Academy of Sciences* (Humanities and Social Sciences Edition), no. 6 (2015): 40–41.

As long as a community for neighborhood security can be realized, there is hope for the creation of the neighborhood community with a shared future.

2.3 Phase 3: Building a community with a shared future

The creation of a community with a shared future needs to be based on a community of interests and a community of security. Since China and its neighboring countries have a strong consensus on values, shared feelings, and shared responsibilities, a community with a shared future can be realized. A neighborhood community with a shared future does not ultimately form a unified country, but should not use coercive methods such as force to resolve their differences. The pursuit of common interests among countries is higher than national interests, and the absolute benefits are higher than the relative benefits. The realization of a neighborhood community with a shared future depends on a high degree of mutual political trust among countries, a high degree of positive public recognition, and a high degree of coordination and integration between mechanisms. A neighborhood community with a shared future means that rules and ethical ties will replace power relations and become the norm for dealing with the relations between neighboring countries.

Rome was not built in a day, and the creation of a community with a shared future cannot be accomplished overnight. Truly realizing it requires China and neighboring countries to continue discussing, building, and sharing.

3 The Main Challenges of Building the Community

Although the neighborhood community with a shared future has planned out the future direction of development for China's neighborhood diplomacy, it will face many challenges in terms of concepts, power, and institutions to realize it.

3.1 Ideological disagreements

With increasingly close exchanges and the intensification of interests between countries, a community with a shared future should be the future direction of development for global society. However, not all countries are able to realize this at the same time. China's proposal of the concept of a community with a shared future for its neighbors is an expectation for the development prospects of its relations with its neighbors as things currently stand. However, not every neighboring country agrees with this. The inconsistency between neighboring countries and China's perceptions is often caused by "historical inertia" and old concepts, according to Chen Xiangyang.[21] It is also due to the multiple differences in political systems, religious beliefs, and development stages of neighboring countries. Differences in concepts have led to differences among countries on whether and how to build a community with a shared future in the neighborhood, which undoubtedly increases the difficulty of building a neighborhood community with a shared future.

3.2 A power game among major powers

For the creation of a neighborhood community with a shared future, the negative impact of the power game between major nations cannot be ignored. Many major powers both inside and outside the region regard the neighborhood community with a shared future as China's attempt to build a sphere of influence or regional dominance, and believe that China is trying to recreate the "tributary system." This makes it difficult for them to view the neighborhood community with a shared future from a pragmatic perspective.

The United States believes that China's creation of a neighborhood community with a shared future is an attempt to build regional hegemony, which will impact the United States' dominion in the Asia-Pacific region. For example, the United States suspects that the new Asian security concept is China's "Monroe Doctrine," aiming to drive the US out of Asia. The United States has yet to accept the BRI, AIIB, and other new diplomatic measures for China's neighboring countries, and has repeatedly blocked its allies from joining AIIB.

Japan has long been wary of China's development, due to its huge impact on Japan's claims to regional dominance. At the same time, there are fears that Japan may retaliate against China when it becomes stronger. Therefore, when it comes to opposing the BRI and the AIIB, Japan has aligned with the United States. For the neighborhood community with a shared future, Japan has also taken interference and boycott measures from time to time.

Russia is an important neighbor to China. However, their differences in geographic traditions and religious beliefs results in Russia not fully recognizing China's community with a shared future.

India is a major country with a strong pursuit for independence. It is not enthusiastic about China's neighborhood community with a shared future, and

---

21. Chen Xiangyang, "Leading the Reshaping of the World Order with a 'Community with a Shared Future for Humanity,'" *Contemporary World*, no. 5 (2016): 20–21.

even has a precautionary attitude to the BRI, believing that this will jeopardize its dominance in South Asia.

The game between major powers will make it harder to build a community with a shared future around them.

3.3 Skepticism towards China in neighboring countries

Not every country surrounding China agrees with the idea of building a community with a shared future, with some expressing skepticism. In recent years, the attitudes of neighboring countries towards China have been quite contradictory. They hope to share China's development dividends and expect it to assume more responsibilities. However, they are worried that China will dominate Asia by squeezing out the development space of other countries and "following the old path of seeking hegemony," as Liu Zhenmin notes.[22]

For the neighborhood community with a shared future, a community of interests is expected to be realized through means such as win-win economic cooperation, but the security concerns of neighboring countries about China are difficult to resolve in the short term. After all, during the long era of the tributary system, China made no shortage of military expeditions against neighboring countries. The fears of neighboring countries towards China will restrict the creation of neighborhood security communities. The economic cooperation between China and neighboring countries, as well the neighborhood community with a shared future will also be affected.

It is impossible to dispel the skepticism of neighboring countries towards China in the short term. However, for the long term, China should uphold the new ideals of friendship, sincerity, mutual benefit, and inclusivity in its neighborhood diplomacy, and do more good in neighboring regions. It should think more about how to realize mutual benefits and win-win cooperation for neighboring countries, and make more of an effort to encourage interconnection among neighboring countries, as well as try to provide more public goods for security cooperation for neighboring countries. This way, neighboring countries are bound to reduce or even eliminate their doubts and misunderstandings about China, and recognize its neighborhood diplomacy and the creation of a neighborhood community with a shared future.

---

22. Liu Zhenmin, "Insist on Win-Win Cooperation and Join Hands to Build a Community with a Shared Future in Asia," *International Studies*, no. 2 (2014): 5.

3.4 Shortcomings of the mechanism of the community for neighborhood security

The community for neighborhood security is key in linking the neighborhood community with a shared future. Although there is no shortage of security mechanisms in the surrounding area, there are many shortcomings. Firstly, it is the fragmented security mechanism. There are various types of security mechanisms in the surrounding areas, such as alliances and security forums, but there is competition among the mechanisms, making it difficult for each one to have a positive effect in terms of convergence. Secondly, the effectiveness of security mechanisms is generally low. Apart from having multiple security mechanisms in the surrounding areas, excluding alliances, the effectiveness of other security mechanisms is generally low, and this can be attributed to their low degree of institutionalization.[23] The security issues in the surrounding areas, such as Cold War legacies and hot-spot issues, are complex. They include traditional security issues like territorial disputes, and non-traditional security issues such as competition for water resources, as well as security dilemmas among large states and asymmetrical security issues between large and small states. Resolving these multiple security issues in the surrounding areas concerns their ability to achieve peace and stability, and whether the development of a community with a shared future in these areas can eventually be realized.

The surrounding areas are China's strategic support for a peaceful rise, and "testing beds" for its strategies and policies, including its peaceful development, the BRI, and a community with a shared future. As the backbone to building a community with a shared future in its surrounding areas, China's strategy needs to be premised on the basis of good relations with neighboring countries and increasing the influence of its mechanisms in neighboring regions to perform its role as a responsible major country, thereby promoting the early realization of a community with a shared future in the surrounding areas.

---

23. Jin Xin, "China-ASEAN Security Governance: Models, Dilemmas and Solutions," *Contemporary World and Socialism*, no. 5 (2016): 141–147.

CHAPTER 9

Endorsing the China-ASEAN Community with a Shared Future

THE CHINA-ASEAN COMMUNITY WITH A shared future is the result of the Chinese government's review of China-ASEAN relations within the concept of the community with a shared future, and constitutes the latest guidelines for China's development of foreign relations with the ASEAN. The concept of a China-ASEAN community with a shared future originated from a speech delivered by President Xi Jinping at the Indonesian Parliament on October 3, 2013. As the first foreign head of state invited to give a speech, President Xi proposed the main framework for China's development of China-ASEAN relations in the new era in his speech entitled "Jointly Building a China-ASEAN Community with a Shared Future." He emphasized that China "wishes to work with Indonesia and other ASEAN countries and make these countries into good neighbors, friends, and partners that will share prosperity and security and stick together through thick and thin. Through our joint efforts, we will build a closer-knit China-ASEAN community with a shared future, bringing benefits to both sides and to the people living in this region."[1]

In a similar fashion, China hopes to build a vision of an ideological community of cooperation in practice for the development of its relations with ASEAN countries.

---

1. Xi Jinping, "Jointly Building a China-ASEAN Community with a Shared Future – Speech Delivered at the Indonesian Parliament," *People's Daily*, October 4, 2013, 2.

Since then, the main theme of China's neighborhood diplomacy and ASEAN-oriented exchanges has been identifying how to raise awareness of the community of shared destiny in neighboring countries through more pragmatic cooperation. In fact, this also constitutes a new driving force for the development of China-ASEAN relations and a basic path for creating the China-ASEAN community with a shared future.

1 China-ASEAN Relations since the 18th National Congress

The 18th National Congress report emphasized that all countries in the world coexist on the same planet, and advocated for the concept of a community with a shared future for humanity. Concurrently, in response to changes in the regional and international situation, the Chinese government has put forward the ideals of friendship, sincerity, mutual benefit and inclusivity in its neighborhood diplomacy, and regards ASEAN as China's priority in neighborhood diplomacy. As the most significant representation of the community with a shared future for humanity in China's surrounding areas, the proposal of a China-ASEAN community with a shared future has become main focus of the Chinese government on the development direction of China-ASEAN relations. In recent years, it has guided China-ASEAN relations from its "Golden Decade" to its "Diamond Decade," and has pushed forward the sustainable and pragmatic development of these relations.

1.1 Political field

In the political field, China-ASEAN relations have entered a new phase of development, starting from the second decade of the strategic partnership between the two sides. The concept of a community with a shared future has become increasingly prominent in China's development of ASEAN relations. The China-ASEAN strategic partnership has progressed from a "Golden Decade" to a "Diamond Decade," while the creation of a community with a shared future and an intensification of bilateral China-ASEAN relations are some the core tasks of the "Diamond Decade" for the two parties.

The proposal of the China-ASEAN community with a shared future has established the ambitious goal of political exchanges between China and the ASEAN, and is a crucial strategic deployment on the part of the Chinese government to endorse the development of China-ASEAN relations in the current regional and international situation.² In addition, the Chinese government has formulated a specific development plan for the China-ASEAN community with a shared future from the perspective of top-level design, to achieve the goal of building a China-ASEAN community with a shared future. Less than a week after the concept was proposed, Chinese Premier Li Keqiang proposed the "2+7 Cooperation Framework" to develop ASEAN strategic partnerships at the 16th China-ASEAN ("10+1") Leaders' Meeting. As such, the Chinese government has clearly stated its two main political positions to the ASEAN on the development of bilateral relations. Firstly, the fundamental goal of endorsing cooperation is to intensify strategic mutual trust and expand neighborly friendships. Secondly, the key to intensifying cooperation is to focus on economic development and increase mutual benefit and win-win cooperation. China also pointed out seven areas of cooperation for discussion:

(1) to explore the signing of the China-ASEAN Treaty of Neighborliness, Friendship, and Cooperation;
(2) to kickstart the process of upgrading the China-ASEAN Free Trade Area;
(3) to accelerate the creation of infrastructure for interconnectivity;
(4) to reinforce financial cooperation and risk prevention in the region;
(5) to continue endorsing maritime cooperation;
(6) to reinforce exchanges and cooperation in the security field;
(7) to intensify cooperation in culture, science and technology, and exchanges.³

According to scholarly interpretations, this framework draws a clear roadmap for launching a "Diamond Decade" of cooperation between China and the ASEAN in future. At the same time, since the framework was suggested shortly after the concept of a China-ASEAN community with a shared future was proposed, scholars regard it as a concrete roadmap for China to seek to build a China-ASEAN community with a shared future.⁴ In terms of ideas, the cooperation framework includes mutual political trust, win-win and mutual beneficial trade relationships, cooperative security

---

2. Lu Jianren et al., eds., *China-ASEAN Cooperation Development Report (2014–2015)* (China Social Science Press, 2015), 4.
3. "Remarks by Li Keqiang at the 16th China-ASEAN (10+1) Leaders' Meeting (Full Text)," Chinese Ministry of Foreign Affairs website, October 10, 2013, http://www.fmprc.gov.cn/mfa_chn/gjhdq_603914/gjhdqzz_609676/lhg_610158/zyjh_610168/t1086491.shtml.
4. "The China-ASEAN 'Community with a Shared Future': Identity Beyond Specific Interests," Guangming.com, October 19, 2013, http://int.gmw.cn/2013-10/19/content_9222775.htm.

relationship, and harmonious social human relationship, which comprehensively covers the basic areas that China-ASEAN should include in creating a community with a shared future.

Subsequently, in the "Joint Statement" commemorating the 10th anniversary of the establishment of the China-ASEAN strategic partnership, Chinese and ASEAN leaders reiterated and emphasized their mutual political support. China stated that a united, prosperous, and vibrant ASEAN was in its strategic interests, and vowed to continue to support the ASEAN's community building, connectivity, and solidarity, and its leading role in evolving regional structure. The ASEAN stressed that "China's development is an important opportunity for the region, and we support its peaceful development."[5]

As the China-ASEAN strategic partnership enters a new decade, the mutual political and strategic trust between the two sides has increased and reached new heights, providing a foundation for the comprehensive intensification and development of bilateral relations. 2016 marks the 25th anniversary of the establishment of China-ASEAN relations. In the "Joint Statement of the China-ASEAN Commemorative Summit," the two sides restated their mutual support and trust in their development while looking back at the progress of bilateral dialogue relations over the past 25 years.[6] As Chinese Premier Li Keqiang said, if China and the ASEAN are each other's longitude and latitude, then mutual trust is the shuttle. Only when the longitude and latitude are closely intertwined can future cooperation be possible.[7] With the continuing development of dialogue and the expansion of their respective influence in regional affairs in recent years, China and the ASEAN have focused their efforts on reinforcing mutual political trust and establishing the concept of eco-systemic development.

---

5. "China-ASEAN Joint Statement on the 10th Anniversary of the Establishment of Strategic Partnership (Full Text)," Ministry of Foreign Affairs website, October 10, 2013, http://www.fmprc.gov.cn/mfa_chn/gjhdq_603914/gjhdqzz_609676/lhg_610158/zywj_610170/t1086485.shtml.

6. "The 19th China-ASEAN Leaders' Meeting and the Commemorative Summit for the 25th Anniversary of China-ASEAN Relations Joint Statement (Full Text)," Ministry of Foreign Affairs website, September 8, 2016, http://www.fmprc.gov.cn/web/gjhdq_676201/gjhdqzz_681964/lhg_682518/zywj_682530/t1395707.shtml.

7. "Remarks by Li Keqiang at the 16th China-ASEAN (10+1) Leaders' Meeting (Full Text)," Ministry of Foreign Affairs website, October 10, 2013, http://www.fmprc.gov.cn/mfa_chn/gjhdq_603914/gjhdqzz_609676/lhg_610158/zyjh_610168/t1086491.shtml.

1.2 Economic cooperation and trade

Since the 18th National Congress, China-ASEAN have entered a period of economic adjustments as the global economic situation deteriorates. Their economic cooperation and trade relations have experienced an in-depth transformation. This is initially reflected in the changes bilateral trade structure, and is specifically reflected in their volume and standing in trade relationships.

China-ASEAN trade volume has fallen after rising since 2012. In 2012, the trade volume between the two countries exceeded USD 400 billion, making China the ASEAN's largest trading partner, while the ASEAN continued to be China's third largest trading partner.[8] From 2013 to 2014, China-ASEAN trade volume continued increasing, hitting USD 480.4 billion by 2014. However, the bilateral trade volume experienced negative growth in 2015, decreasing to USD 472.2 billion. According to China's mid-2016 statistics, its total import and export trade with the ASEAN was USD 173.57 billion from January to May 2016 – a year-on-year decrease of 7.1%. In 2016, China-ASEAN trade volume fell by 4.2% compared to previous years.[9] With China becoming the ASEAN's largest trading partner, its share in ASEAN countries' foreign trade has been growing, and its economic importance to major ASEAN countries has become increasingly prominent. At the same time, the structure of bilateral China-ASEAN economic and trade exchanges has also shown significant changes, with 2012 being a watershed year., Although ASEAN countries had a surplus before 2012, the volume reached its peak in 2004, and it showed a general downward trend. Since 2012, the growth of China's exports to ASEAN countries has been significantly faster than imports, and the scale of exports is significantly greater than imports. As a result, China has a surplus at this stage. In terms of investment, structural changes in investment relationships between the two sides also reflected the changes in China-ASEAN status. Before 2014, the scale of the ASEAN's investment in China was much larger than that of China's domestic investments. For example, the mutual China-ASEAN investment structure still reflected this trend until 2012.[10]

---

8. "China-ASEAN Trade Volume Exceeded 400 Billion US Dollars in 2012, 7.3 Times that of 2002," *People's Daily Online*, July 23, 2013, http://finance.people.com.cn/n/2013/0723/c1004-22292436.html.

9. "State Council Information Office Introduced China-ASEAN Economic and Trade Cooperation Situation and the 13th China-ASEAN Expo," Chinese government website, July 19, 2016, http://www.gov.cn/xinwen/2016-07/19/content_5092696.htm

10. Statistics show that as of 2012, the cumulative two-way investment between China and the ASEAN reached USD 100.7 billion, of which China accounted for 23.4% and the ASEAN accounted for 76.6%. In 2012, the two-way investment amounted to USD 11.489 billion, of which China accounted for 38.5% and the ASEAN accounted for 61.5%.

With the continuing expansion of Chinese enterprises' investment in the ASEAN in recent years and its growth rate being higher than the ASEAN's investment in China, the proportion of China's two-way investment has continued expanding. By 2014, China's proportion exceeded that of ASEAN for the first time.[11] The in-depth adjustment of the structure of the economic relations between the two sides has major political implications and a deep impact on China-ASEAN political relations and security cooperation.

1.3 Security cooperation

In the field of security cooperation, China and the ASEAN have focused on three aspects in recent years. The first is maritime rules in the South China Sea, i.e., the formulation of institutional norms. The second is the pragmatic actions by China and Southeast Asia for security dialogue and cooperation, which include the China-Malaysia exercise. The third is that more Southeast Asian countries, such as Malaysia, Thailand, and the Philippines, are willing to purchase weapons and equipment from China. China and the ASEAN countries have undergone significant changes and adjustments in security cooperation since the 18th National Congress.

In-depth adjustment is the biggest change in China-ASEAN relations. This is partly the result of ever-increasing dialogues between the two sides over the past 20 years, and partly the reality of China-ASEAN relations – the basis and new starting point for dialogue and cooperation between the two sides to improve the quality of their relations. In fact, this also constitutes the fundamental background for the creation of the China-ASEAN community with a shared future, and the starting point for endorsing the realization of the community with a shared future in Southeast Asia.

2 Main Approaches to Building the Community

The community with a shared future is a new social concept that the Chinese government has emphasized in recent years.[12] In essence, it is a political concept with

---

11. In 2014, two-way China-ASEAN investment totaled USD 12.405 billion, of which China's total investment in ASEAN countries was USD 6.255 billion, accounting for 50.42%; ASEAN countries' total investment in China was USD 6.15 billion, accounting for 49.58%. See Lu Jianren et al., *China-ASEAN Cooperation Development Report (2014–2015)* (China Social Science Press, 2015), 9.

12. Qu Xing, "The Value Basis of a Community with a Shared Future for Humanity," *Qiushi*, no. 4 (2013): 53.

strong social attributes. Community means that in the interactions between people or countries, the identity and role of each have been developed under specific conditions or fields. While these identities can be universal or partial, people or nations are less arbitrary, questionable, or dangerous when an identity or role is established. However, if a person or country has difficulty establishing an identity or role while interacting with others, it will "lose this stability to encourage others with certainty."[13] Renowned German sociologist Ferdinand Tönnies was a major contributor to the community theory, which defines a community as "people who form a certain relationship," in which the will of the individual is combined in an organic way. When there is mutual affirmation, there will always be community in one way or another.[14] In terms of ideas, community awareness includes two important aspects, namely the awareness of pragmatic cooperation in reality, and the awareness of a symbiosis of destiny at the ideological level.

As such, the foundation of community-building goes down two key paths: the path of consciousness, and the path of pragmatic and mutually beneficial cooperation in reality. The main goal of the path of consciousness is to build an ideological community premised on the idea of the two parties having each other, as well as learning from each other and seeking common interests and values. On the pragmatic and mutually beneficial cooperation path, the community hopes to build a relationship of win-win cooperation and common interests between countries, and to face, negotiate, and solve global problems such as food security, terrorism, financial crises, and climate change together, as well as endorsing mutual interests through greater cooperation and realization of diverse and inclusive development among countries. These two aspects form the basis of the concept of a community with a shared future.[15] Evidently, this provides the most critical path of inspiration for the creation of a China-ASEAN community with a shared future. The realization and demonstration of the consciousness of a community with a shared future in Southeast Asia is illustrated in the creation of the China-ASEAN community with a shared future.

---

13. Sigismund Bowman, *Community*, trans. Ouyang Jinggen (Jiangsu People's Publishing House, 2003), 77.

14. Ferdinand Tönnies, *Community and Society: Basic Concepts of Pure Sociology*, trans. Lin Rongyuan (Peking University Press, 1999), 43.

15. "China's Peaceful Development," Chinese government website, September 6, 2011, http://www.gov.cn/jrzg/2011-09/06/content_1941204.htm.

2.1 Enhancing mutual political trust in China-ASEAN relations

Since the China-ASEAN strategic partnership is the precursor and foundation of building a China-ASEAN community with a shared future, an important way of realizing it in Southeast Asia should be the enhancement of mutual China-ASEAN political trust. For more than 20 years after establishing relations, mutual China-ASEAN political trust has been consistently improving. It has reached a new height since the turn of the century, especially after the two sides signed the "Declaration on the Conduct of Parties in the South China Sea" and joined the "Treaty of Friendship and Cooperation in Southeast Asia." With these serving as a policy basis, the ASEAN sees China's development increasingly as an opportunity and the product of a constructive force to ensure regional security balance.[16] At the same time, the Chinese government sees the ASEAN as the driver of regional cooperation and the organizer and coordinator of the "10+3" mechanism.[17] There is also growing interest in the outcome. During the 10th anniversary of the establishment of the China-ASEAN partnership, China proposed signing the "Treaty of Neighborliness and Friendly Cooperation" with the ASEAN. Although the negotiation and signing face many difficulties and challenges, the process of jointly negotiating and dealing with the problem is in essence a process of accumulation and continuing enhancement of mutual China-ASEAN political trust.

2.2 Maintaining and endorsing the multicultural China-ASEAN relationship of peaceful coexistence

Maintaining and endorsing the multicultural China-ASEAN relationship of peaceful coexistence is the fertile soil and cornerstone for building a China-ASEAN community with a shared future. The concepts of peaceful coexistence and inclusive development are also included in the realization of the community with a shared future in Southeast Asia. The China-ASEAN community with a shared future can be regarded as a regional community because the two sides are friendly neighbors. However, it should fundamentally be a relational community, which requires the two sides to consistently enhance mutual recognition through exchanges. In terms of

---

16. Rodolfo C. Severino, "Southeast Asia in Search of an ASEAN Community: Insights from the Former ASEAN Secretary-General," *Institute of Southeast Asian Studies* (2006): 278.

17. Ruan Zongze, *The Rise of China and the Transformation of the East Asian International Order: The Shaping and Expansion of Common Interests* (Peking University Press, 2007), 311.

value awareness, we not only recognize its consistency, but also recognize and respect the two sides' differences in social culture and development methods, allowing for an inclusive mentality and peaceful coexistence in the relationship.

The China-ASEAN community with a shared future is also largely a community of cooperation, requiring both sides to be pragmatic in endorsing mutual cooperation, and to negotiate, resolve common issues, and intensify their cooperation on the basis of mutual benefit and a sense of togetherness. This was first illustrated when the mutually beneficial China-ASEAN economic cooperation and trade relations were upgraded. As a measure proposed by China to implement the building of a China-ASEAN community with a shared future, the upgraded version of the China-ASEAN Free Trade Area is an important measure through which the two sides can push forward economic and trade relations to achieve in-depth development. In addition, as the joint building of the "21st Century Maritime Silk Road" has achieved consensus among most countries in China and Southeast Asia, China and the ASEAN countries have a greater willingness to cooperate and reciprocate in the fields of production capacity and connectivity. In addition, as represented by the Lancang-Mekong Cooperation, bilateral and multilateral cooperation mechanisms between China and the ASEAN countries have become more pragmatic and reciprocal, demonstrating the symbiotic links between the two sides.[18] The "Sanya Declaration" is a political symbol of the Lancang-Mekong Cooperation mechanism. While pointing out the operational modalities of the Lancang-Mekong cooperation, namely government guidance, multi-party participation, and project orientation, it also proposed 26 practical measures under the three pillars of cooperation (political security, economic and sustainable development, and social and cultural cooperation). It includes five priority cooperation areas in the initial stage of Lancang-Mekong cooperation, namely connectivity, production capacity, cross-border economy, water resources and agricultural progress, and poverty reduction. Mutually beneficial and win-win economic and trade relations are the most important, and have been a prominent part of the friendly and cooperative relations between China and the ASEAN for more than 20 years.

---

18. Ge Hongliang, "The Lancang-Mekong Community with a Shared Future Is Created by Pragmatism," *Guangxi Daily*, March 25, 2016, 7.

2.3 Establishing a mutually helpful China-ASEAN relationship for security cooperation

The sense of togetherness and mutual assistance between China and the ASEAN countries are also important aspects of the China-ASEAN community with a shared future. In this regard, President Xi Jinping stated in his speech that he believed that China-ASEAN should "look out for and help each other" in maintaining regional security.[19] This regional security concept is the embodiment of the cooperative and communal security that China has always advocated for, and also includes the idea of cooperative security as emphasized by the ASEAN.

The China-ASEAN community with a shared future is based on the consistent improvement of the mutual political and strategic trust between the two parties. One of the key illustrations is that China-ASEAN security cooperation can be established and intensified while jointly negotiating and addressing regional security challenges. This is undoubtedly conducive to enhancing the ASEAN's leading position in regional security and reinforcing the forum's status and role, which will in turn be beneficial in endorsing the regional security mechanism in Southeast Asia.[20]

At the bilateral level, China and the ASEAN countries have established relevant cooperation mechanisms, resulting in an expansion of cooperation areas from low-sensitivity areas such as non-traditional security to high-level political areas such as traditional security.[21]

The creation of the China-ASEAN community with a shared future covers both ideological and material features, which constitute the direction of development. As such, pushing forward ideological and cooperative development among China-ASEAN countries constitutes the main task of building a China-ASEAN community with a shared future. However, for historical and practical reasons, the journey is not a smooth one, and many issues remain that deserve attention, focus, and in-depth thinking by the two parties.

---

19. Xi Jinping, "Jointly Building a China-ASEAN Community with a Shared Future – Speech to the Indonesian Parliament," *People's Daily*, October 4, 2013, 2.

20. Nie Wenjuan, "China and the ASEAN Regional Forum (ARF): From Active Participation to Innovative Practice," *Southeast Asia Aspects*, no. 11 (2013): 20–22.

21. In recent years, with China's increasingly prominent role in regional security, Southeast Asian countries such as Malaysia and Thailand have sought to purchase weapons from China, and have also reinforced their defense cooperation and exchanges with China.

3 Main Challenges of Building the Community

Since the 18th National Congress, developments in bilateral China-ASEAN relations and the ever-changing regional and international situations have demonstrated a strong sense of pragmatic cooperation between the two parties in the process of building a China-ASEAN community with a shared future, and have also constituted a new starting point for future development. Its creation is a composite process of building consciousness and cooperation, requiring China and the ASEAN countries to form a symbiotic link. In reality, challenges can be overcome together, and more pragmatic and mutually beneficial cooperative relationships can be formed. However, through the development of China-ASEAN relations in recent years, the creation of a China-ASEAN community with a shared future still faces a series of challenges such as structural imbalance.

3.1 The imbalance of development between China and the ASEAN countries

ASEAN countries have always regarded China as "a rising giant."[22] With China's increasing influence in the regional and international arena, ASEAN countries regard it more as simply a "giant." In this regard, renowned American scholar Evelyn Goh has written that the ASEAN's perception of China's rise is more realistic, and it is faster and more tangible than that of other countries.[23] ASEAN countries' perception of China's rise is reflected on two levels.

(1) The change in China's diplomatic behavior. Although China has repeatedly emphasized its support for ASEAN countries' leading the regional multilateral framework, and has always had a positive attitude towards it, ASEAN countries have felt the changes in China's diplomatic approach and its impact on regional affairs amid the rise of debates over whether China's diplomatic approach has indeed changed in recent years, among which China's behavior in the South China Sea dispute is the most significant. Recently, China's rights protection in the South China Sea – particularly the "981" platform incident in the southern part of Zhongjian Island and the subsequent reinforcement

---

22. Cao Yunhua, "Managing Between Major Powers: A Review of the ASEAN's Strategy for Balancing Major Powers," *Jinan Journal* (Philosophy and Social Sciences Edition), no. 3 (2003): 19.
23. Evelyn Goh, "Southeast Asian Perspectives on the China Challenge," in *Managing the China Challenge: Global Perspectives*, eds. Quansheng Zhao and Guoli Liu (London and New York: Routledge, 2009), 177.

and expansion of islands and reefs in the Nansha Islands – has been widely regarded by ASEAN countries as a threat to regional security.[24] In addition, the skeptical attitude of some Southeast Asian countries towards the joint development of the BRI also shows that these countries have not yet fully understood and adapted to China's proactive approach to foreign affairs.

(2) The change in status of economic and trade relations between China and the ASEAN has also highlighted the unbalanced development between the two parties. In this context, the intensification of mutual dependence between China and the ASEAN countries will inevitably entangle some ASEAN countries in existing problems related to bilateral economic and trade, and they are worried that they will be constrained by the intensifying dependence on China in their foreign exchanges. For example, ASEAN leaders have more than once expressed their dissatisfaction with China's competing with them for foreign direct investment in the international market.[25]

In reality, as far as ASEAN countries are concerned, the imbalance in its development compared with China's has become an important reference in their assessment of its future development.

3.2 ASEAN countries' misunderstandings and prejudices towards China's future development

In a sense, the misunderstanding and prejudices in ASEAN countries' perception of China's future development form an important challenge for the two sides in building a community with a shared future. Rather than whether China can rise, ASEAN countries are more concerned about how it will behave after its rise. They are worried that it will become a hegemonic country that relies on its strong economic and military power to change the status quo and recover territories by force.[26] In terms of influencing factors, ASEAN countries' perception of China's future development is affected by history, culture, and the actual international situation. For decades, post-war ASEAN countries have viewed their "northern neighbor" as a

---

24. Zhang Jie, *Assessment of China's Neighborhood Security Situation: The Belt and Road Initiative and Peripheral Strategy (2015)* (Social Science Literature Publishing House, 2015), 135.

25. Ian Storey, *Southeast Asia and the Rise of China: the Search for Security* (London and New York: Routledge, 2011), 81.

26. David C. Kang, "Getting Asia Wrong: The Need for New Analytical Frameworks," *International Security* 27, no. 4 (2003): 83.

threat to regional security and stability. Vietnamese scholar Chang Pao-Min once said that due to the influence of profound historical, cultural, and ideological factors, the ASEAN's distrust of China is likely to persist in the short term.[27] In reality, due to the widening gap in economic development between China and the ASEAN countries, China's growing international influence, and the misunderstanding and prejudice against China as a result of international public opinion, some ASEAN countries are concerned about the uncertainty and possible hegemonic tendencies of China's future development. To these countries, China will undoubtedly pose the biggest and most direct threat to ASEAN national security when such a situation occurs. As such, it is difficult for the ASEAN's political trust in China to increase significantly in reality, which undoubtedly has an extremely negative impact on China and ASEAN countries' negotiation and signing of the "Neighborliness, Friendship, and Peace Treaty," and cooperation in building a community with a shared future.

3.3 The unresolved South China Sea dispute

In the early 1990s, the South China Sea dispute began as a regional hotspot issue, at least from the ASEAN's perspective. However, due to the turbulent situation, the ASEAN became concerned about a potential regional conflict. The dispute then became a focal point and driving force of the ASEAN's regional security practice, and it is still a key issue in its dialogue with China. It has also been on the agenda in regional multilateral frameworks and security dialogues. Although ASEAN countries have launched a series of efforts to solve the South China Sea issue, the persistence of the unresolved disputes casts a looming shadow. With the enhancement of China's national strength and expansion of its influence, the ASEAN is worried about its strong and increasingly normalized rights-defense behavior and island reef creation in the South China Sea, as well as China's use of force or threats thereof in the disputes. However, the South China Sea situation is undermined by power plays among major nations, which also profoundly affects the ASEAN's security demands in the region. With the intensifying involvement of countries such as the United States, Japan, and India in the South China Sea, the issue has become an important fulcrum of the regional policies of these major powers. Under such circumstances, the South China Sea has become the focus of competition and games among major powers and regions. The ASEAN has also achieved its goal of internationalizing the

---

27. Chang Pao-Min, "Vietnam and China: New Opportunities and New Challenges," *Contemporary Southeast Asia* 19, no. 2 (1997): 145.

issue. However, the situation is inevitably undermined by the complex relationships among major powers. In recent years, due to the imbalance of development between major powers and the intensification of competitive relations, security in the South China Sea has shown unprecedented complexity and has become more unstable and uncertain. Undoubtedly, this impacts and challenges the principle of self-dominant regional security, as well as the need to avoid allowing a major power to dominate the region.[28] As such, with the South China Sea dispute remaining unresolved, the realization of the community with a shared future in Southeast Asia is bound to face challenges, as is more substantial and practical cooperation between China and the ASEAN in the South China Sea.

3.4 Can political trust be increased?

The building of a China-ASEAN community with a shared future is a process in which the relationship between the two sides has shifted from quantitative increase to qualitative change. In this process, the creation of a China-ASEAN community with a shared future fundamentally depends on whether the mutual political and strategic trust between the two sides can be consistently enhanced. Dialogue and interactions on issues such as the South China Sea dispute and China-ASEAN economic and trade cooperation are beneficial in enhancing the political trust between the two parties. However, whether the interaction can enhance mutual goodwill and trust between them depends on the negotiation and outcome during the interactions. The creation of a China-ASEAN community with a shared future is no longer a simple process of quantitative increase, but a process in which the two sides pursue a more mature and qualitative change in their bilateral relations. Evidently, this process is much more difficult and more complicated than the previous quantitative increase. In view of this, it is difficult to build a China-ASEAN community with a shared future. It requires that the two sides maintain political patience and demonstrate greater political knowledge.

However, the constantly evolving regional situation and the international situation results in a lack of patience and knowledge in some ASEAN countries when developing their relations with China. Undoubtedly, this has a deep impact on the willingness and progress of both sides in building a China-ASEAN community with a shared future.

---

28. Evelyn Goh, "Southeast Asian Perspectives on the China Challenge," in *Managing the China Challenge: Global Perspectives*, eds. Quansheng Zhao and Guoli Liu (London and New York: Routledge, 2009), 179.

The China-ASEAN community with a shared future is a new concept proposed in the process of the two sides' advancement of their strategic partnership. The strategic China-ASEAN partnership has entered a phase that focuses on quality.[29] Therefore, by implementing and endorsing the creation of the China-ASEAN community of shared destiny, the strategic partnership should be able to achieve more significant and substantive progress. However, the creation of a China-ASEAN community with a shared future faces many problems yet, and whether they can be overcome will determine whether the relationship can achieve a qualitative change in future.

As the regional and international landscape evolves, the roles of China and the ASEAN are constantly changing, which is most notably characterized by China's growing influence on regional and international affairs. After more than 20 years of dialogue and development, China and the ASEAN countries have started new cooperations in the "Diamond Decade" characterized by qualitative change after the "Golden Decade" of quantitative growth. Hence, the dialogue and cooperation between China and the ASEAN countries are bound to undergo significant adjustments, meaning that there will be more challenges in developing bilateral relations in future. In this context, the Chinese government has proposed the concept of a China-ASEAN community with a shared future based on the wider concept of a community with a shared future. It hopes that in the process of upgrading the China-ASEAN Free Trade Area and endorsing the "21st Century Maritime Silk Road" with the ASEAN countries, greater awareness of the community with a shared destiny will be implemented in Southeast Asia, and a more pragmatic bilateral cooperative relationship will be formed.

The creation of the China-ASEAN community with a shared future is a move in the right direction, and also has a significant influence on the development of China-ASEAN relations. It is a regional practice within the concept of a community with a shared future for humanity. It reflects the two sides' awareness of the necessity to share both joy and hardship, and to weather difficulties together in the era of interdependence. It also echoes China's ideas about international power, shared interests, regional cooperation, and common governance in the era of mutual dependence and cooperation.

---

29. Cao Yunhua, "On the Regional Order in Southeast Asia," *Southeast Asian Studies*, no. 5 (2011): 8.

CHAPTER 10

Facilitating the Development of a Sino-African Community with a Shared Future

Sino-African relations have a long history, with over 2,000 years of exchanges. During the Spring and Autumn Period and the Warring States Period, nomadic people in northern China established indirect connections with Africa through other nomads on the Eurasian steppe. African gems and spices were sold to China by land, and Chinese nephrite jade was introduced to Egypt. Chinese sailboats went by sea to the coast of Zanzi (East Africa) after the 7th century. The merchant fleet led by Zheng He, fleet admiral of the Ming Dynasty, visited the Indian Ocean seven times, and made several visits to the east coast of Africa, resulting in a peak in Sino-African maritime exchanges.[1] Ancient China was famous for silkworm farming and silk weaving. During east-west exchanges, the Silk Road was an important trade channel between China and Africa by sea and land.

After the People's Republic of China was founded, China saw great significance in exchanges with African countries, and supported their struggles for national independence against colonialism. When the Cold War ended, the international community – especially Western countries, which generally held a pessimistic

---

1. Shen Fuwei, *China and Africa – Two Thousand Years of Sino-African Relations* (Zhonghua Book Company, 1990), 11–12, 447–452.

attitude towards Africa as the world's least developed continent – doubted the Africans' ability to manage themselves, which led to "African pessimism." Unlike Western countries, China has always insisted on being an all-weather friend to Africa by advocating for a new international political and economic order, and helping African countries eradicate poverty and backwardness. The convening of the Forum on Sino-African Cooperation in 2000 reinforced the friendly cooperation between China and African countries in the new situation, and formed a framework for the two sides to deal collectively with the challenges of economic globalization and seek common development.

Since the 18th National Congress, Xi Jinping's CPC Central Committee has set the community with a shared future as its core guiding ideology for diplomacy. Building a Sino-African community with a shared future has become another important goal of developing Sino-African cooperation. Since the 18th National Congress, it has entered a new phase of development and has shown some new characteristics.

1 Sino-African Relations since the 18th National Congress

As a model of South-South collaboration, Sino-African cooperation is building a community with a shared future – an important part of an overall community with a shared future for humanity. The development of Sino-African relations shows the following characteristics within the framework of the community with a shared future.

1.1 Frequent high-level exchanges between China and Africa, which increase mutual political trust

Since the 18th National Congress, high-level exchanges between China and Africa have been frequent. In particular, the number and frequency of Chinese leaders' visits to African countries have been increasing significantly. President Xi Jinping visited Africa twice, in March 2013 and December 2015 respectively, demonstrating the sincerity of the Chinese leadership in promoting Sino-African cooperation and helping Africa. During his visit in March 2013, Xi stated that China and Africa share common historical experiences, development tasks, and strategic interests, and are a community with a shared future, sharing both good and bad. In his speech at the Nyerere International Conference Center in Tanzania, he said that it is necessary to treat African friends truthfully, cooperate with sincerity, reinforce Sino-African friendship, and solve cooperation issues. Sincerity, real results, friendship, and good faith are important principles by which China manages its relations with Africa, and have received high praise from African countries such as Tanzania.² At the Johannesburg Summit and the Sixth Ministerial Forum on Sino-African Cooperation, Xi Jinping presided over the signing of two important documents: the "Declaration of the Johannesburg Summit of the Forum on Sino-African Cooperation," and the "Forum on Sino-African Cooperation-Johannesburg Action Plan (2016–2018)," which upgraded the relationship to an all-round strategic partnership.

Chinese Premier Li Keqiang, who visited Africa in May 2014, went to the AU headquarters and delivered a speech. He also attended the plenary session of the World Economic Forum Africa Summit. During his visit, Li proposed Sino-African cooperation initiatives across "six major projects" and "three major networks," drawing a blueprint for Sino-African cooperation. Since 2014, Foreign Minister Wang Yi has visited Africa every year, with two visits in January and May 2017.

African leaders have also visited China frequently, expressing their desire to cooperate and seek assistance. In 2014 alone, 13 African leaders visited China.³ As the most important platform for Sino-African cooperation, the Forum on Sino-African Cooperation has played a central role in endorsing the rapid development of Sino-African relations and the economic and social development of Africa since it was established more than a decade ago. More importantly, during the forum and the summit, the heads of state, government, and other senior officials on both sides conduct intensive visits and meetings, which resulted in the Forum being the most important platform for developing Sino-African relations.

Frequent high-level mutual visits are of great significance for the development of Sino-African relations. Firstly, in international relations, they have extremely important symbolism for bilateral relations. They are premised on friendly two-way relations and mutual political trust. The mutual visits of Chinese and African leaders send positive signals to African countries and the international community, and have great significance in intensifying the mutual political trust between China and Africa.

Secondly, high level visits between China and Africa will help China understand the current situation in Africa's development. At present, there are 54 member states of the African Union, and the political systems, social and economic development status, and resource endowments of each country are very different. Communication between Chinese and African officials can enhance the Chinese government's

---

2. "Xi Jinping's Speech at the Nyerere International Conference Center in Tanzania (Full Text)," Xinhuanet, March 25, 2013, http://news.xinhuanet.com/politics/2013-03/25/c_124501703_2.htm.

3. "13 African Leaders Visit China in 2014, a Record," Ministry of Foreign Affairs website, December 30, 2014, http://www.fmprc.gov.cn/web/wjb_673085/zzjg_673183/fzs_673445/xwlb_673447/t1224531.shtml.

understanding of the actual situation in African countries. It is necessary to accurately grasp the development needs of China and Africa, and form a development consensus that will help China to provide more targeted assistance to Africa and enhance Sino-African cooperation.

Finally, high-level mutual visits are conducive to African countries learning from China's development experience. African officials and leaders visit China and see the achievements of its Reform and Opening-up and economic development through on-site visits, and then replicate them in their own countries.

1.2 Enhancing the status of Sino-African trading partners and rapidly increasing investments in Africa

Sino-African bilateral trade has been impacted by the worsening global economic environment, and has been fluctuating since 2013. However, the status of Africa and China as trading partners has been improving, alongside their trade structure and quality. In 2013, Sino-African trade increased by 5.9%, and the total value exceeded USD 200 billion, reaching USD 210.2 billion. In 2014, Sino-African trade reached USD 221.8 billion at a growth rate of 5.5%. Negatively affected by the 2008 international financial crisis, the global economy – especially international trade – has experienced sluggish growth in recent years. According to statistics released by the United Nations Conference on Trade and Development (UNCTAD), the global trade growth rate in 2015 was -13.23%, lower than the global economic growth rate during the same period.

In 2015, Africa's total import and export trade was USD 873.8 billion, a year-on-year decrease of 27.2%, while exports dropped sharply by 34.9%. As a result, Sino-African trade declined in 2015 and 2016, totaling USD 179 billion and USD 149.1 billion respectively.[4]

Specifically, the economic growth of African countries has slowed down and total exports have declined due to the continued fall in global commodity prices such as oil, the economic growth of major world powers, and the spread of the Ebola virus, drought, regional conflicts, and terrorism. As a result, Sino-African trade has been facing downward pressure. Compared with Africa's total foreign trade, Sino-African trade still performed well. In 2016, China's trade volume with African countries reached USD 149.2 billion, of which USD 92.3 billion was exported to Africa and

---

4. Sino-African trade statistics obtained from the General Administration of Customs, http://www.customs.gov.cn.

USD 56.9 billion was imported from Africa. China has been Africa's largest trading partner for the eighth consecutive year.[5] In the long run, Sino-African trade still reflected rapid growth. From 2001 to 2015, the average annual growth of Sino-African trade, total exports to Africa, and total imports from Africa were 23.0%, 23.7%, and 23.2% respectively.

In terms of investment, with the in-depth implementation of China's "go global" strategy in recent years, the scale of direct investment in Africa has been greatly increased, and both the stock and coverage of investment in Africa have shown rapid growth.

From 2012 to 2015, China's direct investment stock in Africa grew at an average annual rate of 21.25%. In 2016, China's direct investment flow to Africa was USD 3.3 billion, and the stock reached about USD 38 billion.[6] From the countries and regions in which it is distributed, investments in Africa show wide coverage but high stock concentration. By the end of 2015, China's investment in Africa involved 51 countries and regions, with a coverage rate of 85%. A total of 2,949 overseas enterprises were established in Africa, in countries such as South Africa, Nigeria, Zambia, Congo (DRC), and Algeria. Among them, South Africa is China's largest investment target country in Africa, with an investment stock of 4.723 billion US dollars, ranking 18th in China's foreign direct investment stock. In terms of the industry distribution of investment, non-direct investment is distributed in mining, construction, manufacturing, finance, scientific research, and technical services.[7]

1.3 Remarkable achievements in China's aid and creation of African infrastructure

Africa is the continent with the most backward infrastructure in the world, and it is one of the main reasons for its limited economic development. In recent years, with the consistent in-depth development of Sino-African cooperation, as well as the active support and assistance of the Chinese government and enterprises, some African countries have achieved remarkable developments in infrastructure, and a series of large-scale projects related to the economy and living standards have been completed.

---

5. "2016 Sino-African Trade Statistics," Ministry of Commerce website, February 22, 2017, http://xyf.mofcom.gov.cn/article/date/201702/20170202520439.shtml.

6. "2016 Statistics of Chinese Investment in Africa," Ministry of Commerce website, February 22, 2017, http://xyf.mofcom.gov.cn/article/date/201702/20170202520441.shtml.

7. Ministry of Commerce, National Bureau of Statistics, State Administration of Foreign Exchange, *2015 Statistical Bulletin of China's Foreign Direct Investment* (China Statistics Press), September 2016.

This has significantly improved the infrastructure status of African countries. At the Johannesburg Summit of the Forum on Sino-African Cooperation in 2015, the Chinese government pledged to provide Africa with a total of USD 60 billion in financial support to endorse cooperation in 10 areas, namely industry, agriculture, infrastructure, finance, green development, trade and investment facilitation, poverty alleviation, public health, humanities, peace, and security.[8] The "Ten Major Sino-African Cooperation Plans" have been the new core guidelines for China's aid to Africa and Sino-African cooperation since the 18th National Congress, which is a milestone for both the development of Sino-African relations and a Sino-African community with a shared future.

Under the guidance of the "Ten Major Sino-African Cooperation Plans," Sino-African cooperation has progressed and has shown some new characteristics. Firstly, China is more active in fulfilling its responsibilities and international obligations as a major power. It formulates and implements practical foreign aid policies according to the country's all-round strength. Undertaking international obligations is an important way for a major country to establish a responsible image, demonstrate the appeal of its diplomacy, and enhance its soft power. Implementing aid to Africa and participating in the creation of large-scale infrastructure projects there pushes forward China's own development, and is an important way for it to participate in global governance and endorse prosperity and stability in Africa and the rest of the world. It is also an important illustration of the combination of development rights and interests of the Chinese people with the common interests of people across the globe.

Secondly, there are innovations in the methods and concepts of assistance. In the 1960s and 1970s, aid to Africa served political purposes, and comprised direct economic and material aid. With these changes, while helping African countries to cope with short-term difficulties, aid began to focus on development assistance based on the idea of "teaching a man to fish." This is embodied in the emphasis on helping African countries to develop and improve their industrial systems, teaching technical and management knowledge, and training personnel. For example, foreign aid helped Sudan and Nigeria develop oil extraction and processing systems, and

---

8. Xi Jinping, "Beginning a New Era of Sino-African Cooperation for Win-Win Cooperation and Common Development – Speech at the Opening Ceremony of the Johannesburg Summit of the Forum on Sino-African Cooperation," *People's Daily*, December 5, 2015, 2.

launched the Congo (DRC) Agricultural Technology Demonstration Center project, as well as setting up vocational and technical schools in Benin.[9]

Thirdly, aid now places more emphasis on the combination of China's experience and the actual situation of African countries. As the largest developing country in the world, China's restructuring and development achievements are obvious to all. China and Africa share the same experience of colonialism, and face common development tasks. Combining China's development experience with the reality of African countries is a useful way for African countries to explore development paths that suit their national conditions and solve development problems.

Thus far, China has made significant progress in a series of engineering assistance and contracting projects in Africa. Projects related to improving infrastructure for the economy and living standards that have been completed are of great significance. Representative projects have been widely used in Africa, and have received praise from the international community. For example, the Kenya Mombasa-Nairobi Railway, which officially opened to traffic on May 31, 2017, is the largest infrastructure project since Kenya's independence, and will greatly improve its transportation. The Gilgel Gibe III Hydroelectric Power Project is the largest hydropower station in Africa, and was undertaken by PowerChina Chengdu Engineering C Corporation with a total installed capacity of 1.87 million kilowatts. It will go a long way in solving the country's power shortage, and will provide it with the support needed for economic development.

Transportation facilities are the basics for the transport of material and personnel exchanges. China has signed a "Framework Memorandum of Understanding" with the African Union to endorse the "three major networks" (high-speed railways, highways, and regional aviation) in Africa as well as cooperation in infrastructure and industrialization. The advancement of related projects will play a key role in Africa's economic development. In addition, in 2016, the value of newly signed contracted projects by Chinese enterprises in Africa was USD 82 billion, an increase of 8% year-on-year, and the completed turnover reached USD 52.1 billion. Africa is China's second-largest supplier of contract projects.[10]

---

9. For specific assistance projects, please refer to the website of the Department of Foreign Aid of the Ministry of Commerce: http://yws.mofcom.gov.cn/article/b/.

10. "2016 Sino-African Contracted Project Cooperation Statistics," Ministry of Commerce website, February 22, 2017, http://xyf.mofcom.gov.cn/article/date/201702/20170202520444.shtml.

1.4 Frequent non-governmental exchanges and cultural and educational cooperation between China and Africa

People-to-people exchanges are the basis of political and economic relations, and are an important part of friendly bilateral ties. Africa is one of the birthplaces of civilization, while China's long-standing culture is famous around the world. Indirect and direct people-to-people exchanges between China and Africa date back many years, and are an important symbol of friendly Sino-African relations. With the increasingly close political and economic ties between the two sides, Sino-African personnel exchanges and cultural and educational cooperation have also become more frequent.

As for education development, the number of African students studying in China has grown rapidly in recent years, with an average growth rate of 34.69%. According to statistics released by the Ministry of Education, the total number of African students studying in China in 2015 was 49,792, accounting for 12.52% of the total number of foreign students in China – an increase of 8,115 over the previous year, or a growth rate of 19.47%.[11] Despite the financial crisis, the slowdown in global economic growth, and the growth rate of international students studying in China, the number of African students studying in China reflects a trend of rapid growth. A large number of international students from Africa read Chinese or related degrees in economics, politics, medicine, and engineering in China through self-funded or Chinese government scholarships. According to the Johannesburg Action Plan of the Forum on Sino-African Cooperation, China will provide African countries with 2,000 academic and degree education places and 30,000 government scholarship places, and want to welcome more young Africans to study in China.[12] Thus far, China has set up 48 Confucius Institutes, 27 Confucius Classrooms, and more than 400 teaching centers in Africa, providing multi-level and multi-demand teaching including business, Traditional Chinese Medicine and martial art for Chinese language learners in African countries.[13]

---

11. "2015 National Data Release of International Students in China," Ministry of Education website, April 14, 2016, http://www.moe.gov.cn/jyb_xwfb/gzdt_gzdt/s5987/201604/t20160414_238263.html.

12. "The Forum on Sino-African Cooperation – Johannesburg Action Plan," the official website of the Forum on Sino-African Cooperation, December 10, 2015, http://www.fmprc.gov.cn/ce/cech/chn/ssyw/t1323148.htm.

13. "2017 Joint Conference of Confucius Institutes in Africa Held in Zambia," Xinhuanet, May 19, 2017, http://news.xinhuanet.com/world/2017-05/19/c_1121002542.htm.

As for cultural cooperation, China and Africa have carried out a series of multi-level cultural exchange projects premised on respecting each other's cultural characteristics, for example, the Sino-African Forum on Cultural Heritage Protection and the Sino-African Cultural Industry Roundtable. At the same time, China and Africa also conducted cultural exchanges to endorse mutual understanding among their cultures. Launched in 2008, the "Culture Focus" event has become a large-scale platform for cultural exchanges between China and Africa. In 2015, South Africa's "China Year" held cultural, educational, and technological exchange events in major cities across South Africa. Led by the Ministry of Culture, the "Happy Spring Festival" event has become an important way for African people to learn about Chinese festivals and customs, and is popular among African people. In addition, China has established five Chinese cultural centers in Benin, Mauritius, Egypt, Nigeria, and Tanzania to carry out Sino-African cultural exchange.

Personnel exchanges between China and Africa have become increasingly frequent alongside the close economic exchanges between China and Africa. In 2014, the number exceeded 3.6 million. As well as a large number of Chinese laborers and students sent to Africa, exchanges between scholars from Chinese and African universities, think tanks, and research institutions have become an important means of high-level personnel exchange. Established in 2011, the Sino-African Think Tank Forum provides an important platform for scholars from China and Africa to exchange ideas. People-to-people exchanges are of great significance in endorsing mutual understanding, respecting cultural diversity, and encouraging cultural prosperity. They also play an important role in establishing a positive image for China and correcting misconceptions about it in Africa. More importantly, non-governmental educational and cultural exchanges and personnel exchanges are conducive to mutual learning and cultural understanding, and lay a strong cultural and social foundation for bilateral relations. Therefore, enhancing non-governmental exchanges between China and Africa is the most basic way to establish friendly relations.

2 Main Path to Building a Sino-African Community with a Shared Future

At present, Sino-African relations have reached a new phase. Although the building of a Sino-African community with a shared future faces a series of problems, the common development tasks, highly aligned strategic interests, and broad prospects for win-win cooperation determine that the Chinese and African people will move forward together. The creation of a Sino-African community with a shared future should continue to explore new paths while following a basic political premise.

2.1 Practicing non-interference in internal affairs, and attaching no political conditions

Both China and Africa have suffered from foreign invasion, colonial rule, and political interference by Western powers. These common historical experiences have caused both to be opposed to foreign political interference. The Chinese government has always practiced non-interference in the internal affairs of other countries as the basic norm of international relations and international law, and has always followed this norm in international exchanges. When China and Africa cooperate to build a Sino-African community with a shared future, the Chinese government follows the principle of non-interference in the internal affairs of African countries, and believes that African issues should be resolved by Africans in African ways.[14]

Africa was the last independent continent in the world, and the African people paid a heavy price for resisting colonial rule. The painful history of being colonized, and the heavy cost of anti-colonialism mean that African people cherish their hard-won political independence. However, Western countries still retain strong political influence there, interfering in the internal affairs of African countries through various overt or covert means. They use unfair international rules and Western values to impose arbitrary pressure on Sino-African cooperation, and place a series of political conditions on their aid to Africa. Against this background, China's insistence on non-interference in internal affairs and attaching no political conditions is particularly precious. For China and Africa to build a community with a shared future, cooperation under the premise of mutual understanding and mutual respect is the best manifestation of respecting the diversity of different cultures and development paths.

For China, non-interference in the internal affairs of African countries aligns with national interests. Firstly, it avoids getting caught up in the internal conflict of African countries. The political situation of African countries is complex, and it is difficult to grasp the various power struggles between religious factions, tribal forces, and political parties. Non-interference in internal affairs can prevent or reduce

---

14. "Special Representative of the Chinese Government on African Affairs: China Upholds the Principle of Non-interference in Africa's Internal Affairs," Xinhuanet, April 19, 2015, http://news.xinhuanet.com/world/2015-04/19/c_1115017101.htm.

the loss of China's interests due to a change of political power in African countries. Secondly, it reduces the suspicion and vigilance of African leaders and people towards China. A long history of colonization has made African countries understandably wary of foreign powers. Following the principle of non-interference in internal affairs can reduce this unnecessary suspicion and psychological vigilance. Thirdly, it prevents exploitation by politicians and media in Western countries. Western politicians often try to sabotage China's political goals in Africa, while Western media outlets (along with some local African media outlets that are influenced by the West) write one-sided and distorted reports on China, exaggerating the so-called "Chinese expansion." A clear principle of non-interference in internal affairs can clarify China's policy proposition and enhance the understanding and trust of African countries and the international community.

2.2 Improving Sino-African cooperation in industrialization

"China's Second Policy Document on Africa" was released in 2015, and stated that "giving priority to supporting industrialization in Africa is the breakthrough and focus of China's cooperation with Africa in the new era."[15] In June 2015, the African Union issued the "2063 Agenda," which stated that the general goal of Africa's industrialization strategy is to push forward its economic transformation through industrialization, in particular the development of manufacturing, to increase the added value of its resources, create high-paying jobs, increase people's income, and generally improve the continent. The share of manufacturing in global value chains will ultimately make Africa a continent of macroeconomic stability, structural diversification, and accelerated and inclusive growth in 2063.[16]

Combining Africa's industrialization needs with China's industrial transfer and upgrading requirement, and improving Sino-African industrialization cooperation will be the main economic path for building a community with a shared future for the two sides. For Africa, industrialization will expand its industrial sectors (especially manufacturing), enhance the industry's status in the economy, and provide African countries with industrial products needed for economic development as well as consumer goods for daily life. For China, the transfer of production capacity to Africa will meet the industrial supply required for African industrialization, and will also

---

15. "China's Second Policy Document on Africa (Full Text)," Xinhuanet, December 5, 2015, http://news.xinhuanet.com/2015-12/05/c_1117363276.htm.

16. See the official AU website: http://www.un.org/en/africa/osaa/pdf/au/agenda2063.pdf.

effectively alleviate China's intense but inefficient production capacity competition. It will also transfer some labor-intensive industries to Africa, which can increase the employment rate of target countries while alleviating the pressure of insufficient domestic labor supply and rising labor prices. Therefore, Sino-African cooperation in industrial docking and production capacity is an improved version of Sino-African economic, trade, and industrial cooperation, and a strategic layout to achieve a win-win situation between China and Africa.

For specific measures, African countries cannot simply follow the traditional industrialization path, but should focus on formulating and implementing practical industrial policies and development plans at different times, using their national conditions and resources to their comparative advantage. In boosting the industrialization process of African countries, China can also leverage its experience to guide them, helping them build exemplary special economic zones, industrial parks, and science and technology parks, drive the development of related industries and their surrounding areas, and improve corresponding industries. To resolve capital issues during the process of industrialization, the provision of financial support to African countries in the form of internal or local financing should be combined with external financing. Micro-credit and bond stock transactions should be encouraged, to prevent Chinese companies from undertaking the whole task and monopolizing it.

In addition, the regional integration process of African countries should be supported to realize intra-regional connectivity, overcome the disadvantages of relatively small land areas and fragmented economies in African countries, and enjoy economies of scale.

2.3 Stressing the importance of developing livelihoods and raising enterprises' social responsibility

Low levels of economic development and lagging industrial progress have resulted in generally low living standards for people in African countries. Improving livelihoods is an important task for the development of African countries. Economic development is closely related to livelihood, and the ultimate goal of economic development is to improve overall national strength and living standards. While building a community with a shared future for China and Africa to achieve common development, the two sides must set improving livelihoods as a strategic priority.

Employment is a prerequisite for raising incomes and improving living standards, and economic growth is the foundation for improving and raising employment levels. As one of the continents with the fastest economic growth and the greatest development potential in the world, Africa's increase in employment levels driven by economic development will be the most important driving force for improving people's livelihood. In the process of Sino-African cooperation to endorse African industrialization and China's industrial upgrading, a planned and purposeful focus on employment will be an important measure to improve living standards in Africa. In terms of bilateral trade, investment and aid to Africa and African infrastructure – considering employment, appropriately tilting towards labor-intensive industries, and recruiting local labor – can achieve mutual development and employment. However, labor-intensive Chinese enterprises should also consider the employment situation in China when transferring to Africa, so as to avoid unemployment in China due to rapid and large-scale transfer of manufacturing industries.

When investing in factories and infrastructure, China-related enterprises should factor in local living standards. They should offer a combination of economic and social benefits by providing locals with roads, drinking water, basic education, and social services such as fundamental medical and health facilities. The purpose of enterprises paying attention to social benefits and social responsibilities when "going global" is to gain the recognition and support of local people and reduce social resistance. Internationally, paying attention to corporate social responsibility can dispel rumors and groundless political accusations against the Chinese government and companies by Western media outlets and politicians. At the same time, enterprises must respect local laws, social customs, and religious traditions, and avoid giving the public the negative impression that enterprises only focus on economic benefits while ignoring social values.

When there are social responsibilities that are difficult for enterprises to bear, the Chinese government should also focus on providing assistance at the public service level when implementing aid to Africa. For example, in terms of public health, the Chinese government has dispatched medical teams to Africa to help prevent or treat infectious diseases such as malaria and AIDS. After the outbreak of the Ebola virus in West Africa, the Chinese government sent medical experts and donated medical supplies to affected countries on many occasions.[17] The government should play a leading role in making up for the lack of corporate capacity and undertaking corresponding social responsibilities.

In summary, by focusing on living standards and corporate social as well as economic development, stronger bonds will be formed and co-existence achieved

---

17. "Fighting Ebola, China's Aid Sees the Truth," *People's Daily Online*, October 10, 2014, http://world.people.com.cn/n/2014/1010/c1002-25800389.html.

2.4 Strengthening security cooperation to boost the Sino-African community with a shared future

Since the end of the Cold War, previously suppressed inter- and intra-state conflicts in Africa have re-emerged. At the end of 2010, political turmoil in Arab countries swept across North Africa at a rapid rate. With the intervention of external forces, the security situation of North African countries deteriorated rapidly. Terrorist forces from and beyond Africa also posed a serious threat to security. Currently, inter-state conflicts, ethnic and factional conflicts, and terrorism are the biggest security problems in Africa. Various types of conflicts and terrorist attacks occur frequently, resulting in many casualties, while internal conflicts often spill over to neighboring countries, causing regional instability. This turbulent situation has made peacekeeping in Africa an arduous task. Currently, the United Nations has a total of 16 peacekeeping missions around the world, of which nine are deployed in Africa.[18]

The building of a Sino-African community with a shared future requires a safe and peaceful environment. Therefore, it is necessary for China and Africa to reinforce security cooperation to boost the building of a Sino-African community with a shared future. In terms of policy, China has always followed the principle of non-interference in internal affairs, and advocates that all parties should resolve conflicts through political and peaceful means. China supports peacekeeping operations under the United Nations framework when it is difficult for Africa to maintain peace on its own. China is the backbone of support for UN peacekeeping operations. At present, it has sent a total of 2,512 peacekeepers, making it the country with the largest number of peacekeepers among the five permanent members.[19] In future, the Chinese government will continue to support African peacekeeping and enhance personnel and financial provisions for African peacekeeping operations. At the United Nations General Assembly held in September 2015, President Xi Jinping pledged to contribute USD 1 billion to the United Nations Peace and Development Fund, and build an 8,000-strong UN peacekeeping standby force, as well as providing the

---

18. See the official website of UN peacekeeping operations: http://www.un.org/en/peacekeeping/operations/current.shtml.

19. See United Nations statistics: http://www.un.org/en/peacekeeping/contributors/2017/may17_2.pdf.

African Union with a total of USD 100 million in free military assistance to support the building of the African Standing Army and the Crisis Response Rapid Response Force.[20]

Implementing diplomatic mediation and encouraging all parties to resolve conflict through peaceful negotiation is another important form of Sino-African security cooperation. As a permanent member of the United Nations, China can play a greater role in conflict mediation and diplomatic mediation. Since the conflict broke out in South Sudan at the end of 2013, China has proposed two meetings. Zhong Jianhua – the Special Representative for African Affairs – has shuttled between the conflicting parties many times, making positive contributions to peace and stability in the region.[21]

3 Main Challenges of Building the Community

The Sino-African community with a shared future is a high-level summary of Xi Jinping's Sino-African relations. China and Africa share common historical experiences, face common development tasks, and share common strategic interests. However, they will still face a series of challenges in the specific process of building a Sino-African community with a shared future. Resolving these challenges will be the key to the overall success of the community.

3.1 Differences in political systems, legal systems, and cultural concepts between China and Africa

Due to colonial rule by European powers for more than 400 years, African countries are deeply influenced by the likes of Britain and France in their political values, legal systems, culture and ideology, and social life – all of which are very different from China. There are currently 54 countries in Africa, and each has its unique characteristics and historical development. In the process of Sino-African cooperation to build a community with a shared future, differences between cultures are unavoidable.

---

20. "China is the Backbone of Support for UN Peacekeeping Operations," Xinhuanet, September 30, 2015, http://news.xinhuanet.com/comments/2015-09/30/c_1116723262.htm.

21. "Peacekeeping, Mediation, Aid, Escort, and Development – Wang Yi Talks about China's Commitment to Peace and Security in Africa with Five Keywords," Ministry of Foreign Affairs website, August 11, 2016, http://www.fmprc.gov.cn/web/zyxw/t1388569.shtml.

Firstly, there are significant differences between the political systems of China and Africa. African countries are at different stages of development, and have huge differences in political systems, with most having directly copied the political systems of former British and French colonial powers. However, the economic and social development of African countries is still relatively low. Western-style democratic and legal systems are not suitable for Africa, and cannot maintain national and social stability. More importantly, in their dealings with China, some African countries assess it on the basis of Western political values. Although China has long insisted that economic cooperation and foreign aid are premised on non-interference in internal affairs, some people in Africa (including members of the elite) still accuse the Chinese government of supporting authoritarian regimes.

Secondly, there are differences between the legal systems of China and Africa. Many African countries have established their own legal systems with reference to metropolitan countries such as Britain and France. As a result, there are huge differences in legislation, particularly for engineering investment and labor protection. When some Chinese companies invest in Africa, they are unfamiliar with the laws of the target countries, and often encounter legal and labor disputes. For example, South Africa – which is China's largest investment target in Africa – follows the legal system of the Commonwealth. The labor protection and trade union system is different from China's. Chinese companies often encounter difficulties in dismissing employees who are slack or incompetent. To protect themselves, Chinese companies can only be cautious in expanding investment and recruiting new employees, slowing down their development.[22]

Thirdly, there are differences in religious beliefs, cultures, and values between China and Africa. Culture is deeply entrenched, and greatly affects people's behavior. Conflicts and clashes caused by cultural differences have a huge effect on Sino-African cooperation. China and Africa belong to different cultural systems, and misunderstandings occur due to cultural differences in the increasingly frequent exchanges. For example, some Chinese personnel in Africa do not respect local religious beliefs and cause antipathy among local people and employees for drinking. In order to ensure or improve production efficiency, Chinese companies require overtime. However, African employees believe that they should enjoy life outside of work, and are reluctant to work overtime even if they are paid for it, which affects the production and progress of Chinese companies.

---

22. Huang Meibo and Ren Peiqiang, "The Impact of the South African Labor Market on Chinese Enterprise Investment," *West Asia and Africa*, no. 4 (2013): 115–130.

3.2 Sino-African trade is unbalanced and badly structured

The imbalance of bilateral trade is one of the main economic factors limiting the creation of a Sino-African community with a shared future. At present, the imbalance of Sino-African trade and investment is exhibited in Africa's large trade deficit with China and the high concentration of Sino-African trade. Since the financial crisis, Africa has experienced a long-term export surplus with China. However, due to factors like shrinking global trade volume and falling prices of bulk commodities such as energy and raw materials, Africa's trade surplus with China has continued to decline, moving from a surplus to a deficit. In 2012, Africa's trade surplus with China was USD 27.85 billion. In 2013, it was reduced to USD 24.62 billion. In 2014, the surplus went down sharply to USD 9.59 billion – a drop of 61%. In 2015, Africa's exports to China turned from a surplus to a deficit, reaching USD 38.30 billion. In 2016, the deficit with China reached USD 35.32 billion.

Apart from being impacted by the global trade environment, the direct cause of the large trade gap between China and Africa lies in the awkward structure of Sino-African trade. Specifically, China's imports from Africa are raw materials such as fossil fuels, iron ore, and precious metals, while its exports to Africa are mechanical and electrical products, mechanical equipment, vehicles, and other industrial products. The characteristics of the commodities of Sino-African trade prove that Africa's exports to China are easily affected by fluctuations in international commodity prices. In addition, the economic development and resource endowment of various African countries are quite different. Nations with greater economic development and better resource endowments (such as South Africa and Angola) have a larger total trade volume with China and a larger trade surplus. However, some African countries with poor economic development and resources have a low total trade volume with China, and suffer trade deficits. In 2016, the total trade volume between China and South Africa – its largest trading partner in Africa – reached USD 35.34 billion, and South Africa alone accounted for 23.7% of the total trade volume between China and Africa.[23]

China's investment in Africa has a high coverage and concentration rate, which is the main factor that impacts Sino-African economic cooperation. In 2015, the top five countries with China's investment stock in Africa were South Africa, Congo

---

23. "December 2016 Import and Export Commodities by Country (Region) Total Value Table (USD Value)," General Administration of Customs, January 23, 2017, http://www.customs.gov.cn/publish/portal0/tab49667/info837870.htm.

(DRC), Algeria, Nigeria, and Zambia. China's investment stock in these five countries reached USD 15.2 billion, accounting for 43.8% of China's investment stock in Africa.

The consequence of unbalanced development of Sino-African trade and investment is that some countries that have a large trade deficit with China will resist China's trade, leading to friction in bilateral exchange. Thanks to the exaggerations and misinformation perpetuated by the Western media, some African countries have misunderstood Chinese investment as "neocolonialism," which has seriously hindered economic cooperation.

3.3 Political instability in Africa

Africa is one of the most politically unstable regions in the world. In the field of diplomacy and international relations, China has long followed the principle of non-interference in internal affairs. However, frequent regime changes and political turmoil in African countries can easily affect political and economic relations with China. Therefore, the creation of a Sino-African community with a shared future faces a relatively high political risk.

As a result of the political and historical problems brought about by long-term colonial rule, the political situations of many African countries are complex, coupled with multiple instabilities. Since gaining independence, most African countries have followed or even directly copied the electoral systems of Western countries, with competitive elections and multi-party systems.[24] However, African countries are at a relatively basic stage of political development. People's ability to participate in politics is not high, with elections being vulnerable to the influence and interference of ethnic groups, tribal factors, and powerful political or military figures. Some African countries are still under the long-term rule of powerful politicians, and the issue of re-election often leads to turmoil. Some African countries have rigid political systems and widespread corruption, and lag behind in terms of political restructuring. The global financial crisis has exacerbated the economic downturn in African countries, and high unemployment and high inflation often lead to intensified social conflicts. In addition, the interference of Western countries is an external factor in the political vulnerability of some African countries. The turmoil that started in the North African

---

24. Xiao Yuhua and Ning Yu, "Overall Trends in Politics and International Relations in Africa (2015–2016)," in *African Regional Development Report (2015–2016)*, ed. Liu Hongwu (China Social Science Press, 2017), 23.

country Tunisia at the end of 2010 quickly spread across the region and into the Middle East. Egypt – a major African political power – has experienced many regime changes, and finds it difficult to regain its former political and economic influence.

Terrorism is another destabilizing factor in Africa. Complicated ethnic and tribal conflicts of interests, religious sectarian conflicts, poverty, and social injustice breed terrorism in Africa. Political conflicts in the Middle East have triggered the development and growth of terrorist organizations such as "Islamic State," which have spread into African countries and exacerbated terrorism there. In West Africa, the terrorist organization "Boko Haram" (which originated in Nigeria) launched a series of terrorist activities under the banner of Islam. In East Africa, the Somali organization "Al Shabaab" (closely related to "Al Qaeda") has long aimed to overthrow the current Somali government. In the Western Sahara region, "Al-Qaeda of the Islamic Maghreb" in Algeria is an important branch of "Al-Qaeda" in North Africa. These terrorist organizations are known as the "three major cancers" of African terrorism, posing serious threats to the governments and people, as well as to the lives and property of Chinese citizens working in Africa.

3.4 External interference

The end of the Cold War brought a disintegration of polarization. The international political landscape has undergone major changes, and the tension caused by competition between the two major groups in Africa has eased. With the decline of Africa's geopolitical status, the international community led by Western powers has given it less attention.

Since the first Forum on Sino-African Cooperation was held in 2000, collaboration between the two sides has increased, becoming more institutionalized. With Africa's rich resources and China's sincere willingness to cooperate, Sino-African cooperation has achieved positive economic results, and African countries have benefited. However, the win-win situation of Sino-African cooperation has attracted criticism from Western countries. China's growing influence in Africa has brought a sense of crisis and urgency to Western countries. Many have reconsidered their indifference to Africa, and have begun to pay close attention to China's activities there. Influenced by traditional political competition and geopolitical thinking, some Western media outlets and politicians have started to attack China's political goals in Africa, accusing it of "neocolonialism."

In reality, Western countries do not genuinely care about the development of African countries. However, they pretend to be "democratic mentors" keen to endorse Western-style democracy in Africa. However, their aid comes with political conditions. In the 1990s, the idea of "new interventionism" based on the theory of human rights over sovereignty became popular, causing interference in the domestic politics of African countries. In the 21st century, Western countries have intervened in the internal affairs of African countries on the grounds of a "responsibility to protect."

Seeing the progress of Sino-African cooperation, Western countries and media outlets perpetuated the concept of "neocolonialism" and the "China threat theory" in Africa and the international community, trying to weaken China's positive influence. Western countries have moved quickly to compete with China in Africa. For example, in January 2014, then-Japanese Prime Minister Shinzo Abe paid a high-profile visit to many African countries and the African Union. In March 2014, the fourth EU-Africa Summit was held. In August 2014, the United States and Africa held the first "US-Africa Leaders' Summit." In April 2014, India also held a summit with Africa. These external interventions from Western countries will inevitably have an adverse impact on the smooth development of Sino-African relations and the creation of a community with a shared future for the two sides.

At a time when the global economic and political landscape is changing rapidly, the building of a Sino-African community with a shared future faces both opportunities and challenges. Seizing the opportunities is of positive significance for China and Africa to develop together to meet global challenges.

The establishment of a Sino-African community with a shared future is not only of economic significance, but also of political consequence to the "forgotten continent." Africa is dominated by small and medium-sized countries with relatively low levels of economic development, which are not valued in world politics. The political significance of building a Sino-African community with a shared future lies in developing Africa's economic level through bilateral cooperation, and improving its political status through the improvement of its economy. Sino-African cooperation is not simply unilateral assistance from China. Its ultimate purpose is to enhance Africa's development capabilities. China's contributions to building and contracting infrastructure in Africa, boosting industrialization, and improving education and health have laid the foundation for the continent's future development.

The building of a Sino-African community with a shared future always follows the concept of justice and interests, pursues mutual benefit, and insists on cultivating Africa's endogenous development capabilities. From this perspective, the building of a Sino-African community with a shared future is of great significance to Africa. For China, it is an important way of taking on more international responsibilities, which will help improve its international image and enhance its status on the global stage. China's contribution to Africa and the rest of the world will earn it respect and international status proportionate to its all-round national strength.

Undoubtedly, the Sino-African community with a shared future will surpass China and Africa and reach global significance. With their total population of 2.3 billion, China and Africa will build a closely connected community with a shared future, which will greatly impact the global landscape. Firstly, the building of a Sino-African community with a shared future is conducive to achieving global sustainable development. Secondly, it is a model of "south-south cooperation" and a way of resolving the contradiction between the global north and south. Thirdly, it is the embodiment of the new global governance concept, and endorses equality and justice. Finally, it is conducive to the establishment of a new international political order and the democratization of international relations. Sino-African cooperation endorses the development of African economies. It will enhance Africa's global representation and voice in international relations, and boost its political status on the world stage. The improvement of Africa's international political and economic status will push forward the democratization of international relations and the establishment of a new international political and economic order.

CHAPTER 11

Forging a Sino-Latin American Community with a Shared Future

SINCE THE 18TH NATIONAL CONGRESS, major changes have taken place in the development goals, policy concepts, and major aims of China's internal and external strategies. Sino-Latin American relations have also entered a new stage of all-round development. President Xi Jinping proposed the new strategic goal of building a community with a shared future for China and Latin America and endorsing their comprehensive strategic partnership. With the intensification of the globalization process, the rise of emerging developing countries, and the continuing integration of the interests of China and Latin America, the two countries have preliminarily established a community with a shared future for mutual development, and are moving towards extending it to politics and security. With the completion of the top-level design of China's strategy for Latin America, the path for building a community with a shared future between the two has become clearer, and faces many challenges and opportunities. China must maintain its strategic determination and patience, and join hands with Latin American countries to build a community with a shared future.

1 China's Relationship with Latin America since the 18th National Congress

Since the 18th National Congress, major changes have taken place in China's domestic and foreign strategies. Internally, President Xi Jinping has proposed the "Two Centenary Goals" for development, to realize the "Chinese Dream." Externally, he proposed a specifically Chinese strategy for major-country diplomacy. As Latin America is an important development partner and a large part of its foreign strategy, China's goals and strategic positioning for it have undergone major changes. On July 17, 2014, when President Xi Jinping met with Latin American and Caribbean leaders in Brazil, he proposed the building of a community with a shared future with Latin American countries.[1] Since then, Sino-Latin American relations have entered a new stage of comprehensive development.

1.1 Frequent high-level visits between China and Latin America

To endorse the development of the comprehensive partnership between China and Latin America, President Xi Jinping visited Latin America three times in the four years following the 18th National Congress, covering ten countries. A number of cooperation agreements were signed, and the collaborative relationships with certain countries were improved. From May 31 to June 6, Xi Jinping visited Trinidad and Tobago, Costa Rica, and Mexico. He held meetings with the leaders of eight Latin American countries that have diplomatic ties with China, and signed a total of 24 cooperation documents. China's relationship with Mexico relationship was upgraded to a comprehensive strategic partnership. From July 15 to 23, 2014, Xi Jinping visited Cuba, Brazil, Argentina, and Venezuela, where he held meetings with Latin America and Caribbean leaders, and signed more than 150 contracts and framework agreements with the four countries involving USD 70 billion. From November 17 to 23, 2016, Xi Jinping visited Ecuador, Peru, and Chile. He signed a series of important cooperation documents with the three countries, and attended the closing ceremony of the Sino-Latin American Cultural Exchange Year and the Sino-Latin American Media Summit. China's relationships with Ecuador and Chile were upgraded to comprehensive strategic partnerships.

---

1. Xi Jinping, "Striving to Build a Community with a Shared Future Together – Keynote Speech at the Sino-Latin American and Caribbean Leaders' Meeting," *People's Daily*, July 19, 2014, 2.

1.2 Increasing the momentum of Sino-Latin American economic and trade relations

In the first ten years of the 21st century, the breakthrough development of Sino-Latin American economic and trade relations was driven by trade. In recent years, China's investment and financial loans to Latin America have continued to increase, becoming a new driving force for the development of Sino-Latin American relations. According to the *China Statistical Yearbook*, China's direct investment flows to Latin America increased from USD 6.17 billion in 2012 to USD 21.46 billion in 2015. During the same period, the inventory investment increased from USD 68.2 billion to USD 126.3 billion. In 2016, China's non-financial direct investment in Latin America amounted to USD 29.8 billion, a 39% increase from the previous year. At the same time, the value of China's engineering contracts in Latin America has increased significantly. In 2015, the cumulative value of contracted projects signed by Chinese enterprises in Latin America reached USD 74.6 billion. In 2016, the value of newly-signed contracts by Chinese enterprises in Latin America reached USD 19.1 billion. Since the 18th National Congress, the total amount of China's financing arrangements for Latin America stands at around USD 88 billion, including concessional government loans to Latin America, a special loan program for Sino-Latin American infrastructure projects, the Sino-Latin American Cooperation Fund, the Sino-Latin American Industrial Cooperation Investment Fund, the China-Brazil Capacity Cooperation Investment Fund, and the Chinese government's concessional loans to the Caribbean.[2] Apart from bilateral cooperation, financial cooperation between China and Latin American countries has been consistently reinforced. Within the BRICS mechanism, countries such as China and Brazil decided to establish the New Development Bank (NBD) and a Contingent Reserve Arrangement (CRA) in July 2014. In December 2015, Brazil became a founding member of the AIIB. Peru, Venezuela, Bolivia, Chile, and Argentina also joined.

1.3 Increasing cultural and people-to-people exchanges

Since the 18th National Congress, China has intensified its cultural and public diplomacy towards Latin America, and has reinforced cultural and people-to-people exchanges and dialogues with Latin American countries. Firstly, cultural and

---

2. Wang Lin, "China's Cooperation Fund Arrangements for Latin America Reaches USD 88 Billion," *China Business News*, April 20, 2016.

people-to-people exchanges have become an important part of summit diplomacy. In June 2013, when President Xi was in Mexico, he visited the ancient Mayan site Chichen Itza. When Premier Li Keqiang visited Colombia and Peru in May 2015, he encouraged dialogue with China.

Secondly, various cultural exchange events were carried out with Latin American countries, such as a "Cultural Month" and a "Cultural Year." The "Cultural Month" between Brazil and China in September 2013 and the "Sino-Latin American Cultural Exchange Year" in 2016 elevated Sino-Latin American cultural and people-to-people exchanges to a new level. Among them, the "2016 Sino-Latin American Cultural Exchange Year" is the largest annual cultural event co-hosted by China and Latin American countries since the founding of the People's Republic of China. From the opening ceremony at Beijing Tianqiao Performing Arts Center in March to the closing ceremony in Latin America in November, extensive exchanges in art, literature, cultural relics, films, and books were held in China and 30 Latin America countries through the "Bringing In" and "Go Global" strategies.

Thirdly, educational exchanges between China and Latin America have been reinforced along with the training of Chinese personnel from Latin American countries. In July 2014, when Xi Jinping met with Chinese and Latin American leaders in Brazil, he said that China would provide 6,000 government scholarships, 6,000 training places in China, and 400 on-the-job master's places to Latin America and the Caribbean from 2015 to 2019. As of December 31, 2016, China had established 39 Confucius Institutes and 18 Confucius Classrooms in 20 Latin American countries.[3]

1.4 Improvements to the Sino-Latin American cooperation mechanism

China's bilateral relations with Latin American countries have been enhanced. As of November 2016, China had established a series of all-round strategic partnerships with Brazil, Mexico, Venezuela, Argentina, Peru, Chile, and Ecuador. From January 8 to 9, 2015, the first ministerial meeting of the China-CELAC Forum was held in Beijing, and China-CELAC relations entered a new phase of cooperation. The meeting adopted three outcome documents, namely the "First China-CELAC Forum Ministerial Meeting Beijing Declaration," the "China-Latin America and Caribbean Countries Cooperation Plan (2015–2019), and "Arrangements and Operating Rules of the China-CELAC Forum." In addition, several organizations have been formed,

---

3. Hanban, "Confucius Institutes/Confucius Classrooms," http://www.hanban.edu.cn/confuciousinstitutes/node_10961.htm.

including the Sino-Latin American Agricultural Ministers' Forum, the Sino-Latin American Scientific and Technological Innovation Forum, the Sino-Latin American Entrepreneurs Summit, the Sino-Latin American Think Tank Cooperation Forum, the Sino-Latin American Political Youth Leaders' Forum, the Sino-Latin American Political Parties Forum, and the Sino-Latin American People-to-people Friendship Forum. The China-CELAC Forum has become a new platform to endorse the development of China-CELAC relations, and China-CELAC cooperation has entered a new phase of cooperation and bilateral relations.

2 Main Approaches to Building the Community

In the 1990s, the end of the Cold War and the development of Internet technology accelerated the process of globalization, and the community with a shared future is the logical interpretation of its continuing development.

As a result of trade and investment expansion among countries and an increase in personnel exchanges, economic interdependence among countries is expanding, and political and security interests are being consistently integrated, forming an interdependent community with a shared future. In this community, "nations are interdependent and share both positives and negatives."[4] The intensified participation of China and Latin America in the process of globalization and the expansion of Sino-Latin American interdependence have laid a solid foundation for China and Latin America to build a community with a shared future.

2.1 Endorsing the Sino-Latin American economic community

The economy is the most important driving force for the progress of globalization. The expansion of trade, growth of investment, and reinforcement of economic cooperation not only encourage the economic growth of certain countries, but also the integration of their development interests, which are the cornerstones of building a community with a shared future. Since the beginning of the 21st century, the economic and trade relations between China and Latin America have leapfrogged. The interests of the two sides have been increasingly integrated, and they have preliminarily built a community with a shared future for mutual development.

---

4. Xi Jinping, "Joining Hands to Build a New Partnership for Win-Win Cooperation and Building a Community with a Shared Future for Humanity – Speech at the General Debate of the 70th United Nations General Assembly," *People's Daily*, September 29, 2015, 2.

Firstly, China and Latin America are important trading partners. From 2000 to 2014, Sino-Latin American trade increased from USD 12.595 billion to USD 263.461 billion. During the same period, Latin America's share of China's total foreign trade rose from 2.66% to 6.12%. China's position in Latin America's foreign trade has also been rising. From 2000 to 2011, China's share of Latin America's total exports rose from 1.1% to 8.9%. During the same period, China's share of Latin America's total imports rose from 1.8% to 13.8%. China has become Latin America's third largest trading partner after the United States and the European Union.[5] Since 2009, China has been the largest trading partner of Chile, Brazil, and Peru. Due to a fall in international commodity prices in 2012, trade between China and Latin America slowed and declined from 2015 to 2016. However, in the context of sluggish global trade, the slowdown in trade between China and Latin America as a whole is lower than that between Latin American countries and other countries and regions in the world.

Secondly, China's investment in Latin America provides opportunities for the economic development of both sides. Latin America has become an important region for Chinese companies to "go global." In 2013, Latin America accounted for 13.4% of China's foreign direct investment flow and 13% of stock investment. China has also become an important source of investment for Latin America. According to data by the Economic Commission for Latin America, China's investment in Latin America reached USD 15 billion in 2010, accounting for 9% of the inflow of foreign direct investment in the region. China has become the third largest source of investment in Latin America, after the United States and Holland.[6]

Thirdly, financial cooperation has created new momentum for Sino-Latin American relations. In recent years, especially after the international financial crisis in 2008, China's loans to Latin America grew rapidly. The loan amount exceeded that of international multilateral institutions such as the World Bank, the Latin American Development Bank, and the Inter-American Development Bank in 2010, 2011, and 2014.[7] According to the latest data from the Economic Commission for Latin America, from 2005 to 2015, nearly 80% of the funds provided by China to Latin

---

5. ECLAC, "The People's Republic of China and Latin America and the Caribbean Dialogue and Cooperation for the New Challenges of the Global Economy," October 27, 2012, http://www.eclac.org/publicaciones/xml/8/48138/ChinayALCdialogo.pdf

6. ECLAC, "Foreign Direct Investment in Latin America and the Caribbean," http://www.eclac.cl/publicaciones/xml/0/43290/Chapter_III._Direct_investment_by_China_in_Latin_America_and_the_Caribbean.pdf

7. OECD/ECLAC/CAF, "Latin American Economic Outlook 2016: Towards a New Partnership with China," OECD Publishing, Paris, 2015, p. 158, http://dx.doi.org/10.1787/9789264246218-en.

America were used to support infrastructure.⁸ Therefore, China's financial loans to Latin America have improved the investment environment there, as well as boosting employment and pushing the development of local economies.

China and Latin America have a high degree of economic dependence. They rely on each other for mutual development. China's economic growth is beneficial to Latin America. When Chinese President Li Keqiang met the Latin American delegation at the first ministerial meeting of the China-CELAC Forum on January 9, 2015, he said that China's economy had maintained a medium-to-high growth rate and was moving towards a medium to high-end level. He vowed that China would provide more market, investment, and growth opportunities for countries around the world, including Latin America and the Caribbean.⁹ He also stated that the prosperity and stability of Latin American countries would help China expand its exports to Latin America and ensure the security of Chinese investment and loans there.

Pushing forward pragmatic cooperation is conducive to enhancing the endogenous power of the Sino-Latin American community with a shared future. Economic and trade relations are the ballast of Sino-Latin American ties. During his visit to Brazil in July 2014, President Xi Jinping proposed a new "1+3+6" framework for practical Sino-Latin American cooperation. The "1" refers to the plan to achieve the goal of inclusive growth and sustainable development and formulate the "China-Latin America and Caribbean Countries Cooperation Plan (2015–2019)." The "3" refers to the three major engines of trade, investment, and financial cooperation as the driving force, encouraging China Latin America's practical cooperation to develop in an all-round way, and striving to achieve a trade volume of USD 500 billion between China and Latin America within ten years, a 10-year investment stock of USD 250 billion in Latin America, and the expansion of local currency settlement and local currency swap in bilateral trade. The "6" refers to six major areas, namely focusing on energy resources, infrastructure, agriculture, manufacturing, scientific and technological innovation, and information technology, and endorsing the integration of China and Latin American industries. The new "3×3" cooperation model for production capacity proposed by Premier Li Keqiang during his visit to Latin America (to jointly build three major channels for logistics, electricity, and information; to implement positive interaction among enterprises, society, and government; and to expand three financing channels for funds, credit, and insurance) has proposed specific goals for

---

8. OECD/ECLAC/CAF, "Latin American Economic Outlook 2016: Towards a New Partnership with China," OECD Publishing, Paris, 2015, p. 158, http://dx.doi.org/10.1787/9789264246218-en.
9. Zhao Minghao, "Maintaining Peace and Stability in the Region and the World and Promoting Overall Sino-Latin American Cooperation for Mutual Benefit and Win-Win," *People's Daily*, January 10, 2015, 3.

pragmatic Sino-Latin American cooperation, as well as key cooperation areas and paths. If these cooperation areas are in place, they will push practical Sino-Latin American cooperation to a new height and improve Sino-Latin American economic and trade relations.

2.2 Building a Sino-Latin American security community

In the era of globalization, the implications of national security have changed. Firstly, with the development of economic and trade relations, the expansion of personnel exchanges, and the smooth flow of information, local security issues are increasingly internationalized, and non-traditional security has an increasing impact on national security. Secondly, the interaction between internal and external factors has led to an increased complexity in some countries' national security environments. Thirdly, the degree of economic interdependence among countries has deepened, and the transmission of various security issues has intensified.

Economic issues may become political issues, and political issues may affect bilateral relations. On April 15, 2014, when Xi Jinping presided over the first meeting of the National Security Commission of the Chinese Communist Party, he stated, "At present, China's national security has greater significance than at any other time in history. The space-time continuum is wider, and the internal and external factors are more complex than ever. We must stick to our overall national security concept with public security as its purpose, political security as its basis, economic security as its foundation, and military, cultural, and social security as its guarantee. We push for international security as we embark on a distinctly Chinese path towards national security."[10] The Latin American region involves many national security issues for China, including the traditional security issue of Taiwan, and many non-traditional problems.

The Taiwan issue within Sino-Latin American relations concerns China's sovereignty, security, and core interests. After the death of Taiwanese politician Chiang Ching-kuo in 1988, Lee Teng-hui began to implement the Taiwanese Independence Policy, pursuing dual recognition in Latin America, and greatly expanding the number of countries with diplomatic ties to Taiwan. In 2000, the Democratic Progressive Party, which pursued the Taiwanese Independence Policy, came to power in Taiwan, and the Chen Shui-bian administration intensified its

---

10. Xi Jinping, "Upholding the Overall National Security Concept and Taking the Road of National Security with Chinese Characteristics," *People's Daily*, April 16, 2014, 1.

efforts to implement it. Therefore, discouraging support for Taiwanese independence in Latin America became one of the most important aspects of China's policy there in the early 20th century. As China has risen, more of the Latin American countries that have diplomatic relations with Taiwan want to establish them with mainland China, and the pressure on China's national security stemming from the Taiwan issue has eased. When Ma Ying-jeou came to power in May 2008, the two sides reached a tacit diplomatic truce, and the issue was temporarily shelved. In May 2016, Tsai Ing-wen of the Democratic Progressive Party came to power, and the Taiwan issue once again became a concern within Sino-Latin American relations. As of June 2017, Taiwan had diplomatic ties with 21 countries, of which 11 were in Latin America – still the main arena for discouraging support for Taiwanese independence.

Securing resources is the biggest non-traditional security issue affecting Sino-Latin American relations. China enjoys high complementarity with some Latin American countries when it comes to certain resource products. The economies of some Latin American countries are highly dependent on the export of oil, minerals, and agricultural products, and China is their main export market. In 2010, soybean exports from Argentina, Brazil, and Mexico to China accounted for 58% of their total exports; Chile's and Peru's non-ferrous metal exports to China accounted for 60.2% of their total exports, and Chile's copper exports to China accounted for 27.5% of their total exports. Brazil's iron ore exports to China accounted for 60.5% of its exports.[11] The high dependence of China and Latin America on resource products gives their economic and trade relations a high degree of sensitivity and fragility.

With the development of economic and trade relations and the expansion of personnel exchanges, public safety has become an issue of concern. The number of business and labor personnel, international students, and tourists traveling between China and Latin America has grown rapidly. At the end of 2014, China had 26,600 laborers engaged in engineering contracting and 35,000 in dispatch work in Latin America. A total of 20,000 Chinese people travelled to Cuba and 40,000 travelled to Brazil or Mexico annually. In 2011, 25,000 Chinese travelled to Argentina.[12] The number of Latin Americans entering China for meetings/business, sightseeing/leisure, visiting family/friends, and service work reached 346,200 in 2014. The safety of citizens overseas has become a concern for all countries. Latin America has the highest murder rate in the world due to a combination of factors including social

---

11. Matt Ferchen, Alicia Garcia-Herrero and Mario Nigrinis TPF, "Evaluating Latin America's Commodity Dependence on China," *BBVA Working Paper*, no. 13/5, January 2013, https://www.bbvaresearch.com/wp-content/uploads/migrados/WP_1305_tcm348-370500.pdf.

12. "Why Don't the Chinese Come to Latin America?" *Tourism Review*, May 5, 2014.

inequality and poor governance. The 2009–2011 murder rate was 27.9 per million, higher than that of Africa (18), Asia (3.9), Europe and North America (2.5), and Oceania (1.1).[13] The issue of violent crime poses a huge challenge to public safety and social development in Latin American countries, and also threatens the safety of Chinese people overseas.

To sum up, building a Sino-Latin American security community has become a crucial element in the establishment of a community with a shared future for China and Latin America.

2.3 Creating a political community with a shared future for China and Latin America

With the progress of globalization and increased interdependence among countries, achieving world peace and development has become the responsibility of all countries in their push for growth. China proposes the creation of a community with a shared future for humanity, the main purpose of which is to establish a new type of international relations with win-win cooperation as the core. However, to achieve this goal, relying on its own strength is not enough. According to Wang Yi, "building partnerships is the main way."[14] China and Latin American nations are developing countries that share a common identity. They have common political missions and responsibilities in pushing for a new international political and economic order, maintaining world peace, defending the interests of developing countries, and restructuring the global governance system. Therefore, the Sino-Latin American community with a shared future is also a community of shared political destiny.

On January 9, 2015, China and Latin American countries reached a basic consensus in the "Beijing Declaration of the First Ministerial Meeting of the China-CELAC Forum," stating that "China, Latin American, and Caribbean countries, as developing nations and emerging economies, wish to achieve world peace and prosperity, and are an important force in endorsing multilateralism, a multipolar world, and the democratization of international relations."[15]

---

13. Citizen Security with a Human Face: Evidence and Proposals for Latin America," Regional Human Development Report (2013–2014), cited from Inés Bustillo and Helvia Velloso, "Insecurity and Development in Latin America and the Caribbean," *PRISM 5*, no. 4, 49.

14. Wang Yi, "Jointly Build a Community with a Shared Future for Humanity," *People's Daily*, May 31, 2016, 7.

15. "Beijing Declaration of the First Ministerial Meeting of the China-CELAC Forum," *People's Daily*, January 10, 2015, 3.

The building of a political community with a shared future between China and Latin America also requires a reinforcement of international cooperation. Globalization and interdependence among countries are the foundations for building a community with a shared future for humanity. However, due to the unbalanced progress of globalization, the economies of European and American countries faced a downturn after the international financial crisis in 2008, and their security is subject to threats such as terrorism and illegal immigration. The wave of anti-globalization triggered by Brexit and Trump's coming to power has brought many uncertainties to the world's political and economic development, as well as to China and Latin America's development. Therefore, China and Latin America should intensify international coordination and endorse global governance. They should build lasting peace, universal security, openness and inclusivity, and common prosperity with green and low carbon considerations, and create a community with a shared future for humanity.

Latin America is an important force in global governance. In recent years, with the rise of emerging markets, Latin American countries (especially middle powers such as Brazil and Mexico) have expressed a greater interest in participating in global governance, and their role has continued to grow. Brazil, Mexico, and Argentina have become members of the G20. Brazil has also formed groups of countries with some emerging market countries. For example, it formed the "Trilateral Dialogue Forum" (IBSA) with Brazil, India, and South Africa, and BRCIS with China, Russia, India, and South Africa, to encourage the restructuring of the United Nations, climate change negotiations, and upgrades to the international system. In September 2013, Mexico, South Korea, Indonesia, Turkey, and Australia established MIKTA, which gathers intelligence and consolidates strength under a large coordinate system where global problems are becoming increasingly prominent and the existing international order is facing reconstruction – a core group that is taking ownership of world peace and prosperity. China and Latin America share many common interests in supporting an improvement to the international order and global governance. They can work together to advance restructuring and build a community with a shared future for humanity.

2.4 Building a Sino-Latin American cultural community

In recent years, China has encouraged cultural and people-to-people exchanges and dialogues with Latin American countries. However, it still has a soft power deficit there, and the quality of these exchanges is low. On June 30, 2014, in an interview with Chinese and Mexican reporters in Mexico City, the then Minister of Culture Cai Wu said that "cultural exchange between China and Latin American countries is relatively small compared to the exchanges between China and neighboring countries, Eurasia, and some other countries in the world, and some obstacles exist."[16] In 2013, President Xi Jinping stated in his speech to the Mexican Senate, "In terms of people, China and Latin America should reinforce cultural dialogue and exchanges. We do not just appreciate our own virtues, but also applaud the virtues of others. This has become a model for disparate cultures to coexist in harmony and encourage each other." On July 17, 12014, when visiting Brazil and meeting Latin American and Caribbean leaders, Xi Jinping proposed a "new five-in-one pattern" of Sino-Latin American relations, and placed mutual learning and appreciation in an equally important position as politics, economy, trade, and diplomacy. He stated that it is only by solidifying the foundation of public support in Sino-Latin American relations that these relations can be consolidated. He also said during his visit to Latin America that "the most important thing is to know each other from the heart," and "only friends connected heart-to-heart can achieve long-term success."

Strengthening cultural and people-to-people exchanges between China and Latin America is conducive to enhancing mutual understanding, building consensus, and endorsing cooperation. At present, the awareness of China's community with a shared future for humanity based on win-win cooperation has been recognized by many Latin American countries, and is inseparable from the increasing frequency of Sino-Latin American cultural and people-to-people exchanges. It also strengthens public support for the building of a community with a shared future between the two sides. While cultural differences between China and Latin America still exist, cultural and people-to-people exchanges can continue to achieve fruitful results and contribute to the building of a community with a shared future, as long as there is mutual respect and education.

3 Main Challenges of Building the Community

Although the building of a Sino-Latin American community with a shared future has a relatively solid foundation, it also faces many challenges due to changes in the international political and economic situation.

---

16. Cai Wu, "China Will Reinforce Cultural Exchanges with Latin America," *China Culture News*, July 2, 2014.

3.1 The current status of China's economy, and difficulties in transforming Sino-Latin American economic and trade relations

China has always been the engine of the world economy and the driving force of Latin America's economic growth. As China's economic development enters a new phase, practical Sino-Latin American cooperation is being transformed and improved, and the sustainability of its economic and trade cooperation has been challenged. China's economy has shifted from high-speed to medium/high-speed development. Coupled with the fall of international commodity prices, Sino-Latin American trade has slowed down or even declined. The bilateral trade volume barely grew from 2013 to 2014, falling by 11% in 2015 and 8.4% in 2016. The shift of China's economic growth rate from high-speed to medium/high-speed is caused by the transformation of growth drivers and structural adjustments, which will also bring about structural adjustments to Sino-Latin American economic and trade relations. This structural adjustment is beneficial to the development of Sino-Latin American relations, but the structural transformation is challenging for the Chinese economy and its economic and trade structure with Latin America.

3.2 Changes in the Latin American political landscape and environment

With the end of the boom cycle for international commodities and the economic slowdown of Latin American countries, the "pink wave" of left-wing governments in Latin America at the beginning of the 21st century has gradually receded, and the political pendulum has begun to turn to the right. Right-wing governments come to power or win elections and become more powerful. On November 27, 2015, center-right politician Mauricio Macri won the Argentinian presidential election, ending 12 years of Kirchner's left-wing government. On May 12, 2016, Brazilian president Dilma Rousseff was impeached by the Senate and ousted from her presidency. A center-right provisional government comprising of the Brazilian Democratic Movement Party and the Social Democratic Party came to power. Venezuela's right-wing opposition won a landslide victory in parliamentary elections on December 6, 2015. On February 21, 2016, leftist president Evo Morales of Bolivia lost a referendum to seek re-election in 2019.

The rightward turn of the Latin American political cycle and changes in the political environment have impacted Sino-Latin American relations in two ways. Firstly, the political and economic stability of the region may affect China's investment environment. The transition of the political cycle in most countries in Latin America has been smooth, but economic, political, and social unrest has occurred in some. From 2014 to 2016, the Brazilian economy experienced significant decline for two consecutive years, plunging into the worst recession since 1930. Venezuela has suffered the deepest recession, and high inflation and food shortages have led to severe social unrest. Secondly, the adjustment of foreign policies and foreign relations may have an impact on Sino-Latin American relations. Right-wing Latin American governments are politically and ideologically close to the United States. This means that they are aligned with the US in regional and international politics such as Venezuela and human rights issues. In foreign relations, reinforcing ties with the United States may become their priority.

3.3 Uncertainty in the global political economy

After the international economic crisis in 2008, developed countries and regions such as the United States and Europe experienced slow economic growth. The world economy has grown too slowly for too long. This has had a significant impact on the economic growth of China and Latin American countries, which in turn has affected their relations. For example, exports from Latin American countries declined due to sluggish external demand. To maintain a trade balance, Latin American countries may increase trade protectionism and anti-dumping measures against China. As Gao Chunyu notes, "In 2016 alone, about one third of the 119 trade remedy investigations China encountered were from Latin American countries and regions."[17]

Creating a Sino-Latin American community with a shared future comes with many challenges and opportunities. In terms of China's development, despite its slowing economy, it is still the world's fastest growing economy and engine for economic development. According to data released by the National Bureau of Statistics on January 20, 2017, China's gross domestic product (GDP) reached the "RMB 70 trillion level" for the first time in 2016, hitting RMB 74.4127 trillion – an increase of 6.7% over the previous year at comparable prices. The World Bank predicts that the global economic growth rate in 2016 will be around 2.4%. Computed at the US dollar's value in 2010, China's contribution to world economic growth in 2016 still reached 33.2%, making it the largest contributor to world economic growth.

---

17. Gao Chunyu, "Sino-Latin American Trade Volume Reached USD 216.6 Billion in 2016," China Military Network, February 18, 2017, http://www.81.cn/gnxw/2017-02/18/content_7492542.htm.

China's development and its desire to take on greater international responsibilities will bring more opportunities to Latin America and the world economy. On June 12, 2017, Panamanian president Juan Carlos Varela announced the establishment of diplomatic relations with China, stating his belief that "China represents the future."[18]

In terms of the international environment, although deglobalization has brought many uncertainties to the development of the global political economy, it has also offered unprecedented opportunities to Sino-Latin American cooperation. When Donald Trump took office, his "America First" policy spread a strong nationalistic attitude. He adopted a strong stance on anti-immigration and anti-multilateral free trade, and reduced the US's international obligations and commitments by announcing its withdrawal from Trans-Pacific Partnership. He renegotiated the North American Free Trade Agreement, and built the US-Mexico border wall, effecting the mass deportation of illegal immigrants, cutting foreign aid, and withdrawing from the UN Paris climate agreement. These policy changes affected Mexico and Latin American countries most severely. As a result, many Latin American countries regarded Trump's coming to power as a complete disaster.

The changes and expectations of Latin American countries in their relationship with the United States provide opportunities for the development of Sino-Latin American relations. Antonio C. Hsiang –

Director of the Center for Latin American Economy and Trade at Chihlee University of Technology in Taiwan – stated that "Trump's policy towards Latin America has made China great in Latin America."[19] This has "allowed China to seize the opportunity to get closer to Latin America, and may also lead Washington's former allies to try to adjust their posture . . . Latin America may even give up multilateralism and focus on developing bilateral relations with China."[20]

However, in both opportunities and challenges, China should maintain its strategic determination and patience. Firstly, it has to be well-prepared. In the new economic situation, the improvement of China's economic structure will be accelerated through supply-side restructuring. This transformation of China's economy

---

18. "Panamanian President-Elect Will Respect Diplomatic 'Truce' with Taiwan" *Latin America Herald Tribune*, Caracas, June 19, 2014.

19. Antonio Hsiang, *Trump Makes China Great in Latin America*, April 21, 2017. http://thediplomat.com/2017/04/trump-makes-china-great-in-latin-america.

20. "Trump's 'Double Abandonment' Endorses Warming of Sino-Latin American relations," CICC Online, January 4, 2017, http://news.cnfol.com/guandianpinglun/20170104/24094429.shtml.

determines whether it will enter a phase of sustainable economic development, and also endorses the improvement of the economic and trade structure between China and Latin America. It will push bilateral economic and trade relations beyond the basic complementary relationship of primary products-manufactured products, and will enhance intra-industry cooperation, realizing the diversification of Sino-Latin American trade and investment.

Secondly, Sino-Latin American cooperation plans in political, economic, and cultural aspects should be implemented, and the integration of interests with Latin American countries should be reinforced in order to consolidate bilateral cooperation. Also, as China upholds the concept of justice and interests, and expands its opening, investment, benefit, and assistance to developing countries in Latin America, it should perform its own risk control, take note, and control the scale of investment. It should guard against investment risks, pay attention to agricultural safety, and reinforce the protection of key agricultural sectors. In addition, China should take advantage of the opportunities brought by the global power transfer to reinforce cooperation with Latin American countries on global governance and endorse the establishment of a new international political and economic order. Finally, it should fortify the connection between the BRI and its Latin America strategy to achieve global connectivity.

CHAPTER 12

Managing Relations among Major Countries

Since ancient times, the great sages and philosophers have tried to visualise the future of mankind. However, the impressive changes that are taking place in the world today have exceeded their imaginations. The occasional flaps of a butterfly in the Amazon rainforest could cause a tornado in Texas two weeks from now. The "butterfly effect" proposed by American meteorologist Edward Norton Lorenz is famous all over the world.[1] From financial crises to climate change, from cyber security to terrorist attacks, from major pandemics to refugee crises, these emerging global issues have closely linked the interests and destinies of every country in the world, forming a community with a shared future that shares both positives and negatives. The relationships among major powers play a pivotal role in endorsing the creation of a community with a shared future. These relationships are also an important factor that determines the international pattern and affects countries' strategic choices. Whether China can achieve peaceful development and achieve the gradual realization of a community with a shared future for humanity depends on the relationships among major powers. Since the 18th National Congress of the Communist Party of China, China has consistently developed its relations with major countries. Through

---

1. "Let the Concept of a Community with a Shared Future for Humanity Illuminate the Future – Written on the Occasion of President Xi Jinping's First Visit in 2017," *People's Daily Online*, January 15, 2017, http://politics.people.com.cn/n1/2017/0115/c1001-29023527.html.

frequent communication between leaders, continuing development of practical cooperation, and ongoing advancement of cultural and people-to-people exchanges, China's relationships with major powers such as Russia, the United States, Europe, and India have generally remained positive.

1 Relations among Major Countries since the 18th National Congress

The new form of international relations, with win-win cooperation at its core, is President Xi Jinping's concept of major-country diplomacy with Chinese characteristics within his overview of the world. More specifically, a new form of international relations with major powers is a priority in China's diplomacy. Against the backdrop of the collective rise of emerging countries led by China, and profound changes in the international landscape, its relationships with major powers such as Russia, the United States, Europe, and India can be viewed as an important cornerstone for building a community with a shared future for humanity.

1.1 Sino-Russian relations

As neighbors, the positive development of Sino-Russian relations serves the interests of both countries, and is also an important guarantee for maintaining an international strategic balance and world peace and stability. Thanks to the unremitting efforts of both sides for the past 20 years, China and Russia have established a comprehensive strategic cooperative partnership, which fully accommodates each party's interests and concerns, while delivering tangible benefits to the people of both countries. History has proved that China and Russia share many similarities in their development blueprints. At present, both are in an important phase of national rejuvenation, and bilateral relations have entered a phase of providing each other with important development opportunities and being each other's main priority partners.

In recent years, the two countries have maintained close high-level political exchanges, and have supported each other on issues concerning core mutual interests such as sovereignty, security, and territorial integrity, thus completely resolving the border issue and laying a solid legal foundation for bilateral relations. During President Xi Jinping's visit to Russia in March 2013, the two heads of state jointly signed the "Sino-Russian Joint Statement on Win-Win Cooperation and Strengthening the Comprehensive Strategic Partnership of Coordination (2013–2016)." During Vladimir Putin's visit to China in May 2014, the two heads of state signed the "Sino-Russian Joint Statement on the New Phase of the Comprehensive Strategic

Partnership of Coordination," which proposed the establishment of a comprehensive Sino-Russian energy partnership.

In May 2015, President Xi Jinping visited Russia again. He and Putin signed the "Joint Statement on Intensifying the Comprehensive Strategic Cooperative Partnership and Advocating Win-win Cooperation" and the "Joint Statement on the Cooperation Between the Silk Road Economic Belt and the Eurasian Economic Union." These two important joint statements marked a higher strategic level in Sino-Russian relations while charting the direction for the development of the strategic partnership between the two countries.[2] In July 2017, President Xi visited Russia again. The two countries reached a high degree of consensus on reinforcing practical cooperation in various fields, intensifying cultural and people-to-people exchanges, and reinforcing communication and coordination on major international and regional issues. Xi and Putin signed and issued a joint statement, and approved the 2017–2020 implementation outline of the "Treaty of Neighborliness, Friendship, and Cooperation,"[3] as well as signing an investment agreement worth up to USD 10 billion, which attracted widespread attention.[4]

Economically, practical cooperation between China and Russia has been expanding and intensifying. The two countries differ in their national conditions. However, as they cooperate closely, learn from each other's strengths, and complement each other's weaknesses, it is in their common interest to develop a cooperative and win-win relationship. At present, China and Russia are complementing each other's national and regional development strategies to create more converging interests and growth areas for cooperation. They should expand their cooperation from energy and resources to investment, infrastructure, technology, and finance, and shift from the import and export of commodities to joint research and production, so as to consistently increase their practical cooperation.

In the context of Western sanctions against Russia, Sino-Russian financial cooperation is particularly prominent. During the 19th regular meeting, the Chinese and Russian prime ministers stated that they should continue to reinforce cooperation in the financial field and the exchange of macroeconomic policies between the two countries. This will reinforce cooperation between the financial institutions of the

---

2. "Xinhuanet Review: Sino-Russian Relations Reach New Heights," Xinhuanet, May 12, 2015, http://news.xinhuanet.com/comments/2015-05/12/c_1115247771.htm.

3. "The Bigger Picture to Sino-Russian Relations," Xinhuanet, July 3, 2017, http://news.xinhuanet.com/world/2017-07/03/c_129645810.htm.

4. "Foreign Media Praise President Xi Jinping's Visit to Europe," *People's Daily Online*, July 8, 2017, http://world.people.com.cn/n1/2017/0708/c1002-29391557.html.

two countries in the mutual provision of export credit, insurance, project financing, and bank cards, while expanding the scope of local currency use in bilateral trade, direct investment, and credit and improving the facilitation of bilateral trade and investment.

On May 26, 2017, Foreign Minister Wang Yi said in a joint press conference with Russian Foreign Minister Sergey Lavrov that, after their talks in Moscow, China and Russia would make every effort to endorse their development strategies, the creation of the BRI, and the linkage and cooperation of the Eurasian Economic Union, as well as accelerating major projects such as energy investment, aerospace, and interconnectivity, so as to achieve substantial progress[5] and continue to create a greater convergence of interests and growth areas for cooperation.[6]

China and Russia are friendly neighbors connected by mountains and rivers, and have a long history of friendly exchanges between their people. Friendship, which derives from close contact between people, holds the key to sound state-to-state relations. The two nations share a common aspiration, and a need to intensify their comprehensive strategic partnership of coordination to consistently reinforce people-to-people exchanges, intensify communication and understanding, and carry forward their peaceable friendship from generation to generation.

Cultural exchanges between China and Russia are in full swing, with the mutual hosting of various year-long events such as the "Year of Tourism," "Year of Culture," and "Year of Language," which have played an indispensable and irreplaceable role in endorsing the Sino-Russian strategic partnership of coordination. Held in 2014 and 2015, the "Sino-Russian Youth Friendly Exchange Year" held more than 300 events, with over 300,000 participants from both countries. In 2016 and 2017, the two countries held the Sino-Russian Media Exchange Year.

The cultural cooperation framework between China and Russia has been improving, and the two countries have established fruitful relationships of cultural cooperation through bilateral and multilateral mechanisms. In short, the scale, level, and quality of cultural exchanges between China and Russia have been constantly improving, with remarkable results.[7] They will continue to intensify the

---

5. "Wang Yi on the Current Sino-Russian Relations," Huanqiu Web, May 27, 2017, http://world.huanqiu.com/hot/2017-05/10750815.html.

6. Ibid.

7. "Cultural Exchanges between China and Russia Heat up with the Creation of the BRI," Guangming.com, April 26, 2017, http://news.gmw.cn/2017-04/26/content_24301015.htm.

comprehensive strategic partnership of coordination between China and Russia, while building a closer community with a shared future between the two countries.[8]

1.2 Sino-US relations

Sino-US relations are increasingly regionalized and globalized. At the same time, this relationship is globally influential and strategically significant. Although the United States' strength declined during the financial crisis, it is still the world's only superpower. Meanwhile, China is the largest developing country and emerging power in the world. As one of the most important bilateral and major country-relations in the world today, Sino-US relations occupy a special and important position in China's diplomatic layout. China has always viewed and handled Sino-US relations from a strategic and long-term perspective, and is committed to making them sound and stable in the long run.[9] Efforts to build an exemplary major-country relationship between China and the United States is a major strategic decision made jointly by the two nations.

Uncertainties are on a rise at a time of major change and adjustment in the international landscape. The role of Sino-US relations as the anchor for world stability has become more significant, and there is a renewed need and urgency to reinforce cooperation between China and the United States. Developing long-term, healthy, and stable Sino-US relations is in the fundamental interests of the two sides, and is also the general expectation of the international community. In 2013, President Xi Jinping met with Barack Obama at Sunnylands, and reached a consensus on jointly building an exemplary major-country relationship based on non-conflict, non-confrontation, mutual respect, and win-win cooperation. In 2014, the leaders of the two countries held a late-night talk at Yingtai, during which they laid out a blueprint for the development of Sino-US relations and launched the Trans-Pacific Partnership.[10] In September 2015, they had a meeting at the White House, and agreed to enhance strategic mutual Sino-US trust and push forward

---

8. "Xi Jinping: Sino-Russian Relations Are the Best among Major-country Relations," *China News Service*, March 23, 2013.

9. "Xi Jinping's Speech at the Welcome Reception for Overseas Chinese in the United States (Full Text)," *People's Daily Online*, September 25, 2015, http://world.people.com.cn/n/2015/0925/c1002-27632490.html.

10. "Overview: How Xi Jinping's 'New and Exemplary Major-Country Relationship' Diplomatic Strategy Was Forged," *People's Daily Online*, February 13, 2016, http://world.people.com.cn/n1/2016/0213/c1002-28120530.html.

a new and exemplary major-country relationship. The two sides reached a broad consensus and made a series of achievements, including 49 that appeared on the list of achievements published by China alone.[11] From April 6 to 7, 2017, President Xi met with US President Trump at Mar-a-Lago in Florida, where they reached an important consensus and charted a direction for the development of Sino-US relations in the new era, thus opening of a new chapter for win-win cooperation.[12]

In recent years, Sino-US economic cooperation has achieved remarkable results, and the areas of cooperation have been comprehensively expanded and intensified. During a meeting with US Secretary of State John Kerry in April 2013, Xi Jinping noted that Sino-US trade cooperation is mutually beneficial in nature. He called for the two countries to create more bright spots for cooperation, leverage converging interests, take active measures to address mutual concerns, and discourage the politicization of economic issues.[13] Although deeply affected by factors such as sluggish economic recovery, the trade between the two countries has maintained an annual volume of USD 500 billion in recent years. Since the establishment of diplomatic relations more than 30 years ago, bilateral trade in goods has increased 207 times from USD 2.5 billion in 1979 to USD 519.6 billion in 2016, and the integration of bilateral interests has continued to deepen. In addition to the steady growth of bilateral trade, Sino-US bilateral investment has also maintained stable and rapid growth. By the end of 2016, the cumulative bilateral investment between China and the United States had exceeded USD 170 billion. Cumulative non-financial direct investment by Chinese companies in the US has reached nearly USD 50 billion, covering 44 states and creating nearly 100,000 jobs in the United States. American investment in China has also brought great benefits to US enterprises. According to the China Business Climate Survey report released by the US-China Business Council in October 2016, 90% of US-funded enterprises are profitable in China. By the end of 2016, the total number of American investment projects in China reached 67,000, with actual investment of USD 79.86 billion, accounting for 7.8% of approved foreign enterprises in China and 4.5% of paid-in foreign investment.

---

11. "Historic Visit Begins a New Chapter in Sino-US Relations," Xinhuanet, September 27, 2015, http://news.xinhuanet.com/comments/2015-09/27/c_1116688329.htm.

12. "President Xi Jinping's Remarks at the Sino-US Summit Were Thought-provoking," People.cn, April 9, 2017, http://world.people.com.cn/n1/2017/0409/c1002-29197702.html.

13. "Endorsing the Building of a New and Exemplary Major-country Relationship between China and the United States – Assistant Foreign Minister Zheng Zeguang Gives a Briefing to Chinese and Overseas Media on the Strategic Dialogue within the Framework of the 5th Round of Sino-US Strategic and Economic Dialogue," Xinhuanet, July 13, 2013, http://news.xinhuanet.com/world/2013-07/13/c_125003758.htm.

American companies have made important contributions to China's employment, tax revenue, and economic growth.

In recent years, cultural and people-to-people exchanges between China and the United States have flourished. The two countries have established more than 220 pairs of sister provinces, states, and cities. There are 350,000 Chinese students studying in the United States, and more than 20,000 American students studying in China. Cultural and people-to-people exchanges are active, as tens of thousands of reciprocal visits happen every day.

In 2016, more than 5 million visits were made between the two countries, expanding the cultural and people-to-people exchanges. According to statistics, an average of 13,000 people travel across the Pacific Ocean every day, with a flight taking off and landing every 17 minutes. Chinese tourists spend about USD 8,000 per person in the United States, bringing in more than USD 21 billion in tourism revenue to the United States. At present, the total number of Chinese students studying in the United States has exceeded 300,000, making it the number one source of international students in the US. Although mainstream opinion in both China and the United States holds that the increase of cultural and people-to-people exchanges is conducive to the development of Sino-US relations, the difference in history and cultures means that the exchanges may require a long period of adjustment, and that the increase in familiarity may even result in mutual contempt and disgust. Both sides should focus on the long term and see the big picture, and not be distracted from the ultimate vision.

1.3 China-EU relations

As the largest developing country and the largest association of developed countries in the world respectively, China and the EU are two major forces for world peace. The two globally important economies are the two major markets that endorse common development. As important birthplaces of Eastern and Western cultures, China and Europe are two major forces in the march of human progress.[14] The China-EU relationship is also one of the most important bilateral relationships in the world. Their cooperation goes beyond the bilateral scope, and has global significance.

Since the establishment of diplomatic relations between China and the EU more than 40 years ago, the consensus between the two sides on maintaining world peace

---

14. "Xi Jinping: China and Europe Are the 'Two Powers' in Maintaining World Peace," Huanqiu Web, November 21, 2013, http://world.huanqiu.com/regions/2013-11/4585604.html.

and endorsing common development has been consistently expanding. The depth and breadth of cooperation also continue to develop, and the strategic significance of China-EU relations is increasingly prominent.[15] In recent years, the leaders of China and Europe have interacted even more frequently, and Xi Jinping's visit to Europe has achieved fruitful results. On April 1, 2014, President Xi delivered a speech at the College of Europe in Bruges, Belgium. He stated that in order to advance China-EU relations, the two sides need to intensify mutual understanding, work together to build the four bridges of peace, growth, restructuring, and culture, and design a comprehensive strategic partnership with greater global impact.[16] At present, the two sides are steadily intensifying the four major China-EU partnerships and seeking new areas of cooperation and growth.[17] With his visits to Switzerland and Finland, Xi Jinping's trip to Europe in July 2017 drew attention to the ever-closer China-EU relationship. During his visit to Germany, he spoke positively with the German leader about the traditional friendship between their nations. The leaders drew a new blueprint, clarified new goals, and planned a new path for the future development of the comprehensive strategic Sino-German partnership. They agreed to intensify mutual political trust, reinforce practical cooperation, intensify cultural and people-to-people exchanges, endorse closer multilateral cooperation, and push forward closer Sino-German relations.[18]

In recent years, China-EU cooperation in trade and economy has made great progress, and the EU has emerged as China's largest trading partner. According to Eurostat, the import and export value of goods between the 27 EU countries and China was USD 565.78 billion. Among them, the EU's exports to China are worth USD 186.16 billion, and the imports from China are worth USD 379.62 billion, making China the EU's second-largest export market and largest import market. The China-EU High Level Economic and Trade Dialogue, which has been held many times, is the highest-level dialogue in the economic and trade domain between the two sides. In addition, China and the EU have established dialogue frameworks in the form of mixed economic and trade committees, trade policies, intellectual property

---

15. "Xi Jinping and EU Leaders Exchange Congratulatory Messages to Celebrate the 40th Anniversary of the Establishment of Diplomatic Relations between China and the EU," Xinhuanet, May 6, 2015 http://news.xinhuanet.com/world/2015-05/06/c_127771586.htm.

16. "China and Europe to Build Four Bridges of Peaceful Growth, Reform, and Culture," *People's Daily Online*, April 2, 2014, http://paper.people.com.cn/rmrbhwb/html/2014-04/02/content_1409807.htm.

17. "Xi Jinping on China-EU Relations: One of the Most Important Bilateral Relations in the World," People.cn, October 16, 2015, http://cq.people.com.cn/n/2015/1016/c365403-26807716.html.

18. "Xi Jinping Meets with German President, Holds Talks with Chancellor Merkel," Xinhuanet, July 6, 2017, http://news.xinhuanet.com/mrdx/2017-07/06/c_136421299.htm.

rights, and competition policy. They have reinforced multi-level cooperation in R&D and production in areas such as energy, science and technology, climate change, and urbanization.

Cultural and people-to-people exchanges have become an important part of the China-EU strategic partnership. In recent years, China and the EU have held the "China-EU Summit" and the "China-EU Year of Intercultural Dialogue." People-to-people exchanges between China and Europe are also increasing. In 2014, over 6 million visits were made between China and the EU, surpassing the number of visits between China and the US for the first time. In 2012, 3.28 million European tourists came to China, which is an increase of 10% year on year.[19] However, there are regional differences between China and Europe. Generally speaking, Southern European countries have a stronger cultural affinity with China, while Northern and Western European countries have greater difficulty understanding it due to their differences in historical experience and cultural habits. However, in contrast to the warm reception from the top and the lively welcome from the public, Europeans generally have a negative impression of China.

In short, China and the EU have achieved a strong political relationship, an efficient and practical economic and trade cooperation, and regular and novel cultural achievements,[20] all of which play important roles in leading and endorsing the major-country relationship. The non-zero-sum game of win-win cooperation has set the tone for China-EU relations, serving as a useful reference for the coordinated development of China and other Western countries as well as between emerging countries and Western countries.[21]

1.4 Sino-Indian relations

China and India are ancient civilizations with long histories. They are also the world's largest developing countries and emerging markets. Their combined population exceeds one third of the world's total. Sino-Indian relations have gone far beyond

---

19. "China's Relations with the European Union," Ministry of Foreign Affairs website, http://www.fmprc.gov.cn/web/gjhdq_676201/gj_676203/oz_678770/1206_679930/sbgx_679934/

20. "Cultural Exchanges between China and Europe in 2016: Frequent and New Forms of Interaction, with More Distinct National Themes," *The European Times*, December 26, 2016, http://www.oushinet.com/ouzhong/ouzhongnews/20161226/250735.html.

21. "Overview: How Xi Jinping's 'New and Exemplary Major-Country Relationship' Diplomatic Strategy Was Forged," People.cn, February 13, 2016, http://world.people.com.cn/n1/2016/0213/c1002-28120530.html.

the bilateral domain, and have important global and strategic significance.[22] China regards India as its strategic cooperative partner, and sees Sino-Indian relations as one of its diplomatic priorities. China is ready to work with India to achieve peaceful, cooperative, and common development, while bringing the Sino-Indian strategic cooperative partnership to a new level.[23]

In recent years, China and India have had more frequent political communication. In September 2014, when President Xi Jinping visited India, the two sides issued a joint statement on building a closer development partnership as the core focus of their strategic relationship.[24] On May 26, 2016, when meeting India's President Mukherjee, Xi Jinping noted that the two countries should maintain the overall direction of their bilateral relationship, maintain neighborly friendship and mutually-beneficial cooperation, expand bilateral cooperation, and cultivate more growth points, so as to achieve faster and better development for Sino-Indian relations and bring more benefits to the people of the two countries. At the same time, Xi stated that the two sides should build a solid foundation for mutual political trust. The leaders of the two countries must maintain strategic communication, and improve the top-level design of Sino-Indian relations, while enhancing mutual understanding and trust through various bilateral dialogue mechanisms. China and India should positively view and support each other's participation in regional and international affairs, and reinforce coordination and cooperation, as well as jointly uphold peace and integration in the region and beyond.[25] As one of the most important bilateral relationships in the world today, Sino-Indian relations will benefit the people of the two countries, and will also have a profound impact on the future direction of Asia and the rest of the world.[26]

The continuing enhancement of bilateral economic and trade cooperation serves the common interests of both countries. In 2016, Sino-Indian trade was worth USD 71.18 billion, and India was China's seventh largest commodity exporter and 27th largest commodity importer. Among India's exports to China, diamonds, cotton thread, iron ore, copper, and organic chemicals top the list. India is China's largest exporter of fertilizers and antibiotics. Meanwhile, China has replaced the United

---

22. "Xi Jinping: Bringing the Sino-Indian Strategic Cooperative Partnership to a New Level," China Net, May 26, 2016, http://news.china.com.cn/2016-05/26/content_38543562.htm.

23. Ibid.

24. "Xi Jinping's Ways to Get Along Between the Great Powers of China and India," Xinhuanet, May 27, 2016, http://news.xinhuanet.com/world/2016-05/27/c_129021216.htm.

25. "Xi Jinping: Bringing Sino-Indian Strategic Cooperative Partnership to a New Level," China Net, May 26, 2016, http://news.china.com.cn/2016-05/26/content_38543562.htm.

26. Ibid.

States and the United Arab Emirates as India's largest trading partner and main source of imports. Based on the principles of mutual benefit and win-win results, China and India seek and expand cooperation in new areas such as industrial investment, infrastructure, energy conservation, environment protection, advanced technology, clean energy, sustainable urbanization, Internet Plus, and production capacity.

Cultural and people-to-people exchanges between China and India have also increased, intensifying mutual understanding between the two countries. A multi-level and multi-domain people-to-people exchange framework has been established between China and India. In 2015, 889,200 visits were made between the two countries, of which 730,600 were from India and 158,600 were from China. The two countries now run direct flights from Beijing, Shanghai, Guangzhou, Chengdu, Kunming, Shenzhen, and Sanya to cities such as New Delhi, Mumbai, Bangalore, and Kolkata, with about 45 flights a week. From 2013 to 2016, China and India formed 13 pairs of sister cities, provinces, and states, encouraging local exchanges and cooperation.

However, the boundary dispute between China and India has not yet been resolved, and has become a stumbling block between the two countries, affecting the sustained and healthy development of bilateral relations. In additional, the geopolitical dilemma of the concurrent rise of the two major neighboring countries is also an important factor affecting Sino-Indian relations.

2 Main Approaches to Improving Relations among Major Countries

The development path of major-country relations can be categorized into bilateral and multilateral levels. The bilateral level is concerned with mutual political trust, economic win-win, mutual security, and cultural exchanges. At the multilateral level, it reinforces international cooperation, such as jointly maintaining international peace and stability, endorsing the peaceful restructuring of the international system, and improving global governance. International cooperation at multiple levels and in various fields will help major countries build a new form of international relations and forge a closer community with a shared future.

2.1 Bilateral level

The development path of major-country relations at the bilateral level is reflected in four aspects: mutual political trust, economic win-win, mutual security, and cultural exchange and mutual learning.

Mutual political trust is the strategic driving force and an important guarantee for major-country relations. The core of mutual political trust lies in mutual respect, mutual understanding, and equality. China and Russia have a high level of mutual political trust, and hold similar positions and opinions on major international issues. However, this trust needs to be translated into broader practical cooperation outcomes. China and Russia should continue to maintain close high-level exchanges and strategic communication, continue to increase mutual political support, and reinforce coordination and cooperation in international and regional affairs.[27] China and the United States need to approach their relationships from a strategic and long-term perspective, enrich the strategic meaning of their cooperative partnership, and embark on a new model of major-country relations that features non-conflict, non-confrontation, mutual respect, and win-win cooperation. However, in general, the strategic mutual trust between China and the United States and the sound development of bilateral relations needs to be improved. Since the 18th National Congress, the leaders of China and the United States have consistently reinforced strategic mutual trust at the Sunnylands summit, the late-night talks at Yingtai, the autumn talks at the White House, and the Mar-a-Lago meeting. They have consolidated a foundation of cooperation, and sought the greatest common ground for their mutual interests. At the same time, the two countries should engage in constructive dialogue and communication to prevent strategic misjudgment, resolve conflicts, manage differences, and strive to build a new and exemplary major-country relationship.

Mutual political trust centered on mutual respect and equal treatment is the most valuable quality of China-EU relations, and also the core factor that determines their shape.[28] Since the 18th National Congress, the intensifying of mutual political trust and practical cooperation between China and Europe have laid a solid foundation for future China-EU relations. In recent years, China and India's efforts to enhance mutual political trust have yielded positive results, but insufficient mutual political trust remains the biggest obstacle to the development of Sino-Indian relations. India has not given a clear response to China's BRI, and is wary of this initiative due to geopolitical considerations. China will continue to prioritize India in its neighborhood diplomacy, and is willing to consult and communicate with it on development

---

27. "Xi Jinping: China and Russia Should Transform High Mutual political trust into Broader Pragmatic Cooperation Results," International Online, April 15, 2014, http://gb.cri.cn/42071/2014/04/15/7551s 4505186.htm.

28. "Political Trust Is the Core Asset of China-EU Relations," Guangming.com, July 3, 2015, http://theory.gmw.cn/2015-07/03/content_16167673.htm.

cooperation between South Asia and the Asia Pacific region. Cooperation within the multilateral framework can to a certain extent alleviate each side's doubts.[29]

The development of major-country relations is also reflected in economic win-win. Reinforcing practical cooperation is conducive to consolidating the comprehensive strategic Sino-Russian partnership of coordination. China and Russia share common aspirations in advancing the alignment of development strategies. The alignment of the BRI with the Eurasian Economic Union will help intensify pragmatic Sino-Russian cooperation and benefit the people of the two countries and other nations in the region.[30] Over the past 30 years since the establishment of diplomatic relations between China and the United States, although the relationship between the two countries has experienced ups and downs, it has maintained an overall stable and continuing momentum. China and the United States have more common interests than differences, and have experienced more achievements than challenges. Economic and trade cooperation has therefore become the foundation and propeller of Sino-US relations.[31] However, the reinforcing of China's economic strength and the improvement of its industrial structure have led to the politicization and strategization of Sino-US economic ties. In addition, the increase in intellectual property rights disputes and trade protectionism in the US have posed major challenges for the stable development of Sino-US relations. The EU has been China's largest trading partner since 2004, and China has remained the EU's second largest trading partner for many years. In 2016, bilateral trade stood at USD 547.09 billion. At a time when protectionism is on the rise and economic globalization is facing headwinds, China and the EU have reaffirmed their firm support for economic globalization and a rule-based multilateral economic and trade order.[32] As the world's largest developing countries, emerging economies, and BRICS members, China and India share similar development goals and are capable of endorsing each other in their development processes. The two sides enjoy huge potential and broad prospects in bilateral and multilateral economic and trade cooperation. According to Chinese customs statistics, bilateral trade volume increased rapidly from USD 2.9 billion in 2000 to USD 70.65 billion in 2014, with an increase of 23 times over the past

---

29. "Sino-Indian Relations Have Entered a New Upward Trajectory, but Mutual Political Trust Is the Biggest Obstacle," ifeng.com, May 4, 2016, http://news.ifeng.com/a/20160504/48676723_0.shtml.

30. "Enhancing Sino-Russian Political and Strategic Mutual Trust," ifeng.com, June 28, 2016, http://news.ifeng.com/a/20160628/49256947_0.shtml.

31. "How to Keep Sino-US Relations on the Right Course," Xinhuanet, January 23, 2017, http://news.xinhuanet.com/world/2017-01/23/c_1120369706.htm.

32. "Finance Watch: China and the EU Will Reinforce Economic and Trade Cooperation," china.com, June 4, 2017, http://news.china.com/finance/11155042/20170604/30643574.html.

14 years. China has become India's largest trading partner, and India's position in China's trade map is increasingly prominent.[33]

Good security relations form the foundation of strategic stability among major countries. China and Russia are each other's largest neighbors, and share a long border. Their development of relations shows that the proper handling of security between two countries is a prerequisite for the stable development of bilateral relations. In recent years, China and Russia fully properly resolved each other's security issues, and have jointly spoken out on major global security issues, expounding the principles and positions of the two countries on major global security issues. The two countries have consistently consulted and cooperated with each other in resolving international hotspots and regional conflicts, and have become important forces in maintaining international peace. China and the United States have broadly agreed that cooperation will benefit them both, while confrontation will hurt them. Maintaining a strategic balance is the only rational choice. This is because, in the nuclear era, neither side can gain absolute superiority or security.

In the domains of non-traditional security and network security, the cooperation between China and the United States is also becoming stronger.[34] No conflict and no confrontation between China and the United States is the consensus of the two governments and people, as well as a blessing for the rest of the world. Despite the geographical distance between China and Europe, the two share many common aspirations for international peace and stability, which has encouraged them to reinforce cooperation on a range of issues, including traditional and non-traditional security matters.

Due to a range of factors, historical and otherwise, the territorial dispute between China and India has yet to be resolved. In recent years, the Chinese and Indian governments have conducted several rounds of dialogue to encourage the settlement of the territorial dispute. Although there is no conclusion at present, it has generally ensured overall stability and crisis management on the border issue between the two countries.

The steady development of major-country relations cannot be achieved without the support of domestic public opinion. Friendship between people holds the key to state-to-state relations. Cultural and people-to-people exchanges are fundamental, pioneering, extensive, and long-lasting. Reinforcing these exchanges among major

---

33. "Sino-Indian Economic and Trade Cooperation Has Huge Potential," Huanqiu Web, May 15, 2015, http://world.huanqiu.com/hot/2015-05/6443865.html.

34. "China and the US Reinforce Cybersecurity Cooperation," Xinhuanet, December 4, 2015, http://news.xinhuanet.com/world/2015-12/04/c_128500279.htm.

countries is conducive to shoring up the social foundation of bilateral relations. Cultural and people-to-people exchanges and cooperation are a highlight of Sino-Russian relations and the foundation for the long-term development of the relationship between the two countries. In recent years, China and Russia have held themed events such as a "Year of China/Russia, "Year of Language," "Year of Tourism," and "Year of Friendly Exchanges" between young people. Cultural and people-to-people exchanges have been intensifying,[35] and educational exchanges and local interactions are developing extensively.[36]

Cultural and people-to-people exchanges between China and the United States are also in full swing. Through seven rounds of the High-Level US-China Consultation on People-to-People Exchange, new achievements and highlights are made every year. For example, during the first round of the consultation, the "Sending 10,000 Students to Study for Doctoral Degrees in the United States" and "Chinese Bridge" programs were launched. In the third round of the consultation, the "Sino-US Young Scientist Forum" was launched. In the fifth round, the "1,000 Schools Together Program" was finalized. These exchanges, most of which continue to this day, have encouraged mutual benefit and trust in people-to-people exchanges between the two countries in all aspects.[37]

Over the years, cultural and people-to-people exchanges between China and Europe have become increasingly frequent, benefiting the people of the two sides in terms of their material well-being, and heightening their recognition of each other's culture and history. In particular, since the establishment of the High-Level China-EU People-to-People Dialogue, exchanges and cooperation between the two sides have yielded fruitful results.[38]

Both China and India are ancient civilizations with long histories. Reinforcing cultural and people-to-people exchanges and enhancing mutual understanding and recognition are also important cornerstones for the development of Sino-Indian relations. In recent years, cultural and people-to-people exchanges between the two

---

35. "Wang Yi: Cultural and People-to-people Exchanges and Cooperation between China and Russia Are the Foundation of the Long-term Development of Bilateral Relations," ifeng.com, April 29, 2016, http://news.ifeng.com/a/20160429/48639810_0.shtml.

36. "Putin: China Is Russia's Main Partner; China and Russia Have a Very High Level of Mutual Political Trust," Huanqiu web, December 14, 2016, http://world.huanqiu.com/exclusive/2016-12/9807510.html.

37. "Sino-US People-to-People Exchanges Embark on a New Stage," People.cn, June 10, 2016, http://opinion.people.com.cn/n1/2016/0610/c1003-28423944.html.

38. "Liu Yandong: The High-level China-EU People-to-People Exchange Dialogue Framework Bears Fruitful Results," China News, September 16, 2015, http://www.chinanews.com/gn/2015/09-16/7525691.shtml.

sides have gained momentum. There has been an increase in high-level exchanges in mainstream media, with frequent exchanges among media practitioners. Various organizations, seminars, and dialogues have intensified communication and understanding between the Chinese and Indian media.[39]

2.2 Multilateral level

The development of major-country relations at the multilateral level is reflected in the cooperation of major powers to jointly maintain world peace and stability, endorse the restructuring of the international system, and restructure global governance. China's major-country diplomacy needs the soul, heart, and responsibility of a major country. As a permanent member of the UN Security Council, China is very aware of its international responsibilities and obligations, and is willing to provide more public goods and play a unique and positive role in solving various problems and challenges in the world according to its ability. China will take a more active part in the handling of international and regional hotspot issues, and will shoulder its due responsibilities in safeguarding world stability and tranquility.[40]

The first step is to jointly safeguard world peace and stability. In recent years, China and Russia have issued several joint statements on the international situation and major global issues. They have exchanged views on the situation in Syria many times, and adopted the same position in the UN vote on the Syrian issue. The two countries have also reinforced coordination and cooperation on pressing international issues such as the situations in West Asia and North Africa, nuclear issues in Iran and the Korean Peninsula, and the situation in Afghanistan. The Chinese and Russian leaders also reached a consensus on reinforcing coordination and cooperation in international affairs, as well as upholding the purposes and principles of the UN Charter and the basic norms of international law. China has also worked for the peaceful settlement of hotspot issues and regional and global peace, as well as stability and development. In recent years, China and the United States have consistently reinforced cooperation on international and regional hotspots and global issues, which has enabled their new and exemplary major-country relationship to be based on closer common responsibilities. As the world's largest developed and developing countries, China and

---

39. "Intensifying Sino-Indian People-to-people Exchanges and Reinforcing Media Communication," NetEase News, September 18, 2013, http://news.163.com/13/0918/09/991TS17R00014AED.html.

40. "Exploring the Path of Major-Country Diplomacy with Chinese Characteristics – Speech by Foreign Minister Wang Yi at the Luncheon at the Second World Peace Forum," Ministry of Foreign Affairs website, June 27, 2013, http://www.fmprc.gov.cn/mfa_chn/zyxw_602251/t1053901.shtml.

the United States are shouldering an increasing share of responsibility to maintain regional and international stability. If they can work together to contribute to world peace and stability and the progress of civilization, it will meet the expectations of the international community, and will also define their new and exemplary major-country relationship.[41]

During meetings, the leaders of China and the United States have expressed their willingness to endorse the proper settlement of international and regional hotspot issues, and to maintain world peace and stability. They have also agreed to reinforce communication and coordination on regional and global issues such as the Korean Peninsula, the Middle East, and South Asia, and work together to meet common challenges and maintain peace and stability.

Chinese and European leaders have also continued to reinforce consultations on international and regional hotspot issues. As comprehensive strategic cooperative partners, both China and the EU shoulder the major responsibility of maintaining world peace and stability. In recent years, China and the EU have communicated and consulted closely on the Syrian issue and the Iranian nuclear issue, and have worked together to endorse international peace and stability. Within the four-pronged partnership framework, China and the EU aim to build a partnership of peace in which both sides reinforce communication and coordination in international and regional affairs, encourage the political settlement of regional hotspot issues, and formulate relevant international regulations.

China and India also share common interests in safeguarding the security of Central Asia and the Indian Ocean. In recent years, the growing Afghanistan issue has become a common concern for both China and India, and has prompted the two countries to cooperate to ensure common security in the surrounding areas. Peace and stability in the Indian Ocean region are also in the interests of the two countries, and they continue to work together to combat maritime crime and launch maritime rescue.

The second step is to push for the peaceful restructuring of the international system, which is undergoing an important period of transition, with a magnitude and scope rarely seen before. Although the original powers are still the dominant forces, non-Western powers are playing an increasingly prominent role. The collective rise of emerging powers is the main driving force for the restructuring of the international

---

41. "How to Build a New Model of Sino-US Major-Country Relations – Foreign Minister Wang Yi's Speech at the Brookings Institution," Ministry of Foreign Affairs website, September 21, 2013, http://big5.fmprc.gov.cn/gate/big5/www.fmprc.gov.cn.

system. As the world's power center shifts to the Asia-Pacific region, an international system dominated by the West is unsustainable. The new international system will move towards shared dominance between East and West, and cooperation between China, Russia, and India will contribute to a smooth and peaceful transition.

Over the past 30 years of Reform and Opening-up, China has integrated itself into the international system, and has become an important participant. The current international system is undergoing profound changes, which bring about a great amount of uncertainty. Identifying how to encourage the peaceful restructuring of the international system is the common responsibility of all major countries. China and Russia have been reinforcing cooperation on this peaceful transformation as well as the restructuring of the United Nations. Enhanced strategic cooperation between the two countries will also help limit US hegemony and unilateralism.

China and the United States are important global powers that share responsibility for maintaining the stability of the international system. As a hegemonic power and rising power respectively, the ways in which the US and China can handle differences and achieve no conflict or confrontation will be of great positive significance to the restructuring of the international system. As important players on the international stage, China and the EU share important strategic consensus on endorsing democratization and multi-polarization of international relations. Increasing high-level visits and strategic communication between China and the EU is vital in supporting the peaceful restructuring of the international system. With neither China's nor India's position in the existing international system matching their own strengths, the two countries can work together to enhance their international status. Their sheer size means that their impact in the world cannot be ignored. If China and India work together, their restructuring efforts will attract global attention.

Europe and America have vested interests in preserving the existing international system. Although their strengths are in decline, they still cling to their stakes in various international political and economic organizations, which greatly limits the transformation of emerging countries' strengths into international influence, making it difficult for these countries to improve their international positions. Therefore, emerging countries should come together to improve their status.

The third step is to jointly support the improvement of global governance. To solve global problems in the long term requires an effective global governance system. The current restructuring of the international system has heightened the urgency of wider global transformation, and also provides an unprecedented opportunity for reorganization and innovation of global governance. The shift of the center of world power has brought about a commensurate shift in the center of global governance:

from the current joint governance of Western developed countries to the future joint governance of Western powers and emerging countries, and from the present Atlantic region to the future Asia-Pacific region. Emerging powers are increasingly part of the global governance leadership. Cooperation between emerging powers such as China, Russia, and India and developed Western countries and regions such as the US and Europe helps to make the global governance system more just and equitable, while supporting the democratization in international relations.[42]

China and Russia have been coordinating their positions and reinforcing cooperation to support collaboration in the international economic and financial systems, making the international economic order fairer and more equitable. China and the United States should reinforce cooperation at the global and regional levels to achieve mutual benefit and common development. At the global level, China and the United States will jointly address challenges such as climate change and cybersecurity, and reinforce coordination and cooperation in multilateral mechanisms such as the United Nations, G20, and APEC. As the world's major economies, China and the United States will reinforce mutual support within the G20 mechanism, work with other economies to support strong, sustainable, and balanced development of the world economy, and make the G20 an important platform for global economic governance.

China and the United States will also work together to restructure the IMF and support the restructuring of the multilateral trading system. They have also agreed to reinforce economic cooperation in the Asia-Pacific region, and have pledged to fortify coordination and cooperation under the APEC framework to jointly endorse economic growth and prosperity in the Asia-Pacific region. Chinese and European leaders have reached consensus on intensifying cooperation at the global and regional levels. China and the EU both support the G20 as the main forum for international economic cooperation, allowing it to play a greater role in global economic governance. Both sides reaffirmed their determination to fulfill their G20 commitments as planned, including in the areas of the global economy, financial regulatory restructuring, IMF capital increase, and IMF quota and governance reorganization. China and India have enormous common interests in terms of improving global governance and endorsing the global order. To improve global economic governance, these two important members of the G20 have played an important role in making it a major platform for the global economy. As major developing countries, China

---

42. "An Inventory of President Xi's Statements on Global Governance," Xinhuanet, November 14, 2015, http://www.xinhuanet.com/world/2015-11/14/c_128428606.htm.

and India have come together to support the continuing development of BRICS countries in order to enhance the status of developing countries in global economic governance. China and India both endorse multi-polarization and democratization of international relations. The two countries are more effective working together than working alone.

In short, enhancing cooperation among major countries in global governance is conducive to the common development and prosperity of the international community. To achieve peaceful development through cooperation and restructuring, China needs to maintain sound cooperative relations with other countries, and work in concert to solve many common problems faced by the international community, while making global governance more just and equitable.

3 Main Challenges of Improving Relations among Major Countries

The international community is developing into a community with a shared future, for which the sound development of major-country relations is an important strategic foundation. Although major-country relations have generally remained stable in recent years, their development is still constrained by a series of factors, such as power politics, limited mutual trust, and differences in ideas.

3.1 Power politics: a bottleneck that restricts the development of major-country relations[43]

Throughout the ages, power politics have been regarded as the essence of international relations. Constant competition for power between countries has become an important driving force for the continuing evolution of international relations. However, power politics are gradually giving way to rule-based politics. The nature of power is changing, moving away from hard power (such as force and capital) towards soft power (such as reputation and ideas), the latter of which is growing in importance. Meanwhile, power is becoming increasingly dispersed. International relations are no longer completely dominated by large countries. Small and medium-sized countries also have a voice. Even non-state actors like international organizations, enterprises, and individuals can play an important role in international relations. At the same time, the ever-increasing number of global problems calls for a democratization of

---

43. Wang Fan, *Great Power Diplomacy: From "Hiding Its Strength and Biding Its Time" to "Great Power Diplomacy," What China Wants to Tell the World* (Beijing United Publishing Company, 2016), 256.

international relations, with rules rather than power becoming the main feature of coordinating international affairs. Power politics still play an important role in major-power relations, but major countries rely increasingly on international cooperation, which means that they need to constantly reinforce coordination based on rules and consensus, and pursue win-win cooperation rather than differentiation and confrontation.

Regrettably, major powers still carry the power politics and zero-sum game mindset, which greatly limits cooperation among them. For example, with the collective rise of emerging countries, major powers such as the United States and Europe hope to incorporate them into institutional frameworks that align with Western interests. However, to maintain their dominance, Western developed countries also suppress the demands of the emerging countries to enhance their international status. Such mindsets are hugely inconvenient for rules-based cooperation between major powers, thus highlighting the obvious obstacles of power politics.

3.2 Limited mutual political trust often limits in-depth cooperation between major powers

Trust is the foundation of friendship and cooperation. The greater the mutual trust, the more room there is for collaboration. To build and enhance strategic trust, it is important to understand the other side's strategic intentions in good faith, and not treat them as the enemy. In recent years, China has put forward a series of new ideas and measures in its diplomacy. It has led the BRI, established the Asian Infrastructure Investment Bank, and pursued its own version of major-country diplomacy based on the principle of win-win cooperation. However, major powers such as the United States, Europe, and Japan worry that a rising China will inevitably seek global hegemony in the future. The United States believes that the security order in East Asia and the Asia-Pacific region, which it has long dominated, is being challenged by China. It also believes that it has been sidelined in the ruling of the world economy and the control of hot-button issues,[44] leading to the emergence of the "China Threat Theory." Limited mutual political trust makes it difficult for major countries to view each other's demands as peaceful and see their cooperation from the perspective of relative benefits rather than absolute benefits. As a result, major countries' first consideration is not how to achieve cooperation successfully, but their own relative

---

44. Wang Fan, *Great Power Diplomacy: From "Hiding Its Strength and Biding Its Time" to "Great Power Diplomacy," What China Wants to Tell the World* (Beijing United Publishing Company, 2016), 233–235.

gains and losses. As a result, cooperation between major countries is greatly limited, and faces greater resistance on some issues or areas that are beneficial to society but have diverging interests among major powers. The half-hearted efforts of the major powers mean that international cooperation lacks core leadership.

3.3 Differences in ideas are another important factor restricting the cooperation between major countries

In today's world, coexistence between multiple cultures is the norm. Significant differences in ideas exist among countries, and this is no exception in major-country relations. Ideological differences are particularly obvious. Although the Cold War is over, and ideology is no longer the mainstream in major-power relations, its influence on major-country relations has not completely disappeared. Ideology is the guiding principle of state-to-state exchanges and relations. Color revolutions are still an important manifestation of major-power confrontations, and global cooperation is still refracted through an ideological lens. In addition, concepts such as religion and identity also have an impact on relationships among major countries. China stands for diversity and does not believe in the so-called universal values that are supposedly applicable to all countries. However, the ideals of fairness, justice, and sustainable development – which are shared values in China – are similarly understood and recognized by Western countries. It is these differences in ideas that affect cultural and people-to-people exchanges between countries. In this regard, it is necessary to face up to these differences, seek cohesion and common ground, and even assimilate differences.

Based on the above considerations, global players need to pay particular attention to the following aspects for the future development of major-country relations. First, they must resolve strategic differences and consistently enhance strategic mutual trust. The importance of the relationships among major powers is clearly reflected in its strategic aspect, which is an important factor affecting the global structure. At present, there are obvious strategic differences between China and some major powers, especially the United States, which require proper handling. It is hard for the US to shake off the Cold War mentality, zero-sum game mindset, and hegemonic strategic logic. The strategic differences between China and the US have become increasingly acute in recent years. In order to defuse possible miscalculations and strategic risks arising from the strategic differences between China and the United States, it is necessary to follow a consensus and reinforce strategic communication and targeted exchanges, as well as endorsing trust through strategic stability, and reinforcing new strategic thinking based on a non-zero-sum mentality. There are also some strategic differences in China's relations with the EU and India. Strategic differences are inevitable in the development of China's major-country relations. The key lies in how to resolve them and enhance mutual trust.

Secondly, global players must continue to heighten pragmatic cooperation and reinforce the foundation and lubricant of major-country relations. The development of major-country relations requires practical cooperation to be constantly reinforced. For example, although the strategic competition between China and the United States has intensified, the reinforcing of practical cooperation between the two countries has limited strategic competition, leading to a complicated situation in which cooperation and competition co-exist. For Sino-Russian relations, the weakness lies in the fact that practical cooperation needs to be improved. Despite strong economic complementarity between China and Russia, the scope and depth of their cooperation are relatively limited, leading to the slow growth of the total economic and trade volume between the two countries over the years. In China's relations with major regions and countries such as the EU and India, practical cooperation should be the driving force. In fact, China's major-country relations should focus on practical cooperation, as should those of the other great powers. It is only in this way that major-country coordination can play a more active role in international relations.

Thirdly, global players must intensify cultural and people-to-people exchanges to lay a solid social foundation for the development of bilateral relations. Friendship between people is the key to positive state-to-state relations. A friendship that is based on money will be dissolved when one side runs out of wealth. A friendship that is based on power will be toppled when one side no longer has power. It is only through genuine and sincere exchanges that a friendship can be long lasting. Cultural and people-to-people exchanges between major countries should be wide ranging, multi-tiered, frequent and in-depth, and of a high level. Such exchanges form the three pillars of major-country relations, along with strategic mutual trust and practical cooperation. At present, China attaches great importance to its cultural and people-to-people exchanges with other major countries, especially exchanges between young people, which bode well for future growth. However, it is not easy to endorse genuine and sincere exchanges through people-to-people interactions. It requires determined efforts over several generations.

To achieve its "Two Centenary Goals," China needs to carry out major-country diplomacy with its own characteristics. Managing relations with major countries is the top priority. To develop Sino-US relations, it is necessary to enhance strategic mutual trust and practical cooperation, seek inclusivity and mutual learning, and achieve common development. The Sino-Russian relationship is China's most important neighborly tie. Close cooperation in strategic and political aspects will enhance the common influence of the two countries. However, there is still a lot of room for improvement, and many difficulties, in the practical cooperation between the two countries in the domains of trade and the economy. China-EU relations are typical of China's regional and major-country diplomacy. Attention should be paid to the dual structure of regional diplomacy and major-country relations. These countries are partners that China can draw on in some areas. In terms of Sino-Indian relations, it is necessary to solve the dilemma of the concurrent rise of two neighboring countries and increase their common interests through pragmatic cooperation. In short, major-country relations should keep pace with the times and follow the prevailing inclinations. Active management of major-country relations is an important element of the international community's concerted efforts to build a community with a shared future for humanity, which will have a profound impact on the continuing development of major-country relations.

PART IV

Participating in Global Governance

Building a community with a shared future for humanity requires the cooperation of the international community in a variety of areas. The only way to achieve this is by improving global governance. Currently, the international landscape is undergoing profound changes. Competition among various powers in the world is becoming more intense and complex, while global problems are on the rise on a daily basis. Multilateral institutions and frameworks are unable to deal effectively with these challenges. Global governance is needed more urgently than ever, but is lacking. Due to differences in actors and disparities in cost and benefit sharing, global governance varies from issue to issue. Good global governance of the economy, security, the environment, and the cyber domains are the key to building a community with a shared future for humanity, and also an important component of the "Five-sphere Integrated Plan" for this community.

CHAPTER 13

Global Economic Governance

Driven by time and globalization, emerging global problems are increasingly intertwined, threatening national development, social progress, and people's well-being. As such, there is an increasingly urgent need for global governance. Global economic governance has always been an important area within this. Since the financial crisis in 2008, its importance has risen to an unprecedented level. At present, global economic governance is at a critical juncture of "progress or retreat."[1] Since the outbreak of the international financial crisis in 2008, the world economic landscape has adjusted even more rapidly, and the global economic governance system has faced profound changes. In President Xi Jinping's keynote speech at the opening ceremony of the World Economic Forum Annual Meeting 2017, he stated that "China should develop a model of fair and equitable governance to keep up with the trend of the times," putting forward China's proposition to improve the global economic governance system, support global economic governance and its transformation, and strive to build a community with a shared future for the well-being of humanity.

---

1. "Global Economic Governance is at a Critical Juncture between Progress and Retreat: Comments on the G20 St Petersburg Summit in 2013," China Reform Forum website, May 30, 2014, http://www.chinareform.org.cn/open/economy/201405/t20140530_198590.htm.

1 The Existing Governance Structure and Its Main Issues

Just as economic globalization is an important part of overall globalization, global economic governance is also an important part of overall global governance. The driving force behind global economic governance lies in economic globalization. In academic circles, there is a general consensus that economic globalization is the main driver for the development of global economic governance.[2]

1.1 The architecture of global economic governance

At the end of 2010, the Secretary-General of the United Nations, member states, and relevant organizations submitted an analysis report to the 66th United Nations General Assembly, focusing on global economic governance and development. The report gave an authoritative definition of global economic governance, emphasizing the role of multilateral institutions and processes in influencing global economic policies, law, and regulations. While highlighting the efficacy of governance, this definition also stressed the critical role of multilateral institutions in governance.[3]

Different understandings and aspirations have given different meanings to global economic governance. The international cooperation that has rebuilt the international economic order since World War II has borne the changes of the times. The G20 summit framework, which was established in response to the 2008 financial crisis, is an institutional framework and an important platform for international cooperation. Establishing a global management system that transcends national sovereignty is a future oriented concept.[4] Therefore, global economic governance refers to the necessary and minimal joint management of the world economy through the creation of international systems and international rules.[5]

---

2. Zhou Yu, "Global Economic Governance and China's Engagement Strategy," *Journal of World Economics*, no. 11 (2011): 26–32.

3. Sun Yiran, "Convergence and Competition of Ideas in Global Economic Governance in the Post-Crisis Era," *European Studies*, no. 5 (2013): 1–21.

4. Zhou Yu, "Global Economic Governance and China's Engagement Strategy," *Journal of World Economics*, no. 11 (2011): 26–32.

5. International institutions and international rules can be divided into (1) Formal multilateral international rules and institutional arrangements, such as GATT and WTO; (2) Informal institutional arrangements consisting of only a small number of countries, such as the Group of Seven; (3) Regional economic governance, that is, the realization of economic integration and the liberalization and harmony of trade and investment among countries in the world and its subregions.

In the face of endless new situations and problems in the development of the world economic order since the 2008 financial crisis, the adjustment of the global economic pattern has accelerated, and global economic governance is in urgent need of restructuring and transformation. The development and evolution of the systematic structure of global economic governance have shown the following characteristics:

Firstly, the subjects of global economic governance are multiple and diversified. Governments and international inter-governmental organizations have always been in the leading position, and multinational corporations and international non-governmental organizations play an indispensable role.[6] In recent years, international NGOs, such as multinational corporations and civil societies, have increased sharply in number and power, exerting a certain level of influence on the decision-making process of global economic governance.

Secondly, the governance framework is multi-tiered. International organizations such as the World Bank, the International Monetary Fund, the World Trade Organization, and the Bank for International Settlements are interconnected but have their own respective functions. Since the outbreak of the international financial crisis in 2008, the G20 has played an important role in the global economic governance system. Its status has risen rapidly, and it has become an important platform for multilateral dialogue and the coordination of macroeconomic policies. In recent years, the rapid development of regional cooperation frameworks such as that of the BRICS has become an important feature in the evolution of the global economic governance system. Regional trade arrangements have also grown sharply, from about 20 in the early 1990s to more than 450 today.[7]

Thirdly, the governance system is evolutionary. Global economic governance is a dynamic concept that is constantly changing with the times. Different historical stages carry different periodical implications:[8]

(1) The evolution of the global economic governance framework mostly follows the principle of increasing complexity, while maintaining an inherent logic of continuous development and improvement.

---

6. Long Guoqiang, "Characteristics and Tone of the Current Global Economic Governance System," People.cn, August 30, 2017, http://theory.people.com.cn/n1/2017/0830/c40531-29503389.html.

7. Ibid.

8. Zhou Yu, "Global Economic Governance and China's Engagement Strategy," *Journal of World Economics*, no. 11 (2011): 26–32.

(2) Technological progress and economic development have created new issues and put forward new requirements for the restructuring of the global economic governance system.

(3) The international influence of individual countries changes with the pattern of global economics and trade, which is bound to impact the existing international economic and trade rules and endorse the restructuring of the global economic governance system.[9]

1.2 Major issues facing global economic governance

Since the 2008 financial crisis, the international community has worked together and made remarkable achievements in global economic governance. However, in the post-crisis era, global economic recovery remains sluggish, and debt levels remain high. International trade continues to slump, sustainable development remains a long and arduous task, and global economic governance faces many challenges.

Firstly, the representation, voice, and decision-making power of developing countries in global economic governance are severely insufficient. As an important area of global governance, global economic governance has been greatly affected by three connected processes, namely the economic division of the world during the Cold War, the possibility of global economic integration brought about by the end of the Cold War, and the re-integration of the world economy in the post-Cold War period.[10] For a long time, Western powers have dominated and even largely monopolized global economic governance, meaning that the word "global" has lost its proper significance and undermined the representation and voice of a vast number of developing countries.

The 2018 financial crisis has since undoubtedly provided a historic opportunity to restructure global economic governance. In order to escape the crisis as quickly as possible, the US and European countries (which were hit hard by the crisis) began to support the restructuring of global economic governance. However, they did not want to give up their long-standing dominance over global economic governance. When they asked emerging countries to shoulder more international responsibilities, they did not give them corresponding powers while attempting to resist measures that were not favorable to them. This has naturally led to one-sided restructuring. At

---

9. Long Guoqiang, "Characteristics and Tone of the Current Global Economic Governance System," People.cn, August 30, 2017, http://theory.people.com.cn/n1/2017/0830/c40531-29503389.html.

10. Pang Zhongying, "Global Economic Governance since 1956 and Its Lessons," *International Observer*, no. 2 (2011): 1–8.

present, the vast number of developing countries, led by China and other big players, are accounting for an increasing proportion of global economic growth, and have even become the main source of that growth. However, their voice and decision-making power in the international economic system remain limited.

Secondly, the current governance rules do not fundamentally reflect the changes and trends of emerging countries. Western countries are absolutely dominant in the formulation and implementation of international rules, while developing countries often have to passively accept them, and find it difficult to play their roles. Early global governance was the product of post-war Western powers working together to plan the world's blueprint. Its rules and frameworks were formulated by developed Western countries, and its essence was imperial and hegemonic governance. When dealing with complex global issues, hegemonism and power politics frequently emerge, marginalizing developing countries to varying degrees. With the gradual increase in the strength of emerging countries, and the continuous improvement of their international status, their cultures and ideas are increasingly affecting the restructuring, innovation, and improvement of international rules. However, the governance rules supported by power and centered around Western countries do not fundamentally reflect the change and development tendency of power distribution.

Thirdly, global economic governance lacks effective international leadership. When a world government is an impossibility and the dilemma of collective action is a serious issue, the key to global economic governance lies in leadership. With profound changes in the global power structure, how can we solve the problem of each country acting in its own way due to the supremacy of national interests? Who will provide global public goods, and who will maintain the world order? Advanced Western countries are neither willing nor able to remain as leaders of global economic governance. However, emerging countries, such as China, are not ready to take on more global responsibilities. New leadership is urgently needed to serve as the backbone and provide the direction for global economic governance, so as to stem the tide of anti-globalization.

Fourthly, global economic governance is ineffective, and there is an urgent need to overcome what Garrett Hardin calls the "dilemma of collective action" and the "tragedy of the commons."[11] Global economic governance is plural in terms of participants, and is based on self-awareness, but it is highly public or common in the problem areas. As global problems increases, the theoretical logic of global economic governance is to establish rules and frameworks to overcome collective

---

11. Garrett Hardin, "The Tragedy of the Commons," *Science*, no. 162 (1968): 1243–1248.

action dilemmas through selective incentives, given the different characteristics of countries that are the main players. Therefore, identifying how to preserve this kind of collective action efficiently and overcome Hardin's "dilemma" and "tragedy of the commons" is one of the most pressing issues in global economic governance.

To judge whether global economic governance is effective or not, it can be initially assessed based on three key criteria, namely economic growth, institutions, and cooperation.[12] According to the assessment of the International Monetary Fund, the average growth rate of the global economy from 2014 to 2019 will remain at low – below 4%.[13] However, the G20, IMF, and WTO – the three frameworks of the international economic governance system – have limited ability to bring new impetus and vitality to global economic governance. Under the principle of the supremacy of national interests, it is difficult to substantively advance global multilateral cooperation. Challenges in international economic cooperation, such as trade and finance, are also evident in the current situation. Therefore, although the financial crisis has raised the importance of global economic governance to an unprecedented height, currently it has not achieved significant results in the three key criteria mentioned above.[14]

In fact, the emergence of this situation has a profound historical background. With the rise of emerging powers and the shift of the center of global power to the Asia-Pacific region, the international system is in an important transitional phase. To a certain extent, the governance system is determined by the power system. The governance system in a certain period cannot contradict or deviate from the power system. The developments and changes of the power system also require that the governance system makes a series of corresponding adjustments. The current power system is undergoing transformation, and the governance system is also in a state of flux.

Of course, understanding global governance from the perspective of power does not offer a complete picture. This is because, to a certain extent, governance itself is a way of existence outside of power. Within the historical context of the world economy, global economic governance is an inevitable requirement for the continuous expansion of economic globalization. Driven by the tide of economic globalization since the late 20th century, developed Western countries have been calling for the restructuring of global economic governance, and the majority of developing countries have made the

---

12. Manuela Moschella and Catherine Weaver, *Handbook of Global Economic Governance* (London: Routledge, 2013), 4.

13. IMF, "Recovery Strengthens, Remains Uneven," *World Economic Outlook*, 2014, 181.

14. David Held and Charles Roger, eds., *Global Governance at Risk* (Nanjing: Polity Press, 2013).

same demands. The old international economic order is no longer suited to the reality and development tendency of the world economy. Restructuring global economic governance has become the consensus of the international community. The key is how to understand and carry out the restructuring.

2 China's Involvement in Global Economic Governance: New Ideas and Measures

Faced with the development and evolution of the world's economic situation, global economic governance needs to keep pace with the times.[15] In the process of participating in global economic governance, China has put forward a series of new ideas and translated them into practical actions, endorsing global economic governance and its transformation.

2.1 China's vision for global economic governance

Since the 18th National Congress, China's diplomacy has made continuous efforts to build a community with a shared future for humanity, guided by its own unique thoughts on major-country diplomacy. China has contributed its unique knowledge and solutions to global economic governance.

First, it has struck a balance between rights and obligations, and has endorsed the restructuring of global economic governance. In November 2012, the 18th National Congress set the principles of "reinforcing exchanges and cooperation with other countries and endorsing the restructuring of global governance" and "balancing rights with obligations and participating in global economic governance" as the main guiding principles and mission of the Chinese government's foreign strategy. On many important international occasions, such as the G20 Hangzhou summit and the speech at the UN headquarters in Geneva, President Xi reiterated the importance of global economic governance, which proves its importance to the Chinese government.[16]

Secondly, China upholds a new concept of international relations based on win-win cooperation and partnership. In March 2013, when President Xi made a speech at the Moscow Institute of International Relations, he called on all countries to work

---

15. "Xi Jinping: Improving Global Economic Governance Together," Xinhuanet, September 3, 2016, http://news.xinhuanet.com/world/2016-09/03/c_129268306.htm.
16. Cai Tuo, "How China Participates in Global Governance," *International Observer*, no. 1 (2014): 1–10.

together to build a new form of international relations with win-win cooperation at its core. Under this guidance, global economic governance should abandon the zero-sum mentality wherein one party has to lose for the other party to win. Instead, it should uphold win-win cooperation, close partnerships of equality, mutual consultation, and mutual accommodation, assuming of due responsibilities and endorsing the development of the world economy in a more balanced, inclusive, and sustainable direction.

Thirdly, China pursues innovative, coordinated, green, open, and shared development, as stated by President Xi at the opening ceremony of the Asian Infrastructure Investment Bank in January 2016. The focus of the agenda will be on supporting innovation-driven development to reinforce new drivers for economic development, as well as allowing supply-side restructuring to adapt to and lead the new normal of economic development, and opening wider to the outside world with more emphasis on advancing high-level and two-way opening up.[17] The five major development concepts are based on a thorough review of development experiences in China and abroad, and also an assessment of local and foreign development tendencies. They reflect China's profound reflection on the laws of economic and social development, and are solutions to its move towards a new economic norm and the sluggish recovery of the world economy.[18]

Fourthly, China upholds a vision of global economic governance that is based on equality, oriented towards openness, driven by cooperation, and aimed at shared benefit. At the same time, it advocates for the building of governance structures in the four major areas of finance, trade and investment, energy, and development. During the successful G20 Hangzhou Summit in September 2016, the Chinese government expounded its view on global economic governance, stating that it should have innovation as a core outcome, placing development in a prominent position in global macro policy coordination, and forming a framework for multilateral global investment rules for the first time. This is China's way of addressing both the symptoms and root causes of the sluggish world economy, leaving an indelible mark on global economic governance.

These new concepts reflect profound changes in the world economic structure, as well as the interests of emerging markets and developing countries. They guide China's

---

17. "Xi Jinping's Views on Global Economic Governance," People.cn, January 17, 2017, http://politics.people.com.cn/n1/2017/0117/c1001-29029711.html.

18. "Implementing the Concept of Innovative, Coordinated, Green, Open, and Shared Development to Achieve the Goal of Building a Moderately Prosperous Society in an All Respects as Scheduled," People.cn, January 7, 2016, http://politics.people.com.cn/n1/2016/0107/c1024-28021893.html.

participation in global economic governance, inject new momentum into global economic governance, and are conducive to the restructuring and transformation of the global economic system. These concepts have also received wide acclaim from the international community.

2.2 New practices for China's participation in global economic governance

At present, global economic governance is at a critical turning point. The international community expects more from China as the world's second-largest economy. To build a community with a shared future for humanity, the Chinese government is responding to the situation and following the trend. In participating in global economic governance, China has shifted from a passive response to general participation, and from active participation to leading participation. In this process, it has become a major player, architect, coordinator, and reformer of the global economic governance system.

Firstly, it has supported the restructuring of the IMF quota. In 2010, the US launched an initiative to restructure international financial institutions in order to escape the financial crisis as quickly as possible, claiming that it would amplify the voices of emerging countries in the IMF and the World Bank and reorganize the old global economic governance structure. However, the United States did not implement this restructuring in a timely and earnest manner, as it has been hesitant about the 2010 IMF quota restructuring plan. China and other emerging countries called for the restructuring of international financial institutions, and were greatly concerned about the slow progress. Faced with an impasse in the restructuring of the IMF, in December 2014, IMF Managing Director Christine Lagarde officially issued a statement: "As requested by our membership, we will now proceed to discuss alternative options for advancing the quota and governance restructurings and ensuring that the Fund has adequate resources, starting with an Executive Board meeting in January 2015." Zhou Xiaochuan, Governor of the People's Bank of China, also made it clear in Washington that he was frustrated and disappointed with the progress of the IMF's restructuring, calling on "all parties to do their utmost to safeguard the credibility, legitimacy, and effectiveness of the IMF." With the continuing efforts of China and other emerging countries, the US Congress finally passed this restructuring plan in December 2015.

Secondly, China has established new international financial institutions. Since the 18th National Congress, it has been working on the "Belt and Road Initiative," which includes the establishment of important international financial institutions such as the Silk Road Fund, the AIIB, and the BRICS Development Bank. These institutions have been created with the aim of exerting checks and balances on the US-led global economic frameworks, and laying a solid foundation to participate more effectively in global governance. These measures have generated strong responses from the international community, garnering the support and participation of European countries. On March 8, 2017, a press conference was held during the fifth session of the 12th National People's Congress. When invited to answer a reporter's question about China's foreign policy and relations, Foreign Minister Wang Yi said that it had pushed for the IMF to include the RMB in its Special Drawing Rights basket, and had established the BRICS Development Bank and the Asian Infrastructure Investment Bank to enhance its institutional rights in global economic governance.[19] The establishment of these new China-led financial institutions is not an attempt to replace existing international institutions, but rather a way to supplement them. It is a major innovation in the restructuring of global financial institutions in the current situation.

Thirdly, China supports global economic governance through domestic diplomatic activities. In recent years, it has made great strides in home diplomacy, and has hosted a series of major diplomatic events, including the APEC Summit, the G20 Hangzhou Summit, and the Belt and Road Forum for International Cooperation. The APEC is an important economic cooperation forum and the highest-level intergovernmental economic cooperation framework in the Asia-Pacific region, and has received consistent attention and support from the Chinese government since its establishment. Following the Shanghai Summit, Beijing hosted the APEC Summit in November 2014 for the first time in 13 years, leaving a deep imprint on the history of the organization. In his speech at the opening ceremony of the APEC CEO Summit, President Xi Jinping stated that as China's overall national strength continues to rise, it will be both capable of and willing to provide more public goods for the Asia-Pacific region and the rest of the world, especially new initiatives, and visions for enhancing regional cooperation. China is ready to work with other countries to advance the BRI and become more deeply involved in regional cooperation, as well as making new contributions to connectivity, development, and prosperity in the Asia-Pacific region.[20]

---

19. "Wang Yi Answers Reporters' Questions on China's Foreign Policy and Foreign Relations," Xinhuanet, March 9, 2017, http://news.xinhuanet.com/mrdx/2017-03/09/c_136114589.htm.

20. "Xi Jinping's Speech at the Opening Ceremony of the APEC CEO Summit" People.cn, November 9, 2014, http://politics.people.com.cn/n/2014/1109/c1001-25999767-2.html.

In September 2016, in his keynote speech at the opening ceremony of the G20 Hangzhou Summit, President Xi Jinping highlighted the current global economic pain points, and stressed the importance of mutual benefit and win-win corporation. He called for the establishment of a community with a shared future for humanity, and emphasized the need for global partnership to meet challenges faced on.[21] He also stated that in the era of economic globalization, no island is completely cut off from the rest of the world. As members of the global village, we need to cultivate awareness of a community with a shared future for humanity.[22] The Hangzhou Summit called for the building of an innovative, invigorated, interconnected, and inclusive world economy, producing a series of pioneering, pace-setting, and institutional outcomes. It has achieved the overall goal of charting the course of the world economy, providing impetus for global growth, and laying a solid foundation for international cooperation.[23] This is the medicine that the Chinese government has prescribed for the world economy in terms of multilateral diplomacy, which will put the world economy on a path of strong, sustainable, balanced, and inclusive growth.

On May 14–15, 2017, the world once again turned its attention to Beijing during the Belt and Road Forum for International Cooperation – the most important diplomatic event of the year for China. It is also an event where the international community can discuss and support the BRI, and share the fruits of mutually beneficial cooperation. It is also an important platform for international cooperation and the synergizing of mutual development strategies.[24] The BRI aims to find more converging interests for all countries, and is part of a major effort to build a community with a shared future for humanity. The initiative links China's development with that of other countries along the routes, and matches up the Chinese dream with the dreams of the people in those countries.

Fourthly, China is reinforcing its interactions with the World Bank. Under the new circumstances, China and the World Bank enjoy even broader space for cooperation. The former has always supported the latter in making positive contributions to global poverty reduction and common prosperity. China hopes that the World Bank will

---

21. "Xi Jinping's 2016 Diplomatic Keyword: A Community with a Shared Future for Humanity," Xinhuanet, January 6, 2017, http://news.xinhuanet.com/world/2017-01/06/c_129434584.htm.

22. Ibid.

23. "Xi Jinping: Reinforcing Cooperation to Support the Restructuring of the Global Governance System and Jointly Endorsing the Peace and Development of Humanity," Xinhuanet, September 28, 2016, http://www.xinhuanet.com/politics/2016-09/28/c_1119641652.htm.

24. "Xi Jinping Presided over the 'Belt and Road' Forum Roundtable Summit and Delivered a Speech Emphasizing that the 'Belt and Road' Initiative Will Benefit the People of All Countries," *People's Daily* (Overseas Edition), May 16, 2017, 1.

join it in keeping pace with the times, innovating new ways forward, expanding and intensifying cooperation, and developing a new type of partnership that features equality, mutual benefit, and win-win cooperation.[25] China also endorses the building of a regional financial cooperation system, and is exploring the establishment of a platform for exchanges and cooperation among Asian financial institutions. It also supports complementarity and coordinated development between multilateral financial institutions such as the Asian Infrastructure Investment Bank, the Asian Development Bank, and the World Bank.[26] In addition, China and the World Bank have made practical explorations into new urbanization and the restructuring of the medical and healthcare system, providing a reference for China's economic and social development and the international community.[27]

With China's growing national strength, this shows how it is contributing new knowledge, endorsing the transformation of global economic governance, and trying to play a leading role as a responsible major country.

3 China's Involvement in Global Economic Governance: Strategic Demands and Policies

Since the Reform and Opening-up, China has become one of the most important components in the globalization of the world economy. Since joining the World Trade Organization, it has economically integrated itself into the world, and into the multilateral system to a certain extent. However, this integration has not yet reached record heights. For example, although China is now the world's second-largest economy, it still ranks behind the United States and Japan in the share of the IMF, proving that it has not yet achieved a reasonable position in the existing global economic governance system. Moreover, some deep-seated contradictions between China and the world economy have been exposed, especially with the existing global economic governance. Therefore, in the new international situation, important and urgent issues include the relationship between China and global economic governance, the role China plays in the transformation of global economic

---

25. "Xi Jinping Meets with World Bank President Jim Yong Kim," Xinhuanet, July 8, 2014, http://news.xinhuanet.com/politics/2014-07/08/c_1111518146.htm.
26. "Xi Jinping: Towards a Community with a Shared Future to Create a New Future for Asia," Xinhuanet, March 28, 2015, http://news.xinhuanet.com/politics/2015-03/28/c_1114794507.htm.
27. "Li Keqiang Meets with World Bank President Jim Yong Kim," Xinhuanet, February 24, 2016, http://news.xinhuanet.com/politics/2016-02/24/c_1118148507.htm.

governance, and the strategic aspiration and policy path of China's participation in global economic governance.

3.1 China's strategic aspirations for participating in global economic governance

With profound adjustments in the current international economic situation, the major problems of global economic governance, and China's own development path, it is necessary to improve global economic governance to make it fairer and more equitable, and jointly enhance the representation and voice of emerging market countries in global economic governance. General Secretary Xi Jinping has given high priority to the issue of global economic governance, and has expressed China's strategic aspiration to participate.

Firstly, China must build a sound and stable international economic environment for its development. The intensification of economic globalization and interdependence have closely linked the economies of all countries. It is impossible for a single nation to develop in isolation. The international economic situation has a huge impact on China's economic development. To realize the "Two Centenary Goals" and the "Chinese Dream" of great national rejuvenation, China needs a healthy and stable international economic environment as an external guarantee. The practice of global economic governance is conducive to supporting the recovery of the world economy and changing the current unbalanced development, as well as promoting China's economic development and peaceful rise.

Secondly, China must assume the responsibility of a major country for the healthy and steady development of the world economy. The 2008 financial crisis and the subsequent European sovereign debt crisis show how such crises are far more complex than before. The world economy is still recovering slowly, and economic growth remains fragile and unbalanced. As the representative of a major emerging power, the largest developing country, and the second largest economy in the world, China bears the responsibility of a major country, and the international community expects more from it. Faced with sluggish global economic recovery and increasing uncertainties, the Chinese government calls for continued macro policy dialogue and coordination in the face of current challenges, pursuing partnerships to endorse mutual aid and win-win cooperation, as well as concentrating its thoughts and energies on pursuing robust, sustainable, balanced, and inclusive growth of the world economy.[28] China's

---

28. "Xi Jinping's Closing Remarks at the G20 Hangzhou Summit," Xinhuanet, September 5, 2016, http://news.xinhuanet.com/world/2016-09/05/c_129270557.htm.

continued rapid economic growth will give hope and add new impetus to the world economy in a period of profound adjustment. At the same time, it will convey China's confidence and expectations to the international community, and will demonstrate the responsibility it takes as a major country.

Thirdly, China must make the international order more just and equitable. Under the US-led hegemonic governance, the legitimate rights and interests of emerging powers and developing countries in international affairs have not been protected effectively. This limited representation and voice are not in line with their growing national power, and there are still many inadequacies in the international order. By participating in global economic governance, China can change international economic rules while increasing the representation and voices of emerging powers and developing countries in international affairs. It can make the international order more just and rational, and support democratization in international relations.

3.2 China's policy for participating in global economic governance

China's participation in global economic governance is also driven by the vision of a common community for the betterment of humanity, and its efforts to support global economic governance through the building of a community with a shared future. This will help countries increase mutual trust, reject a zero-sum mentality, and seek win-win cooperation. It is a good way for the international community to address global economic issues and achieve mutual benefit. China should play a leading and coordinating role as a major country in international economic affairs, and advance the process of global economic governance through the comprehensive use of various policy paths.

Firstly, China must shift from being governed to performing active governance. The idea of transforming global economic governance implies that China is governed by the world, but can also govern the world as part of the transformation of global economic governance.[29] Since joining the IMF in the 1980s and the World Bank in the 2000s, China has undergone a long-term process of being economically governed under the influence of these international financial institutions. However, China today no longer hides its strength and bides its time, but rather seeks to make a difference. It is no longer just an object of governance, but is beginning to govern

---

29. Pang Zhongying, "Transformation of Global Governance: From the World Governing China to China Governing the World?" *Foreign Theoretical Trends*, no. 10 (2012): 13–16.

the world.[30] For example, the IMF, European Commission, and European Central Bank intervened together as a "trio" during the European sovereign debt crisis, and the G20 also played an important role. As a result, through reinforcing the existing international economic system, China and other emerging powers embarked on the unprecedented act of intervening in European economic governance. The G20 Hangzhou Summit was an important attempt by China to lead the top-level design of global economic governance. It was also a sign that global economic governance had entered a new stage of seeking sustainable development.[31]

Secondly, China must focus on the leadership of global economic governance and assume the leading role of a responsible major country. This also provides an important strategic opportunity for China to play a leading role as a major country in global economic governance.[32] In fact, strong international leaders can use resources such as political influence and material power to provide global public goods for all countries in the world, maintain the existence of the international system, and endorse the smooth development of the collective action of global economic governance.[33] Therefore, with world government far from the reality, the establishment of effective international leadership has become the key to global economic governance. In the new situation, the emerging powers led by China have increasingly become part of the leading institutions of global economic governance, bringing greater diversity to the multi-level governance body. Innovation and development in this regard will lead the global governance system to develop in a more just and reasonable direction, and will support the democratization of international relations.[34] The concepts of a new model of international relations and a community with a shared future for humanity will help China play a leading role in global economic governance as a responsible major country. This leading role is also one of its strategic demands for its participation in global economic governance.

---

30. Pang Zhongying, "Transformation of Global Governance: From the World Governing China to China Governing the World?" *Foreign Theoretical Trends*, no. 10 (2012): 13–16.

31. "Chinese Think Tank Launches Series of Monographs to Elaborate on G20 and China's Contribution," People.cn, July 28, 2016, http://world.people.com.cn/n1/2016/0728/c1002-28592730.html.

32. Pang Zhongying and Wang Ruiping, "Global Governance: China's Strategic Response," *International Studies*, no. 4 (2013): 67.

33. Pang Zhongying, "Ineffective Multilateralism and International Leadership Deficit: China's Leadership Responsibility in International Collective Action," *World Economics and Politics*, no. 6 (2010): 8; Quoted from James MacGregor Burns, *Leadership*, trans. Chang Jian, Sun Haiyun, et al. (Renmin University of China Press, 2006), 6–13.

34. "An Inventory of President Xi's Statements on Global Governance," Xinhuanet, November 14, 2015, http://www.xinhuanet.com/world/2015-11/14/c_128428606.htm.

Thirdly, China must focus on multilateralism and leverage the advantages of multilateral diplomacy. Another key to global economic governance is the management of relations among great powers. Multilateralism plays a key role in resolving the economic policy conflicts among great powers, having significantly eased the clashes between the US, Western Europe, and Japan after the Second World War[35]. Multilateralism will continue to play an important role in the current and likely future "economic cold war" between emerging and Western powers. Supporting a diversity of voices on the world stage is an important step towards effective global economic governance, and one of the most important differences between pluralistic and hegemonic governance.

Since the 18th National Congress, the Chinese government has conveyed its vision and aspiration to participate in global economic governance through major international organizations such as the United Nations and the IMF, through diplomatic meetings at home such as the APEC Summit in Beijing and the G20 Hangzhou Summit, and through multilateral summits such as the East Asia Summit. These multilateral diplomatic activities have supported the democratization of international relations and the transformation of global economic governance.

China's new international development institutions and platforms, such as the Belt and Road Initiative, the BRICS Development Bank, the Contingent Reserve Arrangement, and the Asian Infrastructure Investment Bank, are also new ways to advance global economic governance. These initiatives have reflected China's knowledge and responsibilities.

In addition to these material global public goods, China also strives to provide conceptual ones, such as restructuring programs for global institutions and global governance norms.[36] President Xi Jinping used his grand vision of building a community with a shared future for humanity to launch the Belt and Road Initiative as a response to the severe challenges facing humanity, such as the deficit of peace, development, and governance. During the Belt and Road Forum for International Cooperation on May 14, 2017, President Xi called for countries to draw strength from the idea of the Silk Road, and urged everyone to make the Belt and Road into a pathway to peace, prosperity, openness, innovation, and culture. This points to the way forward for the future development of the Belt and Road, and also reflects

---

35. Pang Zhongying, "Global Economic Governance and Its Lessons since 1945," *International Observer*, no. 2 (2011): 1–8.

36. Pang Zhongying and Liu Jingwen, "G20 and the Transformation of Global Economic Governance," *Contemporary World*, no. 8 (2016): 9–11.

new thinking on global governance under the current circumstances, and represents China's innovative approach.[37]

Overall, global economic governance should become an integral part of the building of a community with a shared future for humanity. Its improvement can achieve a virtuous circle of mutual reinforcement.

Development is the dominant theme in the world today. Global economic governance turns the international community into a closer community with a shared future, and advances the development of a more just and equitable international economic order, while supporting the building of a community with a shared future for humanity. China's outstanding performance in global economic governance has expanded its circle of friends, and also helps it to play a leading role as a responsible major country in building a community with a shared future for humanity. The building of this community will also help enhance the international community's sense of solidarity, and will change the status quo of the legitimacy, effectiveness, and power deficit of global economic governance, while supporting the smooth development of the collective action of global economic governance.

At this stage, the world economy is still unbalanced, and in a period of profound adjustment, with the anti-globalization trend still prominent. However, in the face of global problems, the countries of the world are ultimately a community with a shared future, while global economic governance is a long and arduous journey. By taking an active role in global economic governance, China should reinforce coordination and cooperation on economic issues, and reduce uncertainties in world economic development. It should also effectively manage and control international financial risks, and make global economic governance more inclusive and effective while realizing its own economic interests.

---

37. "Xi Jinping's Speech at the Opening Ceremony of the Belt and Road Forum for International Cooperation," People.cn, May 14, 2017, http://politics.people.com.cn/GB/n1/2017/0515/c1024-29274490.html.

CHAPTER 14

Maintaining Global Peace and Security

THE COMMUNITY WITH A SHARED future for humanity is a comprehensive "five-in-one" concept covering politics, security, development, culture, and ecology. One of its basic implications is a security arrangement based on fairness, justice, co-creation, and sharing. Building a world of lasting peace and universal security is an inherent requirement for building a community with a shared future for humanity. Although peace and development are still relevant themes today, the international security situation is complex and ever-changing. At the same time, traditional and non-traditional security issues continue to emerge, threatening world peace and stability. As General Secretary Xi Jinping has stated, "The world today is far from peaceful and tranquil, as international hotspots continue to flare up. It is therefore imperative to reinforce global security governance."[1] In the process of global security governance, China has become an active participant and an important supporter, contributing ideas and solutions to governance practices that are rich in Chinese knowledge.

---

1. "Xi Jinping Attends a Leaders' Meeting on the Iranian Nuclear Issue within a Six-part Framework," Xinhuanet, April 2, 2016. http://www.xinhuanet.com/2016-04/02/c_1118517888.html.

1 The Existing Security Infrastructure and Its Main Issues

According to Elke Krahmann, the first scholar to put forward the theory of "security governance," global security governance is a structure and process formed through interrelated policy decisions and their implementation in the absence of central authority. Within the anarchic state of the international system, global security is a common concern of the international community. It cannot be maintained through the rule and management of the central authority, but can be achieved by the common governance of international actors. Faced with a series of traditional and non-traditional security challenges in the global security environment, relevant actors led by dominant states have created a complex governance system through long-term security interaction. The basic structure of this system is the platform and foundation for China to participate in the practice of global security governance, while the inherent difficulties highlighted in its participation have become the background and premise of China's contribution to the notion of global security governance.

1.1 Global security governance: a complex system

Global security governance is a multi-layered and multi-agent structure, forming a loose but relatively complete governance system during its application. This system consists of three basic elements, namely the subject, object, and framework of governance.

As for the subject of governance, the participants of global security governance (including both sovereign states and various non-state actors) are highly diverse. The non-state actors include intergovernmental international organizations as well as international non-governmental organizations and transnational corporations. Among them, sovereign states and inter-governmental international organizations are the core subjects of global security governance, playing a major role in the process of governance. Coordination and cooperation among sovereign states are the basis for achieving and advancing global security governance. Inter-governmental international organizations, ranging from global organizations such as the United Nations to regional organizations like the European Union, the African Union, the ASEAN, and the Shanghai Cooperation Organization, also play an important role in global security governance.

The object of global security governance refers to the threats and challenges faced by global security, including traditional and non-traditional security issues.

To be specific, traditional security threats that are the objects of global security governance include wars, international conflicts, domestic armed conflict, arms races, and weapon proliferation. Non-traditional security threats concern terrorism, transnational crimes, economic security issues, environmental security issues, and international public health issues. Security issues in new international frontiers such as oceans, polar regions, space, and cyberspace are also important issues for global security governance.

The framework of security governance consists of a series of institutional arrangements that have the function of addressing regional security issues. The framework and institutional arrangements of global security governance include the establishment of relevant principles, norms, laws, and regulations as well as corresponding strategies, decisions, and actions.[2] The architecture of security governance framework consists of multiple layers:

(1) A global security governance framework, including global institutions and frameworks in the field of international security, such as the United Nations' collective security frame and the international nuclear non-proliferation regime. It also includes comprehensive multilateral frameworks, such as the G20 framework and the BRICS framework, which play an active role in global security governance.
(2) A regional security governance framework. For example, Europe's security governance has established a multi-pillar governance structure jointly governed by NATO, the European Union, and the Organization for Security and Cooperation in Europe. Comprehensive regional frameworks such as the ASEAN Regional Forum, the East Asia Summit, and the Asia Cooperation Dialogue have also provided dialogue and consultation channels for East Asian countries in their security governance practices.
(3) A security governance framework for bilateral relations. For example, a series of dialogue and communication frameworks, such as diplomatic and security dialogues, maritime security consultations, and cyber security dialogues established between China and the United States, have played a positive role in managing differences and enhancing cooperation between the two countries.

---

2. Li Dongyan, "Global Security Governance and China's Choice," *World Economics and Politics*, no. 4 (2013): 42.

1.2 Major issues facing global security governance

The current global security governance has established a multi-level governance system, and has achieved remarkable results in safeguarding world security, peace, and stability. However, there are some problems in the governance structure and process, which have caused a series of difficulties for the development of security governance.

Firstly, there is a contradiction between the subjects of security governance. Although the diversity of governance subjects is an important attribute of global security governance, sovereign states are currently still the core subject of governance. The reality of state-to-state relations, especially among major powers, has important implications for global security governance. Global security governance involves all countries in the world, and there are inevitably contradictions and differences of varying degrees among these participants. From the structural contradictions between China and the United States, to the differences between the United States and Russia, China and Japan, and Russia and Europe, to the gap between developed and developing countries, the ubiquity of conflicts of interest among governance subjects restricts the development of governance practices. In particular, the divergence of interests on security issues makes global security governance more vulnerable to difficulties.

The willingness of the governance subjects to cooperate is the decisive factor for the advancement of governance action. However, countries in an anarchic international system follow the logic of self-help, and their behavior is determined by rational interest. The strength of conflicts of interest between countries determines the difficulty of cooperative action in governance practice. On non-traditional security issues such as global climate change and cyber security issues, the contradictions and differences between developed and developing countries are obvious. On traditional security issues, some countries have conflicts of core interests such as sovereignty and territorial disputes, making it difficult to coordinate interests and cooperate in security. The G20 is an example. As scholars have revealed, the G20 is still a group dominated by economic cooperation. It has obviously failed to overcome internal differences in security, and has not been able to carry out substantive cooperation in the field of security.[3] Antagonism and competition in national interests may also lead to crises and conflicts between countries, as well as increasing the uncertainty of

---

3. Li Dongyan, "Global Security Governance and China's Choice," *World Economics and Politics*, no. 4 (2013): 42.

the international security situation, and affecting the smooth operation of the global security governance system.

Secondly, there is an insufficient supply of security governance. In the world today, with globalization and the transformation of the international system, global security issues are growing more complex, leading to a constant demand for security governance. Issues in traditional security include occasional international wars, a rise in internal conflicts, and the simultaneous internationalization of domestic security issues and the internalization of international security issues. In terms of non-traditional security, there is the growing threat of terrorism, the increased severity of climate change and ecological damage, cyber security challenges that cannot be ignored, and a lack of effective control of issues such as transnational crime. These security threats and challenges concern all countries, and require the joint governance of the international community. However, the current supply of global security governance is insufficient. Coordination and cooperation in the security field are unable to meet the actual needs of international security, and there is an imbalance between supply and demand in the governance process. As noted by Oran R. Young, a well-known American scholar, governance is needed at the international level, but the supply of governance is severely insufficient.[4] This non-negligible deficit in the current global security domain is another inherent problem of the governance system.

Thirdly, security governance is suffering a lack of development. In the process of global security governance, social and economic foundations have an important impact on security and peace-building. It is of great practical significance to handle the relationship between security and development correctly. However, the traditional governance model led by Western countries overemphasizes the function of political systems in security governance to resolve conflicts and build peace, ignoring the roles of economic development and livelihood issues. Based on the prejudiced "democratic peace theory," European and American powers believe that the root cause of disturbances and conflicts in developing countries is the lack of a democratic system, and place their hope of security governance on the promotion of a Western-style liberal democracy. This strongly ideological approach and method of governance ignore the fundamental role of development in security. Social and economic problems, such as the gap between rich and poor in domestic society and uneven development among countries, are some of the root causes of security threats. The cause of many global problems, including terrorism, the proliferation of weapons of mass destruction, and

---

4. Oran Young, *Governance in World Affairs*, trans. Chen Yuguang and Bo Yan (Shanghai People's Publishing House, 2007), 2.

climate change, can be attributed to the fact that development issues have not been noted and addressed. The development deficit has become a significant defect in the process of global security governance.[5] Supporting the common and balanced development of all countries has become an urgent requirement to guarantee security and resolve conflicts.

Fourthly, there is a lack of justice in security governance. For a long time, a few developed countries have dominated the global security governance system, which has caused many governance practices to lack fairness and justice. These countries, especially the hegemonic nations, put themselves above other countries in security affairs, while endorsing hegemonism and power politics. When resolving internal conflicts in developing countries, they favor pro-Western forces, interfere in internal affairs, and even regard regime change as the goal of governance. In the governance of security issues, some have unilaterally circumvented the legitimate framework of the United Nations and infringed upon the sovereignty and territorial integrity of other countries. The interests of developing countries have not been effectively reflected in the global security governance system. Supporting the democratization of security governance and realizing fair governance of global security are unavoidable in the development of global security governance.

2 China's Involvement in Maintaining Global Security: New Ideas and Measures

Since the 18th National Congress, China has participated more extensively and intensely in global security governance, playing the role of a responsible major country in building a security framework based on fairness, justice, co-contribution, and sharing for a community with a shared future for humanity. China has become an active participant and an important endorser of global security governance, contributing its knowledge to the restructuring of governance concepts, and shouldering its responsibility in the development of governance practices.

2.1 China's vision for global security governance

The development of global security governance, especially the resolution of various inherent problems, requires the joint participation of the international community,

---

5. Lu Jing, "The Institutional Dilemma of Current Global Governance and its Restructuring," *Foreign Affairs Review*, no. 1 (2014): 117.

particularly emerging powers such as China. As General Secretary Xi Jinping has stated, "The world is very big, and there are so many problems. The international community expects to hear China's voice and see China's solutions. China cannot be absent."[6] The building of a community with a shared future for humanity, with all its security implications, provides a constructive plan for the development of global security governance. Under the guidance of the vision of a community with a shared future for humanity, China has formulated a series of concepts and proposals for global security governance in its diplomatic practice, and has made its voice and knowledge heard when addressing various inherent difficulties in the governance system and practice, exerting a positive influence in the international community.

Firstly, China is pursuing a new type of international relations featuring win-win cooperation. Building a community with a shared future for humanity is inseparable from this. Also important are partnerships that feature equality, mutual consultation, and mutual accommodation. The basic principles of win-win cooperation and the building of a partnership based on mutual consultation and accommodation have charted the direction and path for resolving contradictions and differences arising from conflicts of interests among the main actors in global security governance. Within the vision of a community with a shared future for humanity, global security governance should be understood as a process of multilateral participation, consultation, and cooperation. It is a win-win process rather than a zero-sum game.[7] To build a new type of international relations and build a community with a shared future for humanity, countries need to replace confrontation with cooperation in security relations, and seek mutual gains instead of a monopolization of interests. Countries should abandon the zero-sum game mentality of "your loss is my gain," achieving mutual and common benefits through the cooperative governance of global security.

Secondly, China is pursuing a new security concept that advocates for common, comprehensive, cooperative, and sustainable security. This new security concept is a reflection of the vision of a community with a shared future for humanity in the domain of international security. At the fourth summit of the Conference on Interaction and Confidence-building Measures in 2014, Xi Jinping proposed a new Asian security concept that incorporates common, comprehensive, cooperative, and sustainable security. Since the 18th National Congress of the Communist Party of

---

6. "President Xi Jinping delivered a New Year's greeting in 2016," Xinhuanet, December 31, 2015, http://www.xinhuanet.com/politics/2015-12/31/c_1117643074.htm.

7. Li Dongyan, "Global Security Governance and China's Choice," *World Economics and Politics*, no. 4 (2013), 54.

China, Xi's CPC Central Committee has adopted a new security concept in addressing international security issues. Xi has stressed the importance of "paying attention to China's own security as well a common security,"[8] while advocating for the need to "respect and guarantee the security of every country." It cannot be the case that one country is secure while the others are not, or that some countries are secure while others are not. More importantly, some countries should not seek so-called absolute security at the expense of other countries' security.[9] The new concept of common, comprehensive, cooperative, and sustainable security calls on all countries to choose a path that features co-creation, sharing, and win-win. This will help nations work together to address global security issues, increase the supply of security governance, endorse the development of global security governance, and safeguard world peace and common security.

Thirdly, China combines security with development. Security guarantees national development, and development also underpins international security. Global security governance requires the avoidance of wars and resolving conflicts while addressing the socio-economic causes of these wars and conflicts so as to safeguard world security. In its participation in global security governance, China opposes the tendency of Western powers to ignore development issues. It prioritizes the role of development in security, and emphasizes the consolidation of peace and security through development. As Xi Jinping has stated, "We should uphold the concepts of seeking safety for development and endorsing development with safety, so that the two objectives can be integrated and reinforce one another."[10] In global security governance, especially in dealing with domestic conflicts in developing countries, China sees the importance of economic and livelihood issues, and makes active efforts to endorse the economic and social development of these countries. China's initiatives for global security governance aim to address the wealth gap, especially the problem of unbalanced development among countries, so as to eliminate the root causes of security threats and ensure the sustainability of security.

Fourthly, China upholds the principles of fairness and justice. In the security landscape, these principles are an inherent requirement for a community with a shared future for humanity. On the issue of global security governance, China

---

8. "The Central National Security Committee Holds First Meeting, Xi Jinping Delivers a Speech," State Council's website, April 15, 2014, http://www.gov.cn/xinwen/2014-04/15/content_2659641.htm.

9. "Xi Jinping's Speech at the Commemoration of the 60th Anniversary of the Five Principles of Peaceful Coexistence (Full Text)," Ministry of Foreign Affairs' website, June 29, 2014, http://www.fmprc.gov.cn/web/ziliao_674904/zyjh_674906/t1169582.shtml.

10. *Xi Jinping: The Governance of China* (Foreign Languages Press, 2014), 254.

emphasizes fairness and justice, and pays attention to safeguarding the interests and demands of developing countries, while opposing hegemonism, power politics, unilateralism, and armed intervention. In recent years, with the transformation of the global economic system, especially with the collective rise of emerging countries, Western developed countries are no longer dominating the global security governance system, as developing countries are playing an increasingly important role. Speaking at the conference marking the 60th anniversary of the "Five Principles of Peaceful Coexistence," Xi Jinping said: "We should all support the rationalization of international relations, and adapt to new changes in the international balance of power. We should advance the restructuring of the global governance system, reflect the concerns and demands of all parties, and safeguard the legitimate rights and interests of developing countries more effectively."[11]

As for the issue of intervention in security governance, China continues to follow the principles of sovereignty and non-interference, and opposes interference in other countries' internal affairs without the authorization of the United Nations. China is also ensuring that its traditional policy of non-interference is keeping up with the times, while increasing its involvement in global security governance. This is not a denial of the principle of non-interference. On the contrary, it is the enrichment, development, and innovation of this principle in the new situation. It is also a lever to correct the unreasonable and unjust order perpetuated by some dominant forces in the world today, and a necessary path to maintain and enhance China's image as a peace-loving, justice-oriented, and responsible major country.[12] This active and constructive intervention avoids unjust and self-seeking third party intervention in the process of conflict management under the leadership of Chinese and Western powers.

2.2 China's practice in global security governance

With the rapid growth of its national strength, China is playing an increasingly important role in international security affairs, and has participated more heavily in the process of global security governance. After the 18th National Congress, China has participated in global security governance with a new approach to foreign policy

---

11. "Xi Jinping's Speech at the 60th Anniversary of the Publication of the Five Principles of Peaceful Coexistence (Full Text), Xinhuanet, June 28, 2014, http://news.xinhuanet.com/politics/2014-06/28/c_1111364206_2.htm.

12. Wang Yi, "Developing the Doctrine of Non-interference in Internal Affairs to Meet the Requirements of the New Era," *International Security Studies*, no. 1 (2013): 9–10.

that embraces the ideology of a community with a shared future for humanity, which advocates for common, comprehensive, cooperative, and sustainable security in Asia. This is China's contribution to the advancement and restructuring of the governance system. China's practice in global security governance has become an integral part of its major-country diplomacy.

Firstly, China is participating in international peacekeeping operations. It has taken part in UN peacekeeping operations in recent years, and has seen a continued increment in the number of peacekeepers deployed and capital resources allocated. Currently, China is a permanent member of the United Nations Security Council with the highest number of peacekeepers deployed, and the main contributor to peacekeeping operations among developing countries. In April 1990, it began its participation in United Nations' peacekeeping operations, with Chinese military sending five military observers to the United Nations Truce Supervision Organization.[13] As of June 2016, China has participated in 24 United Nations peacekeeping operations, and has deployed more than 31,000 peacekeepers. Eleven peacekeepers have given their lives to safeguard world peace.[14] Among the 16 peacekeeping operations carried out by the United Nations around the world, China has participated in nine, in the Democratic Republic of Congo, Liberia, South Sudan, Darfur, Lebanon, Mali, the Middle East, Western Sahara, and Côte d'Ivoire. Xi Jinping announced at the UN General Assembly that "China will join the new United Nations Peacekeeping Capability Readiness System, having decided to take the lead in setting up a permanent peacekeeping police squad and building a peacekeeping standby force of 8,000 troops."[15] This would make up more than half of the planned manpower for the United Nations Peacekeeping Standby Force. As global security governance develops and China's participation increases, it will play an increasingly important role in international peacekeeping operations.

Secondly, China is helping to mediate and resolve armed conflicts. Since the 18th National Congress, its foreign policy has shifted towards a more proactive stance that strives for achievements. China has participated in the mediation and resolution of domestic armed conflicts globally, and has facilitated dialogues and

---

13. "Timeline of Activities at UNPKOs," Ministry of Defense website, May 29, 2015, http://news.mod.gov.cn/headlines/2015-05/29/content_4587298.htm

14. "Performance of Chinese Peacekeepers Highly Appraised by Other Countries," *Wen Wei Po*, June 10, 2016, 4.

15. Xi Jinping, "Working Together to Forge a New Partnership of Win-win Cooperation and Create a Community of Shared Future for Humanity – At the General Debate of the 70th Session of the UN General Assembly," *People's Daily*, September 29, 2015, 2.

negotiations endorsing the peaceful settlement of disputes. In recent years, it has played an active role in the mediation of conflict in regions such as Sudan, South Sudan, Afghanistan, Libya, Syria, and Myanmar. For example, China invited the Syrian opposition to Beijing in the hope of facilitating a dialogue among all parties in the conflict. Chinese Foreign Minister Wang Yi also proposed five principles to resolve the Syrian crisis. During the conflict in northern Myanmar, China played a constructive role in achieving peace by holding talks with armed ethnic organizations in Northern Myanmar to endorse peaceful negotiations between them and the Myanmar government.

Thirdly, China is helping to maintain the safety of international sea routes, which is both an inherent need within global security governance, and a crucial element of China's economic and overseas interests. Since December 2008, China has dispatched naval escort fleets to conduct regular escort operations in the Gulf of Aden and the waters off Somalia to combat piracy and maritime terrorism. The Chinese naval escort taskforce has also established positive communication with the navies of many countries. As the White Paper on "The Diversified Employment of China's Armed Forces" notes, it has been "carrying out joint escort operations with Russia, and carrying out joint anti-piracy exercises with South Korea, Pakistan, and the US naval fleet ... participating in meetings and conferences organized by various groups and international organizations."[16] It has also been jointly maintaining the security of international sea routes through communication and cooperation. China signed the Regional Cooperation Agreement on Combating Piracy and Armed Robbery Against Ships in Asia, and participated in the establishment of Asia's first inter-government network on maritime security. China has also played a proactive role in the establishment of bilateral exercises to ensure the safety of international sea routes. For example, it holds joint patrol exercises with Vietnam at Beibu Gulf biannually.

Fourthly, China is helping to maintain global nuclear security, adopting comprehensive measures on nuclear security domestically, and participating in international cooperation for nuclear security governance. It has established dialogues with the US on nuclear security, and has achieved effective cooperation with Russia and Kazakhstan on trafficking of nuclear raw materials, while significantly increasing its donations to the IAEA Nuclear Security Fund. General Secretary Xi Jinping's CPC Central Committee takes nuclear security governance very seriously. Xi proposed new concepts at both the 2014 and 2016 Nuclear Security Summits. During the March

---

16. "White Paper on 'The Diversified Employment of China's Armed Forces' (Full Text)," Chinese government website, April 16, 2013, http://www.gov.cn/jrzg/2013-04/16/content_2379013.htm.

2014 summit at the Hague, he proposed a "sensible, coordinated, and balanced" approach to nuclear security, and advocated for the building of an international nuclear security system featuring fairness and win-win cooperation.[17] During the April 2016 summit at Washington DC, Xi proposed the adoption of "an open and inclusive spirit to forge a community with a shared future on nuclear security." On the summit's goals to reinforce the international nuclear security system and endorse global nuclear security governance, Xi Jinping made proposals to step up on areas such as political commitment, national responsibility, international cooperation, and the culture of nuclear security.[18]

Fifthly, China provides humanitarian aid. Humanitarian crises caused by domestic conflicts or natural disasters are hugely challenging, and cannot be ignored in the issue of global security. In recent years, China has reinforced its humanitarian assistance abroad, providing various forms of assistance such as supplies, cash, rescue, and medical teams to countries according to their needs. For example, since the start of the Syrian conflict, China has assisted Syria and its neighboring countries many times, providing supplies and rolling out humanitarian projects. To aid West African countries in their fight against the Ebola virus, China has dispatched nearly 600 medical teams to Africa. In 2014 alone, it provided four rounds of humanitarian aid amounting to RMB750 million to 13 African countries.[19] It also provided nearly 50 batches of humanitarian supplies worth RMB1.2 billion over a period of three years. These supplies were a response to humanitarian disasters such as the Haiti earthquake, the catastrophic flood in Cambodia, the earthquake in Myanmar, the flood in Pakistan, the hurricane in Cuba, the war in Libya, and the unrest in Syria.[20] China also helped these countries improve their emergency rescue, disaster prevention, and disaster relief capabilities through means such as training.

---

17. Xi Jinping, "Statement at the Nuclear Security Summit at the Hague, the Netherlands," *People's Daily*, March 25, 2014, 2.

18. Xi Jinping, "Reinforcing Global Nuclear Security Architecture and Endorsing Global Nuclear Security Governance – Remarks at the Nuclear Security Summit in Washington D.C." *People's Daily*, April 3, 2016, 2.

19. "China Provides Four Rounds of Aid Worth RMB750 million in the Fight against Ebola," China News, November 18, 2014, https://www.chinanews.com.cn/gn/2014/11-18/6787591.shtml.

20. "White Paper on Chinese Foreign Aid (2014), "State Council Information Office website, July 10, 2014, http://www.scio.gov.cn/zfbps/ndhf/2014/document/1375013/1375013_1.htm.

3 China's Involvement in Maintaining Global Security – Strategic Demands and Policies

The most important issues in China's foreign policy today are how to play a more pragmatic role in global security governance, and how to endorse and improve the governance system and its efficiency. Participation in global security governance must stem from its strategic needs and national interests. China must first be clear on its national needs and interests as well as its strategic goals for participation before taking part in global security governance. Stemming from this, it must have a broad plan and considerations before it chooses which direction to choose in its participation in global security governance.

3.1 China's strategic needs to participate in global security governance

China has two strategic needs to participate in global security governance. The first is to create a peaceful and stable environment for national development. In today's era of globalization and interdependence among countries, each nation is an integral part of the international system and cannot develop independently from the international environment. Turbulence in international affairs and tension in the surrounding regions will disrupt China's development. There is no way for China to restructure and modernize socialism without a peaceful and stable international environment. As Deng Xiaoping stated, "striving for peace is what people worldwide need. It is also what we need for development. Without a peaceful environment, what is there to develop?"[21] The threat of war and conflict is the most serious external challenge to national development. The current international environment is complex, peppered with conflict and unrest. To realize the "Two Centenary Goals" and the "Chinese Dream" of national rejuvenation, China needs international security as an assurance. It needs to seize important strategic opportunities, maintain world peace, endorse common development, and create a peaceful and stable international environment. Secretary General Xi Jinping has emphasized the need to "develop oneself by striving for a peaceful international environment, and to maintain and endorse world peace through one's development."[22] Practicing global security governance will help China

---

21. *Selected Works of Deng Xiaoping*, vol. 3 (People's Publishing House, 1993), 116–117.
22. *Selected Articles from Secretary General Xi Jinping's Speeches* (Central Party Literature Press 2016), 25.

resolve its security problems and manage and control its security crises. It will also ensure China's peaceful development.

China's second strategic need is to assume the responsibility of a major power for the common security of the international community. The development of all countries in the world and the progress of humanity is inseparable from a safe international environment. While peace and development are dominant in the world today, the international situation remains unstable. Since the beginning of the 21st century, wars and conflicts have been increasingly common, such as the war in Afghanistan in 2001, the civil war in Côte d'Ivoire in 2002, the Iraq War in 2003, the Russo-Georgian War in 2008, civil war in Libya in 2011, and the ongoing Syrian war. The road towards maintaining global security is a long one, and countries need to reinforce their cooperation to achieve common governance. According to Xi Jinping, "No country in the world can enjoy absolute security. A country cannot have security while others are in turmoil, as the threats they face may haunt it also."[23] To endorse the building of a community with a shared future for humanity in the light of common security challenges requires a major power like China to shoulder the responsibility of ensuring security, and to contribute more to world peace and stability. China needs to demonstrate its responsibility as a major power in maintaining global security, building a positive international image and enhancing its international influence through participation in security governance.

3.2 The Direction of China's policy for participation in global security governance

China's participation in global security governance should uphold the concept of a community with a shared future for humanity, and must be committed to supporting the development of security governance with this ideology. A community with a shared future for humanity is an important policy and iconic example of major-power diplomacy from the 18th National Congress. It is also an effective solution to global security issues. China needs to support the establishment of a community with a shared future for humanity and push for global security governance system to improve in a virtuous cycle where establishing this community interacts with the development of security governance.

---

23. "Speech by President Xi Jinping At the United Nations Office at Geneva," Xinhuanet, January 19, 2017, http://www.xinhuanet.com/world/2017-01/19/c_1120340081.htm.

The global security governance bodies are still facing obstacles caused by conflicts of interest and lack of mutual trust. Establishing a community with a shared future for humanity would help resolve these conflicts of interest and mutual distrust among countries, and in turn endorse security cooperation, resolving the inherent difficulties in global security governance. The creation of the community would make all countries into highly interdependent stakeholders and enhance common interests. It would also help to reinforce the collective identity among countries and improve mutual trust. Following this ideology, with reinforced common interests and trust, countries would be able to consider the security interests of other nations when they pursue their own, thus resolving the issue of working in tandem. Putting this ideology into practice would make it easier for countries to come to a consensus at specific security conferences, thereby ensuring an adequate supply of public goods for international security.

To be specific, China needs to play its role as a major power in global security affairs, and participate in global security governance. It should also use a variety of policy means to endorse the development of security governance.

Firstly, China needs to enhance cooperation between major powers in security affairs as an important approach to global security governance. Major powers play a pivotal role in global security affairs, and influence its direction. Cooperation between major powers is the key to improving governance system and efficiency. In the current system, such cooperation is lacking. China needs to push for its development through new relationships among major powers.

Among the major powers, the Sino-US cooperation in global security governance is particularly significant. China and the United States are currently the two largest powers in the world. Maintaining global security is inseparable from their cooperation. International peace and security can only be assured through the establishment of a new major-power relationship between China and the United States to endorse win-win cooperation. China should step up its dialogue and communication with the United States to push for major-power cooperation, fulfilling the responsibilities of major powers together and providing global security and public goods. Although the two countries have opposing views and compete with each other, they share common interests in global security governance. This new major-power relationship will create opportunities for China and the United States to coordinate and cooperate in the area of global security. With Sino-US cooperation as its core, China can develop extensive bilateral and multilateral cooperation and endorse international cooperation that assures common and comprehensive security to resolve international conflicts, manage and control security crises, and maintain the global security order.

Secondly, China needs to support the development of a system for security governance with safety mechanisms as the basic tools. Currently, global security governance lacks a security mechanism, leading to poor governance systems in many areas, and many security governance issues also lack institutional guarantees. As such, China should become a firm supporter and active participant in the establishment of an institutional system for global security governance. It should reinforce communication, consultations, and cooperation on global security issues with relevant countries, and take positive measures to intensify the concept of a community with a shared future for humanity. With this, China can endorse the coordination of interests and cooperation on various security issues, and build an all-round, multi-level, and cross-domain cooperation network. With this as the foundation, China can endorse the establishment of safety mechanisms and institutionalize them. It is only with an institutionalized security governance system that sustainable security in global security field is assured.

The institutionalization of global security governance can form a series of universally binding principles, rules, and norms on international security, to regulate the security behaviors of other countries and improve the predictability of security relations between states. It can also help to endorse a change in countries' views and the coordination of interests, hence improving international security cooperation. Through these arrangements, governments can achieve dialogue, consultation, and cooperation, eliminating security threats and maintaining international peace. Pushing for the institutionalization of global security governance would also help countries cope with common security threats, achieve effective prevention and control over regional conflicts, and ensure lasting international peace and sustainable regional security.

Thirdly, China needs to build mutual trust in the security field. Mutual trust among governments is an important assurance for global security governance. Presently, many countries lack mutual trust, and there is distrust and even mutual suspicion and fear. This lack of mutual trust has adverse effects on global security governance, and should not be neglected. China should engage in dialogues with other countries to intensify cooperation and build mutual trust and confidence. Through increased frequency in dialogues and improving communication and understanding, suspicion between countries can be reduced and even eliminated. On the basis of dialogue and consultation, China also needs to push for mutual trust bilaterally and multilaterally, and insist on a new security concept that enables communication and builds long-term mutual trust. This will reduce differences, dispel doubts and worries, reduce friction and conflict, and resolve the issues facing international security.

The concept of a community with a shared future for humanity has multifarious security implications. It firmly advocates for building and sharing a universally safe world together, and endorses fairness and justice along with comprehensive, common, and sustainable security. The restructuring and development of the global security governance system should be an integral part of the building of a community with a shared future for humanity. Within this framework, China should reinforce coordination and cooperation on security issues through its participation in global security governance. It can also push for the improvement of the security governance system and security governance capabilities, and play a greater and more constructive role in security governance. Through effective security governance, uncertainties in global and regional security can be eliminated, and international security risks can be managed in good time, thereby fulfilling national security interests and ensuring the stability of the global security order.

CHAPTER 15

Addressing Global Environmental Issues

SINCE THE 18TH NATIONAL CONGRESS, China's participation in global environmental governance has also entered a new phase. The growing domestic pressure for environmental protection and the international call for China to play a greater role requires it to re-position itself in global environmental governance. As global environmental governance and China's participation transform, Xi Jinping's concept of a community with a shared future for humanity answers the questions above, i.e., to use the concept of the community to look at global environmental issues and review existing governing rules, to use this ideology as the new value orientation, and to set an example to support the improvement of global environmental governance in the process of practice. This is the result of China's in-depth understanding of the world's situation, and its relationship with global development. This is also the solution to China's ecological needs, and offers knowledge and proposals to the solving of global environmental issues.

1 The Existing Governance Structure and Its Main Issues

Since the UN Conference on the Human Environment was held in 1972, the international community has gradually become more aware of environmental protection, and the concept of sustainable development has started to take root.

Countries have made a lot of progress in the coordinated development of their economy, population, resources, and environment. International cooperation in the field of global environmental protection has continued to intensify, and the governing system for global environmental governance has improved, with the UN as the main governing body. International treaties on global environmental issues have been passed. However, the current governance system is unable to meet the huge demand for governance, and the global environment continues to deteriorate.

1.1 Global environmental governance: an complex and evolving system

Global environmental governance began in the 1970s. After decades of development, it is now an important issue in the field of global governance. Its main features are diverse governing bodies, the systemicity and complexity of its target audience, and an issue-centric governing mechanism.

As for diverse governing bodies, in the 1960s, the environmental protection movement in the West triggered the emergence of international environmental protection. Therefore, since the beginning of global environmental governance, there have been a variety of groups and governing bodies. Presently, these governing bodies can be classified into five groups:

(1) UN agencies and programs. There are more than 30 UN agencies and programs dealing with environmental issues. The highest decision-making bodies are the UN General Assembly and UN Economic and Social Council, and the UN Environment Program is the main working body. Other agencies and programs include the UN Food and Agriculture Organization, the World Health Organization, and the UN Educational, Scientific, and Cultural Organization (UNESCO).

(2) Non-UN affiliated international organizations such as the Global Environment Facility, the World Bank, and the World Trade Organization.

(3) Sovereign states. As there is no governance in the international community, sovereign states are the main bodies that formulate and implement global systems and rules, and thus play a major role in global environmental governance.

(4) International trade associations and enterprises such as the International Association of Independent Tanker Owners.

(5) Non-governmental organizations and institutions. Such organizations are increasingly participating in and influencing the formulation and implementation of global environmental rules, and their influence is growing.

The second feature is the systemicity and complexity of the target audience. Global environmental problems refer to issues that are unfavorable to human survival, and are caused by human activities. Their influences cross national boundaries, and transnational approaches are required in the process of solving them. These problems include climate change, depletion and destruction of the ozone layer, the water crisis, deforestation, a sharp loss of biodiversity, and land desertification.

Global environmental issues have the following characteristics: Firstly, they are holistic. By the second half of the 20th century, environmental issues had become globalized, and had a distinctive feature of being omnipresent. From the ozone layer to groundwater bodies, and from the global climate system to genetics, there are worrying signs of degradation or deterioration all round. Due to the complex interrelationships between the various factors in environmental issues, a slight change will affect everything else.[1] Secondly, global environmental issues are comprehensive and complex. They are diverse and affect the world on many levels, and also affect other issues such as industrial production, food, population, and trade. A global and orchestrated coordination mechanism is required to coordinate policy implementation from various agencies and departments.

The third feature is the issue-centric governing mechanism. Because the world has started tackling environmental issues based on urgency, international treaties and negotiations on environmental issues often aim at dealing with immediate and visible threats, making them appear fragmented and short-termed.

Presently, global environmental governance is divided into areas such as air pollution, ozone protection, water pollution, oceans, biodiversity, desertification, and transfer of hazardous waste for management. This divide-and-conquer approach enables specific policies to be formulated for each area, making it relatively easy for countries to reach agreements and implement them. However, from a broader perspective, this approach cuts off the connection between each area, and there may be neglected problems or overlaps in issues, which may lead to contradicting regulations

---

1. Sun Kai, "The Evolving Global Environmental Governance System," *Journal of the Ocean University of China* (Social Sciences), no. 4 (2006): 37.

on the same issues in different treaties. This hinders the effective implementation of the treaties.²

1.2 The main issues in global environmental governance

Presently, the issue of the lack of global environmental governance persists. The deterioration of biodiversity and environmental pollution have yet to be fundamentally reversed,³ and the "Millennium Development Goals" have not been fulfilled in time. Issues such as global financial crises, climate change, food and energy crises, and natural disasters have bogged down developing countries' pace of achieving sustainable development. The imbalance between demands for global environmental governance and the current governing system has brought about more problems for global environmental governance.

The first problem is the disagreement between various bodies in the global environmental governance system. The current system and rules for global environmental governance are determined through plenary discussions by nearly 200 sovereign countries in accordance with the principle of consensus. In these discussions, each country has a different set of considerations and varying demands due to their domestic conditions and development levels. As a result, the core topic of global environmental protection is often drowned out by the competing demands.

The main disagreement at present is the difference in environmental demands between developed and developing countries. Despite decades of work, the imbalance in development has not changed, and an ever-widening gap still exists. Many developed countries have achieved clean production and better environmental quality domestically, and have adopted higher pollutant discharge and environmental quality standards, because their unsustainable industries and production methods have been transferred to developing countries. People in countries are still leading a high-consumption lifestyle. Developing countries at the bottom of the international industrial chain are trapped in the traditional development model, and have difficulty with their economic transformation. They face multiple challenges such as alleviating poverty, enhancing employment, and ensuring environmental protection. These challenges are more complex than those faced by developed counties.

---

2. Wang Hua, Shang Hongbo, An Qi, and Li Liping, "China's Strategic Approach to Participating in Global Environmental Governance," *Environment and Sustainable Development Journal*, no. 6 (2012): 11.

3. "Global Environment Outlook 5: Environment for the Future We Want," UN Environment Program, http://www.unep.org/geo/sites/unep.org.geo/files/documents/geo5_chinese_0.pdf.

Unbalanced development has led to significant differences in the expectations and implementation of global environmental governance among countries, and various stakeholders have therefore been delayed in reaching an agreement on the priority issue of global environmental governance. One of the most important issues in global environmental governance is how to allocate manpower, money, and materials into various environmental issues. Current global environmental issues such as climate change, biodiversity, governance of international waters, and desertification are being raised by developed countries. They are not the main concerns for many developing countries. One of the most serious problems faced by developing countries is the lack of safe drinking water, but this has not become a clear global environmental problem, and there is a lack of corresponding international assistance.

The second problem is that there is insufficient governance on global environmental governance. This is reflected in two areas:

(1) Some countries have failed to fulfil their commitments to global environmental governance, the most prominent example of which was at the UN Conference on Environment and Development in 1992. In order to help developing countries improve their environment, developed countries promised to provide 0.7% of their gross national product (about USD 120 billion a year), but these commitments have not been fulfilled.

(2) As the main institution of current global environmental governance, the UN lacks the necessary coordination and supervision capability. Within the UN, agencies related to global environmental governance include the UN Environment Program, the UN Development Program, the World Food and Agriculture Organization, the World Meteorological Organization, and UNESCO. There is a certain degree of competition among these agencies. For example, the UN Environment Program, the UN Development Program, the World Meteorological Organization, the OECD, and the World Bank are all conducting research projects related to climate change, but there is little coordination and cooperation among them.

The third problem is the crisis of ethical values that lies hidden behind the current global environmental crisis. When reflecting on global environmental governance, we should start by making the ethical values clear or clarifying whether they are based on nationalism or globalism. The impact of human activities has spread across the globe. In recent years, scientists have come to agree that humanity has entered a new geological era – a "man-made" era known as the Anthropocene, where the effect of human activities is becoming the main force in changing the Earth. These changes are long term, and some are irreversible.[4] Nationalism believes in upholding national interests, and holds that interests outweigh morality, and efficiency comes before fairness. These values are reflected in the current plight of global environmental governance, where many countries involved in the governance of global environmental issues put their short-term interests ahead of the common and long-term interests shared by the rest of the world.[5]

The fourth problem is that the change in the global situation in recent years has exacerbated the difficulty of global environmental governance. Firstly, the core forces in global environmental governance have been diluted. The collective rise of emerging countries has greatly impacted the original governance structure. Traditional powers are less willing to assume international responsibilities, and their distrust of emerging countries has increased. Global environmental governance has gradually evolved into a field where countries compete with each other.

Secondly, the interests of all parties in global environmental governance have become increasingly diverse, and governance is becoming more complex. Within opposing camps, countries also have increasingly different views. Among the developed countries and regions in the global north, Europe, the United States, Japan, and Australia are coming to oppose many issues. This is similar for developing countries too. For example, Latin American countries have doubts about green economy issues, while some African countries are strongly supporting them. It is becoming increasingly difficult to coordinate and reach consensus on global environmental governance.

2 China's Involvement in Resolving Global Environmental Issues: New Ideas and Measures

Chinese philosophy has many environmental protection concepts. Confucianism supports the idea of harmony between man and nature, while Daoism advocates the concept of following the ways of nature. Buddhism has the theory of origin and the precepts of abstaining from killing and protecting life. These philosophies emphasize the cohesion and unity of man, nature, and society. However, in modern times,

---

4. "Global Environment Outlook 5: Environment for the Future We Want," UN Environment Program, http://www.unep.org/geo/sites/unep.org.geo/files/documents/geo5_chinese_0.pdf.

5. "Global Environment Outlook 5: Environment for the Future We Want," UN Environment Program, http://www.unep.org/geo/sites/unep.org.geo/files/documents/geo5_chinese_0.pdf.

industrialization has put increasing pressure on the environment, and environmental protection has not been given enough attention. Environmental protection is like an imported product to China – something new that arrived when the country opened its doors, and was quickly accepted and adopted. China has moved from passive acceptance to active participation, and it has even started contributing its thoughts and knowledge to the topic. The community with a shared future for humanity is a major achievement for China in its participation in global environmental governance. It has pushed for developments in various fields of environmental protection both within its borders and elsewhere.

2.1 China's ideals of global environmental governance

The characteristics of global environmental problems determine that solutions to these problems require the participation of multiple members of the international community.

With the development of its economy and its increasing participation in globalization, China has become an important player in the field of global environmental governance. The 17th National Congress of the Chinese Communist Party put forward calls to "assist and cooperate with other nations in conservation efforts to take good care of the Earth, the only home of human beings" and to "enhance our capacity to respond to climate change and make new contributions to protecting the global climate." The community with a shared future for humanity is a rich, comprehensive, and highly significant theory. It will become the core diplomatic strategic ideology for the new generation of leaders, guiding them in all aspects of China's foreign affairs. China has contributed a series of ideologies and knowledge to the field of global environmental governance under the guidance of this concept.

The first contribution is to introduce the concept of the ecosystem into the international order. During the general debate at the 70th session of the UN General Assembly in September 2015, President Xi Jinping delivered a speech titled "Working Together to Forge a New Partnership of Win-win Cooperation and to Create a Community with a Shared Future for Humanity," proposing an all-inclusive advancement layout that included building an ecosystem that put nature and green development first.[6] This speech integrates the new concepts of China's diplomacy

---

6. "Statement by Chinese President Xi Jinping at the General Debate at the 70th Session of the UN General Assembly," Xinhuanet, September 29, 2015, http://www.xinhuanet.com/world/2015-09/29/c_1116703645.htm.

since the 18th National Congress, and systematizes the theory of a community with a shared future for humanity. It integrates the new form of major-country diplomacy and international relations with a new concept of justice and interests, governance through consultation, new concepts of common, comprehensive, cooperative, and sustainable security, and development that is green, low-carbon, circular, and sustainable into an all-inclusive advancement layout to transform it into a complete system.[7]

In theory, the ecological environment is an important part of a community with a shared future for humanity. It is the result of the transformation of China's domestic governance, and provides guidance for its participation in global environmental governance. It is China's way of shaping global environmental governance in the new era.

The second contribution is the concepts of sharing benefits, joint responsibility, and win-win cooperation. As President Xi Jinping stated in his speech at the UN in Geneva:

> "There is only one Earth, and humanity has only one homeland ... Earth is still our only home, so to care for and cherish it is the only option for us. There is a Latin motto inscribed in the dome of the Federal Palace of Switzerland that says 'Unus pro-omnibus, omnes pro uno' (One for all, and all for one). We should not only think about our own generation, but also take responsibility for future generations."[8]

Regarding which principle to adopt to deal with global issues such as climate change, President Xi Jinping noted that the Paris Conference should stop playing a zero-sum game and call for all countries, especially developed ones, to share more and shoulder more, so as to achieve mutual benefits and win-win results. To improve the status and role of international law in global governance, countries must ensure that these international laws are in place and adhered to. Countries should also uphold democracy, equality, and justice, and contribute to the international rule of law. They should also advocate for the concept of cohesion in diversity, and allow each other to find solutions that best suit their national needs.

---

7. Chen Xulong, "The Status and Significance of the Theory of a Community with a Shared Future for Humanity in Xi Jinping's Diplomatic Thought," *Contemporary World*, no. 7 (2016): 10.

8. Xi Jinping, "Working Together to Build a Community with a Shared Future for Humanity – Speech at the UN Office in Geneva," *People's Daily*, January 20, 2017, 2.

The third contribution is to integrate development with global environmental governance. As President Xi Jinping stated:

> "We should make our world clean and beautiful by pursuing green and low-carbon development. We coexist with nature, which means that any harm to nature will eventually come back to haunt us. We hardly notice natural resources such as air, water, soil, and blue sky when we have them. But we won't be able to survive without them. Industrialization has created unprecedented material wealth, but it has also inflicted irreparable damage on the environment. We must not exhaust all of the resources passed down to us by previous generations, leaving nothing to our children. Nor must we pursue development in a destructive way. Clear waters and green mountains are as good as piles of gold and silver. We must maintain harmony between man and nature and pursue sustainable development. We should pursue a green, low-carbon, circular, and sustainable way of life and production, and advance the 2030 Agenda for Sustainable Development in a balanced manner, exploring a model of sound development that ensures growth, better lives, and a good environment."[9]

He also stated that:

> "The situation where the rich get richer and the poor get poorer is unsustainable, unfair, and unjust. We have to stay open minded, and support mutual assistance and mutual benefit … The international community should work to achieve ecological progress, with the following principles to guide it: respecting nature, awareness of environmental protection, and the determination to pursue green, low-carbon, renewable, and sustainable development."[10]

2.2 China's practice in global environmental governance

After the 18th National Congress, the Chinese government established a more positive view of responsibility. At the Fifth Plenary Session, it was suggested that

---

9. Xi Jinping, "Working Together to Build a Community with a Shared Future for Humanity – Speech at the UN Office in Geneva," *People's Daily*, January 20, 2017, 2.

10. "Xi Jinping's Speech in the Peruvian Congress (Full Text)," Xinhuanet, November 22, 2016, http://www.xinhuanet.com/world/2016-11/22/c_1119962937.htm.

China actively undertake its international responsibilities and obligations. This sent an important message to the rest of the world that China would play a more active and constructive role on the international stage and provide more public goods to the world. As the world's second largest economy, China's actions have an increasing impact on the global environment, and its participation in global environmental governance has continued to expand. Since the 18th National Congress, China has taken a series of positive measures both domestically and elsewhere to endorse the development of global environmental governance and have a positive impact on the international community.

The first measure is at the domestic level. The rapid development of China's economy in recent years has had two impacts on the global environment. The first is that a considerable part of China's huge demand for energy resources needs to be imported from abroad. While this has driven up global commodity prices, it has also caused problems such as depletion of resources in the export countries, threats to animal and plant habitats, and conflicts with local communities. This is also the main focus of international criticism of China.

Secondly, China's extensive growth model has also caused serious air, water, and soil pollution problems, and has affected some neighboring countries. To resolve this, the Chinese government has made it a priority to endorse a low-carbon transition in the country, including restricting the development of coal-fired power plants and developing renewable energy. At the same time, it has reinforced the supervision of corporations, and has started a blacklist to severely punish illegal corporations that are contributing to environmental pollution. The enforcement of environmental laws and regulations has been reinforced, and environmental courts have improved the hearing of environmental cases, providing legal guarantees for a clean environment. China is also endorsing waste recycling and electric vehicle projects across the country. In Beijing and Shanghai, recycling systems for electronic waste and batteries are rapidly taking shape. In Shenzhen, government departments are encouraging the replacement of electric taxis in an effort to allow citizens to enjoy cleaner air.

More importantly, China has made great efforts to transform its own development path. Its "13th Five-Year Plan" emphasizes improving ecology, and it has developed a series of policies such as having an optimized industrial infrastructure, a low carbon energy system, the construction of green buildings, a low-carbon transport system, and establishing a national carbon emissions trading market. These will be achieved by following the concepts of innovation, coordination, going green, staying open, and sharing development ideas. China hopes to establish a new stage of development where people and nature and develop alongside one another. In its INDC (Intended

Nationally Determined Contributions) towards the UN Framework Convention on Climate Change, China proposes that its carbon dioxide emissions will peak around 2030, but strives to achieve this as soon as possible. In 2030, carbon dioxide emissions per unit of GDP will be reduced by 60% to 65% compared to 2005, and non-fossil energy will account for 20% of its primary energy consumption. It will also increase its forest stock volume by approximately 4.5 billion cubic meters as compared to 2005.

Presently, China is the fastest country in the world in the development of renewable energy. According to BP's Statistical Review of World Energy 2017, global hydropower generation increased by 2.8% in 2016, with China as the largest country with an increment of 4.0%, accounting for 28.9% of the world's total generated hydropower. Global wind power generation had an annual growth of 15.6%, generating 959.5 TWh of energy, of which China is the largest contributor. It showed an annual growth of 39.4%, and generated 241.0 TWh of energy, accounting for 25.1% of the world's total generated wind power. The total global photovoltaic power generation was 333.1 TWh, with an annual increase of 29.6%. Among them, China accounted for 19.9% of the total global energy generated. The United States trailed behind, accounting for only 17.1%.[11] In addition, China's renewable energy export is increasing due to its reputation for being cheap and high quality. Renewable energy is expected to become China's fourth achievement in manufacturing exports, after high-speed rail, nuclear power, and UHV.

The second measure is on an international level. The concept of a community with a shared future for humanity provides a new perspective on global environmental issues, emphasizing its global and holistic characteristics as well as ideas such as mutual benefit, mutual respect, and shared responsibility. This perspective is applied to deal with the lack of responsibility and lack of global environmental governance, and to come up with solutions to tackle these issues. More importantly, this concept of a community with a shared future for humanity points to a direction for future development for global environmental governance, and determines its value. This is China's answer to global environmental governance, and its participation in transformation. Following this concept, since the 18th National Congress, China has adopted a more active attitude to global environmental governance, and has made

---

11. "BP's Statistical Review of World Energy," June 2017, http://www.bp.com/content/dam/bp-country/zh_cn/Publications/StatsReview2017/2017%E7%89%88%E3%80%8ABP%E4%B8%96%E7%95%8C%E8%83%BD%E6%BA%90%E7%BB%9F%E8%AE%A1%E5%B9%B4%E9%89%B4%E3%80%8B%E6%8A%A5%E5%91%8A%20%E4%B8%AD%E6%96%87%E7%89%88.pdf.

great contributions to sustainable development, climate change, green development, wildlife protection and other fields.

For sustainable development, China announced a series of major measures to endorse international cooperation and help developing countries achieve their goals at the 2015 UN Sustainable Development Summit. This included the establishment of the "China-UN Peace and Development Fund" and the "South-South Africa Cooperation Assistance Fund," increasing investment in the least developed countries. It also offered forfeiture of interest-free intergovernmental loan debts due by the end of 2015 for the least developed countries, landlocked developing countries, and developing small island states. It proposed 100 projects for poverty reduction, agricultural cooperation, aid to boost trade, ecological protection, climate change, medical facilities, and educational training for developing counties over the following five years. These projects include the International Development Knowledge Centre and the South-South Cooperation and Development College.

As for climate change, China follows the concept of justice and interests, and participates in international cooperation on climate change. Over the years, the Chinese government has implemented its policy commitments on South-South cooperation in the field of climate change, and has supported developing countries (especially the least developed countries, landlocked developing countries, and small island developing states) in addressing the challenges of climate change.

To increase support, in September 2015, China announced the establishment of a RMB20 billion China South-South Cooperation Fund on Climate Change. In 2016, it launched a cooperation project for ten low-carbon demonstration zones, 100 climate change mitigation and adaptation projects, and 1,000 climate change training locations in developing countries. It has also continued to endorse clean energy, disaster prevention and mitigation, ecological protection, adaptive agriculture, and the creation of low-carbon smart cities on an international level, and has helped these countries improve their financing capabilities.[12] President Xi Jinping has pledged that the Paris Agreement is a milestone in the history of global climate governance, and this achievement should not be wasted. All parties should jointly endorse the implementation of the agreement. China will continue to take action to address climate change and undertake 100% of its obligations.[13]

---

12. "Xi Jinping's Speech at the Opening Ceremony of Climate Change Conference in Paris (Full Text)," Xinhuanet, December 1, 2015, http://www.xinhuanet.com/world/2015-12/01/c_1117309642.htm.

13. Xi Jinping, "Building a Community with a Shared Future for Humanity Together – Speech at the United Nations Headquarters in Geneva," *People's Daily*, January 20, 2017, 2.

As for green development, China has promised to build a green Belt and Road. In May 2017, the Chinese government issued the "Guiding Opinions on Promoting the Creation of the Green Belt and Road" (hereinafter referred to as the "Opinions"). The "Opinions" stated that endorsing the creation of a green Belt and Road is an inherent requirement for sharing the concepts of ecological progress and achieving sustainable development. It is a form of practical global environmental governance, and supports the concept of green development. It aligns with global trend of a green, low-carbon, and circular economy, and is an effective way of enhancing the momentum of sustainable and healthy economic development. As global and regional ecological and environmental challenges become more severe, a good ecological environment has become the basic condition and common demand for the economic and social development of all countries. Prevention and control of environmental pollution and ecological damage is also the common responsibility of all countries. Hence, endorsing the creation of a green Belt and Road is a win-win situation for economic development and environmental protection. It serves the community with a shared future for humanity in terms of endorsing mutual benefits, shared responsibility, and shared destiny.[14]

For the protection of wildlife, the General Office of the State Council of China issued the "Notice on Stopping the Commercial Processing and Sale of Ivory and Its Products" at the end of 2016, and confirmed that it would stop a batch of designated ivory processing units before March 31, 2017. The processing and sale of ivory and its products in units and designated sales venues will be completely stopped before December 31, 2017. This historic decision advances the joint commitment of the United States and China, and will make a significant contribution to protecting wild elephants and stopping ivory smuggling. China has become a pioneer in wildlife conservation.

China has also taken a positive approach in other areas. It has signed the Minamata Convention on Mercury, which aims to prevent birth defects and diseases caused by harmful industrial mercury pollutants. China played a constructive leading role at the 28th Conference of the Parties to the Montreal Protocol, leading to global adoption of amendments to cut HFCs. In addition, China has ratified the Nagoya

---

14. "Guiding Opinions on Promoting the Construction of the Green Belt and Road," Ministry of Environmental Protection, April 26, 2017, http://www.mep.gov.cn/gkml/hbb/bwj/201705/t20170505_413602.htm.

Protocol to help protect biodiversity.[15] It is also the country that contributes the most to the protection of the ozone layer, and the phase-out of ozone-depleting substances accounts for more than 50% of the total phase-out among developing countries.

3 China's Involvement in Resolving Global Environmental Issues: Strategic Demands and Policies

China's participation in global environmental governance is shifting towards an active approach. This is a response to the transformation of global environmental governance and its own role, and is also the result of the repositioning of its relationship with globalization. After experiencing rapid expansion, globalization has entered a new period of adjustment. Fairness, justice, and sustainable development are becoming the consensus of the international community, and the importance of environmental issues is rising. China's participation in global environmental governance complies with this situation. It is assuming its responsibility as a major developing country, endorsing coordinated domestic and international development, and leading the global economy. Moreover, the next five to 10 years will be a strategic window of opportunity for China to participate in the restructuring of global governance mechanisms. China's active participation is significant and necessary.

3.1 China's strategic needs to participate in global environmental governance

China has three strategic needs in global environmental governance. The first is to support the persistence of global environmental issues as a major issue of global concern. From the disregarding of environmental issues to the concern shown at the UN Conference on the Human Environment; and from concern about environment and development issues to today's sustainable development, environmental factors have become part of global governance in decision making. One of the most important issues facing the world today is identifying how to solve global environmental problems. Environmental sustainability is the major issue that leaders from around the world discuss at conferences nowadays. However, the global environmental situation looks grim. According to research into planetary boundaries, humans have pushed

---

15. "Executive Director of the UN Environment Program: China's Huge Effort to Push for Global Environmental Governance," Xinhuanet, February 10, 2017, http://www.xinhuanet.com/world/2017-02/10/c_129474969.htm.

four of the nine key planetary support systems beyond safe operating boundaries. These include climate, ecosystem integrity, nitrogen and phosphorus cycling, and land use. The research also shows that human activity has had a massive impact to the planet, and is pushing it to extremes.[16] The WWF's Living Planet Report 2016 also revealed the scale of human activity and its impact on the biosphere. We are using 1.6 times the Earth's resources to create the products and services we need every year, and the global wildlife population has reduced 67% in the 50 years from 1970 to 2020.[17]

The international community diverted its attention to global environmental governance in 2015. In September 2015, 193 UN member states formally adopted "Transforming Our World: The 2030 Agenda for Sustainable Development" at the Sustainable Development Summit. All nations are committed to stopping the degradation of the planet, including by consuming and producing in a sustainable manner, managing the planet's natural resources, and taking immediate action on climate change so that the Earth can meet the needs of present and future generations.[18]

Environmental sustainability has received unprecedented global attention. The 2030 Agenda locks in the environmental goals for global development in the next 15 years, and the international climate agreement reached at the Paris Climate Conference also points to 2030. In the next 15 years, these two goals will support each other and be implemented simultaneously, which will make tackling climate change and managing other environmental issues a key element of national economic and social development plans and strategies.[19] China's active participation in global environmental governance, especially climate change, is the result of conforming to this development trend.

Secondly, China must assume the responsibility of a major power for the future of global sustainable development. President Xi Jinping has stated many times:

---

16. "2017 Outlook on Global Environmental Issues," FT Chinese Web, January 10, 2017, http://www.ftchinese.com/story/001070919?full=y.

17. WWF, "Living Planet Report 2016," http://www.wwfchina.org/content/press/publication/2016/%E5%9C%B0%E7%90%83%E7%94%9F%E5%91%BD%E5%8A%9B%E6%8A%A5%E5%91%8A summary%E2%80%94%E2%80%94final%E4%B8%AD%E6%96%87.pdf.

18. "Transforming Our World: The 2030 Agenda for Sustainable Development," https://sustainabledevelopment.un.org/content/documents/94632030%20Agenda_Revised%20Chinese%20translation.pdf.

19. Dong Liang and Zhang Haibin, "Implications of the 2030 Agenda for Sustainable Development on Global and Chinese Environmental Governance," Chinese Population, Resources and the Environment, no. 1 (2016): 13.

"China's development cannot be separated from the world, and the world's development also needs China. We will continue to pursue a mutually beneficial and win-win strategy of opening up, devote ourselves to our own development, and emphasize our responsibility and contribution to the world to benefit the Chinese people, and the people of all countries."

Currently, the interaction between China and the rest of the world is growing closer, and the relationship between sharing opportunities and destiny is becoming increasingly prominent. "Chinese people share both prosperity and adversity with people from other countries. Their dreams are interlinked with each other." A community with a shared future for humanity means that the destiny and interests of humanity are becoming even more closely related. China follows the policies of taking the world's benefits as its own benefits, combining the interests of its people with the common interests of the people of all countries, and considering the legitimate concerns of other countries when pursuing its own interests, as well as endorsing the common development of all countries in the pursuit of national development.

China is a large country, and its own environmental issues have a great impact on global environmental problems. Its allocation of resources in the global market has raised international issues for the environment and resources, and the international community is now paying close attention to the impact of China's development on the global environment and resources. China has become the world's largest consumer of energy resources and one of the major polluters. It is also facing various global environmental problems, including greenhouse gases, acid rain, biodiversity, and the management of transboundary waters. At the same time, China ranks first in the world for the emissions of many pollutants, such as sulfur dioxide, nitrogen oxides, greenhouse gases, and mercury. In the next 20 to 30 years, China will continue to have a greater impact on global climate change and other environmental issues, and international pressure will continue to increase. China's more active participation in global environmental governance is a manifestation of the responsibility of a major power.

Thirdly, China's domestic ecological governance requires transformation. This is an important part of the national governance system, and the core of its transformation is to establish and improve the institutional system for the ecological environment so that it meets the needs of the modernization of national governance. However, the essence of modern environmental governance is a social system that constrains the balance of interests between social and natural ecosystems, and the move towards this goal would have to be a comprehensive and long-term process.

Currently, China is still in the initial stage of transition from traditional to modern environmental governance. In terms of system creation, environmental protection technology, environmental protection standards, and sharing of advanced experience, China needs to learn from the achievements of the international community.

3.2 China's policy's direction for participation in global environmental governance

Currently, the trend of global environmental degradation has not been reversed, and the existing system is too weak to deal with it. New concepts and solutions are urgently needed for global environmental governance. Using the concept of a community with a shared future for humanity, China can continue to endorse global environmental governance in the following areas in the future.

Firstly, it can reinforce cooperation between major powers in the field of global environmental governance. Cooperation between China and the United States on climate change is a model in this area. During former President Barack Obama's visit to China in November 2014, the two nations issued the "China-US Joint Statement on Climate Change," which stated that the acceleration of climate change has had a serious impact; higher temperatures and extreme weather events are damaging food production; rising sea levels and more destructive storms are exacerbating the dangers facing our coastal cities; and the effects of climate change are already taking their toll on the world economy, including in China and the United States. These are issues that must be addressed as a matter of urgency.

China and the United States have important roles in addressing global climate change – the greatest threat to humanity – and the two countries need to work together in a constructive manner for the common good. During President Xi Jinping's visit to the United States on September 25, 2009, the two countries issued another joint statement on climate change, expressing the need to reinforce bilateral coordination and cooperation, and to endorse sustainable development along with the transition to a green, low-carbon, and climate-resilient economy. In view of the scale and influence of these two major economies, the intent of this cooperation will undoubtedly set an example for other countries. It will have an important impact on the global emission reduction pattern, and will also effectively push for international negotiations on climate change. However, when former President Trump announced the US withdrawal from the Paris Agreement, the Sino-US climate cooperation was deeply affected.

Secondly, China must endorse North-South dialogue in global environmental governance and encourage major countries to take responsibility. China believes in common but differentiated responsibilities, reinforcing North-South dialogue and East-West consultation. Countries have unique national conditions, and are in different stages of development. In its concept, system design, and professional knowledge, the current global environmental governance is dominated by developed Western countries. However, as the main victims of global environmental problems, developing countries' experiences, perspectives, and concerns are also particularly important, and this requires sharing information and knowledge on the basis of mutual respect to solve global environmental problems. Major powers must be self-disciplined. They must take the initiative to assume international responsibilities, provide developing countries with financial and technical support within their capabilities, and play a leading role in global environmental governance. Therefore, it is necessary to establish a governance mechanism that includes all parties, and a principle of equal participation. It is also necessary to increase support for disadvantaged parties, and make full use of their respective strengths and capabilities through co-governance, so as to leverage their respective advantages and potential. This would allow all participating countries to share the benefits of global environmental governance more equitably.

Thirdly, China must support the creation of a global environmental governance system, and pledge to solve environmental problems with other countries. In his speech at the 27th collective study session of the Political Bureau of the CPC Central Committee, President Xi Jinping stated all countries are now being called upon to work together on solving global issues through consultation. Establishing international mechanisms, abiding by international rules, and pursuing international justice is the consensus for majority of the nations. Global challenges require countries to work together to address them. As the number of global challenges increases, it is only natural to reinforce global governance and endorse the restructuring of the global governance system. In a written interview with the *Wall Street Journal*, President Xi Jinping emphasized the fact that the global governance system is jointly built and shared by the world, and cannot be controlled by one country alone. Maintaining world peace and supporting common development requires cooperation among countries, and is an effective international governance system.[20] At the same time, it is also very important to make comprehensive use of existing global environmental

---

20. "Xi Jinping's Wall Street Journal Interview and Its Positive Impact to the World," Xinhuanet, September 23, 2015, http://www.xinhuanet.com/world/2015-09/23/c_1116658352.htm.

governance mechanisms. In addition to the UN system, multilateral platforms such as the BRICS, OECD, and G20 have paid increasing attention to environmental issues. These are important platforms for China to express its own ideas and endorse its own propositions. For example, the G20 made green finance a priority area after encouragement from China. In recent years, China has also led the establishment of institutions such as the Asian Infrastructure Investment Bank and the Silk Road Fund. These institutions are important platforms to practice its own governance philosophy.

Since the 18th National Congress, China has portrayed itself as a defender and reformer of the existing international order. It has done its best to manage the global situation, taking on responsibilities, and attempting to make the biggest compromise with other countries based on their national situations in the hope of achieving a win-win situation. The community with a shared future for humanity is China's solution. Its creation is a comprehensive process that needs to be advanced through political, economic, security, cultural, and ecological exchanges with other countries. Among them, the environmental dimension is particularly and increasingly important. It is a good testing ground for the building of a community with a shared future for humanity.

Global environmental issues are vital for current and future generations. The governance of the global environment is not just an environmental issue. It is essentially the impact of human industrial production on the global natural environment. The fundamental solution requires changing the production habits and lifestyles of society in order to create a balanced and sustainable common future. Therefore, the holistic view of a community with a shared future can help integrate the fragmented global environmental governance. Its respect and concern for others are conducive to breaking the practice of stakeholders starting from their own interests. Most importantly, the community with a shared future's focus on the future determines its long-term vision, which aligns with the future-oriented feature of global environmental governance.

CHAPTER 16

Internet Governance

THE INTERNET HAS BEEN INTEGRATED into every aspect of daily life, connecting the world and making it into a global village. Based on the ICT Facts and Figures 2016 by the International Telecommunication Union, internet users account for approximately 47% of the world's population. The coverage rate of mobile data is much higher than that of the Internet, of which 2G data coverage reaches 98% (covering 7 billion people), and 3G or above reaches 84%. Over the past three years, LTE network coverage has increased rapidly, benefiting nearly 4 billion people (53% of the global population).[1] The rapid development of the global network has also brought about many unexpected incidents, from the "Snowden incident" to Hillary Clinton's email controversy, from personal data leakage to the Arab Spring, and from cyber terrorism to cyber-colonialism. Internet security issues are not only about personal information and property security; they may even threaten national sovereignty and international security. Although network governance is becoming a worldwide problem that cannot be solved by a single country alone, there are currently many differences between countries in terms of global network governance, and existing institutional arrangements cannot deal with the emerging situations. According to Xi Jinping, "Without cybersecurity, there will be no national security, and without informatization, there will be no modernization."[2] As a major cyber

---

1. "ICT Facts and Figures 2016," International Telecommunication Union, June 2016, http://www.itu.int/en/ITU-D/Statistics/Documents/facts/ICTFactsFigures2016.pdf.
2. "Xi Jinping: Transforming China from a Major Cyber Country into a Major Cyber Power," Xinhuanet, February 27, 2014, http://www.xinhuanet.com/politics/2014-02/27/c_119538788.htm.

country, China needs to assume its responsibilities in global network governance, contribute its knowledge, and solve world problems.

1 A Tough Nut to Crack: Governing the World Wide Web

The term "cyberspace" comes from the American writer William Gibson's science fiction novel *Neuromancer*, which talks about connecting the human brain to a computer through a device to create a vast space. The book was published in 1984, at a time when computers and the Internet were booming, and people began to use this popular concept to describe the information environment that people rely on to survive in the information age. Although cyberspace is often referred to as the fifth space for human existence, it is different from the land, sea, and sky, and has its own unique attributes. According to Harvard Law School Professor Lawrence Lessig, the Internet consists of a physical layer, a regulatory layer, and a content layer. The operation of cyberspace depends on the coordination of these three layers, which are not natural creations, but the crystallization of human technology and wisdom. As countries develop their Internet independently, it has resulted in a differentiation between nations that started early and those that started late. This also gives rise to problems.

1.1 Problems with material infrastructure

Material Infrastructure for global network governance includes infrastructure, key technologies, and frontier technologies. In general, there are two main problems with regard to the material infrastructure of global network governance.

The first problem is the gap between developed and developing countries. Although the number of netizens in the world is quite large, the network coverage and usage in developed countries in the West are far better than those in developing countries. According to the International Telecommunication Union, 81% of the population in developed countries use the Internet, while Internet users in developing countries account for 40% of their total population, which is even lower than the global average. In the least developed countries, Internet accessibility is only 15.2%, which means that only one in seven people use the Internet.[3] In countries with a lower proportion of Internet users, Internet development often lags behind,

---

3. "Xi Jinping: Transforming China from a Major Cyber Country into a Major Cyber Power," Xinhuanet, February 27, 2014, http://www.xinhuanet.com/politics/2014-02/27/c_119538788.htm.

and it is difficult to balance the level of network science and technology with the country's right to speak. In the area of network infrastructure and key resources such as submarine optical cables and root servers, developed countries in the West are also far ahead of developing countries, and are in an absolutely dominant position. Although root servers are not owned by any country or individual in essence, the basic information about the main international top-level geographic domain name server and its managers shows that out of the 13 main root servers, American companies and US government agencies own three each, US universities own two, and a US non-profit private institution, a European company, a European private institution, and a Japanese institution each owns one.[4] Before October 2016, the United States held the management rights of ICANN (Internet Corporation for Assigned Names and Numbers), which is responsible for the management of root servers. In October 2016, the US government handed over ICANN, citing internalization of critical network resources as its reason. However, institutions managing ICANN after the transfer are still based in the United States and operate in accordance with US laws. The President of the United States has the power to shut down the Internet at any time based on national interests.[5] Having control over these institutions allows the United States to dominate the network, and it is unsurprisingly determined to hold onto this dominance.

The second problem is that the current Internet technology is unable to deal with many cyber threats. A computer's own hardware and software systems cannot stop cybercriminals, and many large companies, institutions, and even governments have been victims of widespread cyberattacks. On May 12, 2017, the global Internet was attacked by a large-scale Bitcoin virus, and the attackers locked key information and used it to extort a ransom. Many public hospitals and medical institutions in the UK were affected, and the campus networks of many universities around the world, including China, also suffered, highlighting how vulnerable cyber networks can be. Another key issue is the inability to trace the root cause of cyberattacks. Current technology can only identify the computer that launched the attack, and it is difficult to trace back to the proxy server that controls the computer. It is challenging to obtain conclusive evidence to convict and sentence cyber criminals.[6] There are many

---

4. Shen Yi, "Global Network Governance in the Post-Snowden Era," *World Economic and Politics*, no. 5 (2014), 150.

5. Hou Yunhao and Wang Fengxiang, "Global Security Governance and Its Chinese Elements," *News and Writing*, no. 1 (2017): 7.

6. Gao Wanglai, "The System Dilemma of Network Governance and China's Strategic Choice," *Journal of International Relations*, no. 4 (2014), 56.

examples of hacking incidents, but few hackers have been brought to justice. Without strong and stable technical support, governance cannot really be implemented.

1.2 Problems with institutional arrangements

Since 2006, the proportion of Internet users from developing countries has exceeded 50%, becoming the majority of global netizens.[7] According to Microsoft's forecast, by 2025, there will be 4.7 billion Internet users worldwide, of which 75% will be from emerging economies.[8] With the rapid development of emerging cyber countries, their power and interests in this field have grown, and the differences with developed cyber countries have become increasingly prominent. Although the world has a common demand for cyber security, the uneven distribution of cyber power and differences in fundamental issues make cooperation difficult, and an effective system cannot be established. In terms of institutional arrangements, the differences between developed and developing countries are reflected in two aspects.

The first is in the disagreement between global public domains and national sovereignty. Some Western countries like the United States believe that is difficult to define the jurisdictional boundaries of national sovereignty in cyberspace, and that regulating cyberspace will infringe on the freedom and interests of the people. They therefore advocate for "freedom of information" and global public domains. At the same time, they have been able to extend their power and influence on other countries by virtue of their leadership in the infrastructure and information industries. For most developed countries, the sovereignty of cyberspace is crucial, and it is directly related to their core national security and interests, as well as their status and right to speak in the field of cyber governance. Professor Xie Xinzhou, Dean of the New Media Research Institute at Peking University, stated:

> "There are two considerations for respecting network sovereignty. Firstly, the Internet is a common achievement shared by people all over the world. Countries should not intervene and attempt any subvert activities. Secondly, there are many

---

7. Shen Yi, "Global Network Governance in the Post-Snowden Era," *World Economic and Politics*, no. 5 (2014), 148.

8. "Exploring the Hybrid Governance of Cyberspace," Rand Corporation, https://www.rand.org/randeurope/research/projects/exploring-the-hybrid-governance-of-cyberspace.html.

problems arising from the development of the Internet. These problems need to be addressed based on equality and not by dominance."[9]

Disputes over global public domains and network sovereignty have been ongoing for a long time, and individual countries have their own opinions based on their national interests. This makes it difficult to reach a common consensus.

The second is in the disagreement on governance rules and mechanisms. Developed countries adopt a multi-stakeholder model, which allows the United States to maintain its cyber dominance. In 2011, the Obama administration issued the International Strategy for Cyberspace, which proposed a multi-stakeholder model with the United States as the center, reinforcing ties and cooperation with Western allies, and utilizing the role of large companies and non-governmental organizations to maintain the United States' and the West's dominance over cyber governance.[10] At the same time, they advocated for developing and improving existing international law and related rules, such as the Convention on Cybercrime.[11] However, the Convention was drafted by the European Union and the United States, and reflects the interests of the major network countries. It lacks democracy, and at the same time bypasses international mechanisms such as the United Nations. The Convention also deviates from the principle of mutual benefit of national sovereignty and cooperation.[12] Further revision of the Convention will not challenge the dominance of Western powers. Developing countries have demanded that the cyber network be regarded as common property for all. It should be utilized in a peaceful manner and regulated by the government, and new international laws should be formulated to meet new needs.

In September 2011, countries including China, Russia, Tajikistan, and Uzbekistan submitted the International Code of Conduct for Information Security to the United Nations. In 2015, they submitted a new draft to encourage working towards consensus,

---

9. "Interpreting Xi Jinping's Speech at Wuzhen: Promoting Global Governance with Internet Governance," People.cn, December 16, 2015, http://ah.people.com.cn/n/2015/1216/c358314-27334850.html.

10. "International Strategy for Cyberspace," White House, May 2011, https://obamawhitehouse.archives.gov/sites/default/files/rss_viewer/international_strategy_for_cyberspace.pdf.

11. In 2001, the European Council adopted the Convention on Cybercrime – the first international convention on global cybersecurity. Following this, the United States formulated a strategy based on its own interests and the Convention, endorsing the American model. The Convention on Cybercrime now has 53 signatories, of which 22 are non-EU member states, but are also mostly pro-Western.

12. Zhang Xiaojun, "The Dilemma and Way Out for Global Network Governance: Based on a Hybrid Governance Mechanism," *Law Review*, no. 4 (2015): 52.

reinforcing cooperation, and establishing Internet governance under the framework of the UN.[13] In December 2012, the International Telecommunications World Congress revised the International Telecommunications Regulations formulated in 1988 for the first time. The revision was supported by 89 countries including China and Russia, but was boycotted by 55 countries including the United States and the United Kingdom. The two sides clashed fiercely on the issue of network management.[14]

Currently, the global network environment is full of dangers. Issues such as data leakage, cybercrime, and cyberterrorism harm the interests of people of all countries, and threaten national security. The need for global network governance is imminent. As the old mechanisms are no longer effective, China needs to assume greater responsibility as a major cyber country, and contribute new ideas from its own knowledge. As ICANN chief Fadi Chehad said, China is starting to take a leadership role in global Internet governance discussions. A truly inclusive global Internet governance ecosystem cannot be built without China's participation.[15]

2 China's Involvement in Internet Governance: New Ideas and Measures

The world is entering a period of Internet reconfiguration. After the Snowden incident in 2013, more attention has been paid to the key role of the state in Internet governance, and China's experience in network governance has begun to be recognised. In recent years, China's national leaders have conveyed Chinese concepts and ideas to the world on various occasions, and the government and enterprises have also participated in global network governance.

2.1 The Chinese concept of global network governance

During the first World Internet Conference, which was held in Wuzhen, China in 2014, President Xi Jinping linked the Internet with the community with a shared future for humanity for the first time, noting that "the Internet has turned into a

---

13. "International Code of Conduct for Information Security," Ministry of Foreign Affairs, March 5, 2015, http://infogate.fmprc.gov.cn/web/ziliao_674904/tytj_674911/zcwj_674915/t858317.shtml.

14. Wang Guifang, "Competition of Major Powers over Network and China's Choice on Network Security," *Security Studies*, no. 2 (2017): 30.

15. "Hot Topics at Wuzhen Summit," Xinhuanet, December 12, 2015, http://news.xinhuanet.com/newmedia/2015-12/12/c_134909168.htm.

global village, and the international community has become more intertwined in this community with a shared future."[16] Subsequent World Internet Conferences have shared the theme of building a "community with a shared future in cyberspace," advocating for interconnection, sharing, and co-governance, driving innovation, and benefiting humanity. The community with a shared future in cyberspace is a new theoretical framework and a multi-governance mechanism that has received positive responses from many countries, and has been interpreted as a "Chinese solution" for cyberspace governance.[17] With the goal of endorsing peace, security, openness, cooperation, and order in cyberspace, China participates in the development and governance of the global Internet while maintaining national sovereignty, security, and development interests.

The first concept is to advocate for multilateral participation while respecting network sovereignty. The concept of "network sovereignty" is essentially Chinese. During Xi Jinping's speech at the opening ceremony of the Second World Internet Conference in 2015, he mentioned four principles to endorse the development and governance of the global Internet,[18] of which the first is respect for network sovereignty. Within the National Cyber Security Strategy, the principle of sovereignty is also clearly placed first. Network sovereignty is related to national security and the equal rights of all countries in governance. It requires countries to respect each other's diversity in terms of network development and management. Cyberspace is secretive and vast, making it a potential hotbed for criminals. As there is no absolute definition of sovereignty, when a crime involves multiple countries, a nation cannot demarcate the management boundary. Laws and regulations are also difficult to apply to other countries, making it hard to punish cybercrime. Furthermore, cyberspace sovereignty is a matter of national security for most developing countries. The blurred network boundary has opened a door for subversive forces and separatist movements. Through the Internet, they can influence a country's citizens by propagating political propositions and value choices. The long-term conduct of such activities will threaten social stability and political security of the country.

---

16. "Full Text of Xi Jinping's Congratulatory Message to the First World Internet Conference," Xinhuanet, November 19, 2014, http://news.xinhuanet.com/zgjx/2014-11/19/c_133800180.htm.

17. Zhang Xiaojun and Sun Nanxiang, "Towards a Community with Shared Future: The Chinese Solution to Internet Governance," *Renming Luntan · Xueshu Qianyan*, no. 4 (2016): 33.

18. The four principles for endorsing the restructuring of the global Internet governance system: respecting network sovereignty, maintaining peace and security, endorsing open cooperation, and building good order. See "Xi Jinping's Speech at the Symposium on Network Security and Informatization," *People's Daily*, April 26, 2016, 2.

The UN Charter, which established the principle of equal sovereign rights, is the fundamental principle of contemporary international relations. It covers all aspects of the diplomatic relationships between states, and should be applied to cyberspace too. China should respect other countries' choice of network development and network management model, as well as their public Internet policies and rights to participate in international cyberspace governance on an equal footing. China should not engage in cyber hegemony, interfere with the domestic affairs of other countries, nor engage in, condone, or support cyber activities that endanger the national security of other countries.[19] Cyberspace is territorial just like airspace and territorial waters; respect for network sovereignty is the basis for further cooperation.

Based on the principle of network sovereignty, the international community should negotiate and formulate Internet rules and order, and encourage development through cooperation. In 2015, Xi Jinping mentioned five propositions for endorsing the restructuring of the global Internet governance system in his speech at the opening ceremony of the Second World Internet Conference.[20] He also mentioned that:

> "International cyberspace governance should maintain multilateral and multi-party participation through consultation, giving respective rights to governments, international organizations, Internet companies, technical communities, non-governmental organizations, and individual citizens, instead of engaging in unilateralism. Countries should strengthen communication, improve cyberspace dialogue and negotiation mechanisms, and study and formulate rules on global internet governance to enable a global governance system that is more fair, reasonable, and balanced in reflecting the wishes and interest of most countries."[21]

At the same time, global network governance depends on and serves developed countries, but must also coordinate the interests of developing countries and encourage them to take more responsibility for maintaining order in cyberspace. Members of

---

19. Xi Jinping's Speech at the Opening Ceremony of the Second World Internet Conference (Full Text), Xinhuanet, December 16, 2015, http://news.xinhuanet.com/world/2015-12/16/c_1117481089.htm.

20. The five propositions for endorsing the restructuring of the global Internet governance system are: speeding up the creation of global network infrastructure, endorsing interconnection, building an online cultural exchange and sharing platform to endorse exchanges and mutual learning, endorsing network economic innovation, new development, and common prosperity, ensuring network security and endorsing orderly development, and building a fair and just Internet governance system. See "Xi Jinping's Speech at the Symposium on Network Security and Informatization," *People's Daily*, April 26, 2016, 2.

21. "Xi Jinping's Speech at the Opening Ceremony of the Second World Internet Conference (Full Text)," Xinhuanet, December 16, 2015, http://news.xinhuanet.com/world/2015-12/16/c_1117481089.htm.

the community with a shared future in cyberspace include sovereign states as well as organizations, enterprises, and individuals. The Internet is the common home of humanity, and all countries should build a community with a shared future in cyberspace together.[22] Leveraging the power of the world, coordinating with each other, and achieving win-win cooperation is the way to global network governance.

The second concept is to maintain order in cyberspace while ensuring the freedom of the Internet. The Internet is a platform with a huge information flow, where hundreds of millions of netizens obtain and exchange information. Cyberspace has become a new channel for public opinion, amplifying ideas from the ground in all fields. It is a place where people's needs are reflected, and innovative ideas are nurtured. Hence, the diversity of online expression must be respected. As Xi Jinping's stated in his speech at the Symposium on Network Security and Informatization:

> "To develop the Internet informatization business, we must implement a people-centric development philosophy ... We must adapt to the expectations and needs of the people, speed up the popularization of information services, reduce application costs, and provide the people with accessible, affordable, and well-used information services, so that hundreds of millions of people have more of a sense of achievement in sharing the fruits of Internet development."[23]

It is only by guaranteeing the rights and freedoms of netizens that the rights and freedoms of the state can be safeguarded. This also applies to the world. The ultimate goal of Internet development and governance is to benefit humanity and achieve the goal of free development for everyone. To this end, the online legal system must be improved domestically, and a reasonable order and arrangement must be established internationally. With these parameters, there will be no conflict of interests. If everyone is free to act without restraint, chaos ensues, bringing only a violation of rights.

Therefore, domestic and global network governance must be carried out systematically. Cyberspace is not an extrajudicial space. It is necessary to follow the rule of law so that the Internet can run healthily. China must formulate legislative plans, and improve laws and regulations such as content management and protection

---

22. "Xi Jinping's Speech at the Opening Ceremony of the Second World Internet Conference (Full Text)," Xinhuanet, December 16, 2015, http://news.xinhuanet.com/world/2015-12/16/c_1117481089.htm.

23. "Xi Jinping's Speech at the Symposium on Network Security and Informatization," *People's Daily*, April 26, 2016, 2.

of critical information infrastructure. It must manage cyberspace in accordance with the law, and safeguard citizens' legitimate rights and interests promptly.

On November 7, 2016, the 24th meeting of the Standing Committee of the 12th National People's Congress passed the "People's Republic of China Cybersecurity Law," which stipulates the rights and obligations of citizens, legal personnel, and organizations, and the development of the industry. This is an important achievement in the process of legislating the Internet.

In the international arena, China is also endorsing the establishment of an Internet order. For example, it has submitted the International Code of Conduct for Information Security to the United Nations, and has signed the International Telecommunications Regulations.

The third concept is to endorse development based on ensuring network security. According to Xi Jinping, "Security is the premise of development, and development guarantees security. Security and development must be endorsed simultaneously."[24] The current cyber security situation is grim, and the politics, economy, culture, social security, civil rights, and even national defense of all countries may be threatened by the Internet. In 2016, about 97,000 Trojans and botnet control servers controlled more than 16.99 million hosts in China. Among them, about 48,000 control servers were from abroad, and controlled more than 14.99 million hosts in China. Most of the control servers were traced to the United States, followed by Hong Kong, China and Japan. The China National Vulnerability Database (CNVD) identified a total of 10,822 general software and hardware vulnerabilities, of which 38.3% were high risk.[25] In addition, malicious programs and apps have caused untold inconvenience to production and daily life.

As well as being exploited by criminals, the Internet can also become an arena for major powers to compete. According to the "Record of US Global Surveillance Operations" published by the China Internet News Research Centre in May 2014, the United States used its dominance in the political, economic, military, and technological fields to monitor other countries, including its allies.[26] This is a serious violation of international law and human rights, and a threat to global cybersecurity.

---

24. "Xi Jinping: Security and Development Should Advance Simultaneously," Office of the Leading Group for Cybersecurity and Informatization of the CPC Central Committee, April 20, 2016, http://www.cac.gov.cn/2016-04/20/c_1118679422.htm.

25. National Internet Emergency Response Centre, "An Overview of China's Internet Network Security Situation in 2016," April 2017, http://www.cert.org.cn/publish/main/upload/File/2016%20situation.pdf.

26. "Record of US Global Surveillance Operations (Full Text)," Xinhuanet, May 26, 2014, http://www.xinhuanet.com/world/2014-05/26/c_1110865223.htm.

Network security problems are constantly emerging, and their forms are changing with each passing day, meaning that rapid development is required to deal with them.

Strong development is the foundation for security, and any development at the expense of security is unsustainable. Encouraging the progress of Internet technology, reinforcing the creation of Internet infrastructure, and enhancing the ability of networks and computers to resist attacks will help deal with the threats and challenges facing the global network. All countries should view having a positive Internet environment as their common interest, and should oppose network hegemony while avoiding "cyber wars." They should jointly endorse the development and governance of the global network. Countries should also keep an open mind, share responsibilities, reinforce exchanges, cooperation, and interaction, and endorse the development and progress of the Internet together. They should improve their ability to deal with crises, and lay a more solid foundation for network security.

2.2 China's practice in global network governance

The community with a shared future in cyberspace that China wants to build should be a community of information interconnection, cultural exchanges and mutual learning, economic prosperity, security and order in development, and fairness and justice in governance.[27] Based on the new ideas and concepts mentioned earlier, the Chinese government actively participates in the institutional arrangements and practices of global network governance at all levels. It also encourages society and enterprises to take greater responsibility and participate in the institutional and technical aspects of global network governance in new ways by becoming a "cyber power," implementing its "Internet+" action plan, and promoting the development of the Internet.

(1) At the government level

Firstly, China needs to participate in network governance through a global platform. Since 2014, the World Internet Conference has been held in Wuzhen – a beautiful town in southern China – every winter. It is an international Internet event initiated and hosted by the Chinese government. It aims to build an international platform that connects China and the world, and a Chinese platform for sharing

---

27. "The Internet Is the Common Home of Humanity: Three Theories on Building a Community of Shared Future in Cyberspace Together," Xinhuanet, December 19, 2015, http://www.xinhuanet.com/politics/2015-12/19/c_128547255.htm.

and co-governing the global Internet. Attendees at the event include politicians and entrepreneurs from all over the world. The theme of the second and third conferences was "Building a Community with a Shared Future in Cyberspace," which received wide support from all over the world. China has conveyed its propositions on global Internet governance at the Conferences, including the "Nine-Point Initiative" to establish a multilateral, democratic, and transparent international Internet governance system and jointly build a peaceful, secure, open, and cooperative cyberspace,[28] as well as the "Four Principles" and "Five Propositions" of Internet Development Governance.

China also participates in cyber governance within global platforms such as the UN framework. In 2006, the UN established the Internet Governance Forum (IGF) – an annual event in which China participates. The China Association for Science and Technology uses this as an important platform for Chinese scientists to speak out. During the 9th UN Internet Governance Forum in 2014, the Association's UN Consultative Information Technology Working Committee conducted two workshops, namely "Data Openness and Data Publishing Supervision in the Era of Big Data" and "Cloud Computing and Mobile Internet: Benefiting Developing Countries."[29] In 2014 and 2016, China also co-hosted two international seminars on cyber issues with the UN. The objective was to provide a platform to build consensus for international rules in cyberspace, and to endorse relevant UN processes and cooperation. China is also a regular participant in other global network governance platforms. It was re-elected as a member of the International Telecommunication Union, and has sent delegations to conferences and meetings such as the Hague International Conference on Cyberspace and ICANN meetings. China makes use of these platforms to communicate with and learn from other countries, to expand its international influence, and to help other countries understand its leadership through these interactions.

Secondly, China hopes to reinforce cooperation with developed countries in the field of network governance. It places great emphasis on communication with the United States in this area. Since 2007, China and the United States have

---

28. The nine-point initiative to jointly build a peaceful, secure, open, and cooperative cyberspace covers: endorsing connectivity in cyberspace, respecting the cyber sovereignty of all countries, jointly safeguarding cyber security, jointly conducting cyber counterterrorism, endorsing the development of cyber technology, developing the Internet economy, spreading positivity, caring about the healthy growth of young people, and endorsing the sharing and co-governance of cyberspace.

29. "Wu Haiying Led a Delegation to Participate in the UN Internet Governance Forum," China Association for Science and Technology, September 17, 2014, http://www.cast.org.cn/n35081/n35473/n35518/15913338.html.

held annual Internet forums to endorse cooperation and exchanges between their Internet industries. In September 2015, when Chinese President Xi Jinping visited the United States, the leaders of the two nations came to an important consensus on cybersecurity issues, and established a joint dialogue mechanism on combating cybercrime and related matters. In December, the first Sino-US joint dialogue on combating cybercrime and related matters was held in Washington. At the dialogue, the two countries drafted the "Guiding Principles for Combating Cybercrime and Related Matters." This was a significant step forward in the consensus that the two leaders established in areas such as establishing a hotline, and the general consensus on issues such as cybersecurity cases, counter cyber terrorism cooperation, and law enforcement training.[30]

In May 2016, China and the United States held the first meeting of the Senior Expert Group on International Rules for Cyberspace in Washington. The two countries had in-depth and constructive discussions on issues such as international rules in cyberspace, including norms of state behavior, and international laws related to cyberspace.[31]

China and the United States belong to a community of shared interests and a shared future. They should bridge differences, reduce friction, respect each other, build mutual trust, and work together to contribute to global network governance. China also has close cooperations with other developed countries. Since 2008, China and the United Kingdom have held Internet Roundtables every year, covering topics such as network technology, economy, security cooperation, digital intellectual property protection, combating cybercrime, and safeguarding the rights of young people. In recent years, China has held several meetings with regions and countries such as the European Union, South Korea, and New Zealand to discuss cooperation and development in the Internet field.

Thirdly, China values cooperation with countries with developing networks. Russia is a developing Internet power, and has a similar position to China on network issues. The two nations cooperate closely in the internet field, with collaborations reaching a peak in 2016. In April that year, China and Russia held the first Cyberspace Development and Security Forum in Moscow. In May, the Russian Presidential Office

---

30. "China and the United States Hold the First High-level Joint Dialogue on Combating Cybercrime and Related Matters," Xinhuanet, December 2, 2015, http://news.xinhuanet.com/legal/2015-12/02/c_128491080.htm.

31. "China and the United States Hold the First Meeting of the Senior Expert Group on International Rules of Cyberspace," People.cn, May 12, 2016, http://world.people.com.cn/n1/2016/0512/c1002-28345675.html.

instructed the Russian Internet Research Association to launch the "Internet + China" project team. The first project to be named after a country, it offers strong support to Sino-Russian strategic network cooperation, and endorses investment among tech companies. On June 26, President Xi Jinping and President Vladimir Putin issued a joint statement on cooperation to support the development of cyberspace. The statement emphasized respecting the sovereignty of the Internet, advocating for the establishment of a peaceful, secure, open, and cooperative cyberspace, and exploring ways to jointly support the development of a set of international norms of responsible behaviors within the framework of the United Nations.[32] The statement highlighted the same proposition and common interests of China and Russia on Internet governance issues, and also indicated that the two nations will have more in-depth exchanges and cooperation in the Internet field.

Countries along the "Belt and Road" are also the focus of China's attention. By providing them with public goods such as information technology and sharing advanced technology to drive Internet development in developing countries, they will be able to achieve common governance. In September 2014, the first China-ASEAN Cyberspace Forum was held at the Nanning International Convention and Exhibition Centre in Guangxi Province, to emphasize the fact that cyberspace cooperation is becoming a new area of cooperation between China and the ASEAN. Under the pretext of ensuring the safety of the Internet, countries should build their network infrastructure, establish an Internet economy with cross-border e-commerce, set rules and regulations to ensure the security of networks, and build a Sino-ASEAN information port.[33] Work started on the information port in 2014, and is expected to open as the "Silk Road of Information" in 2017. China also plans to cover the ten ASEAN countries with the BeiDou Navigation Satellite System, sharing its high-tech information technology with them. In September 2015, the China-Arab States Expo's Cyber Silk Road Forum was held in Yinchuan. The forum stressed the need for innovative technologies such as Big Data and cloud computing, and increased service support such as e-commerce and online finance. It also called for the establishment of an online Silk Road for China to link up with the West, to set

---

32. "Joint Statement of the President of the People's Republic of China and the President of the Russian Federation on Collaborative Promotion of the Development of Information Cyberspace (Full Text)," Xinhuanet, June 26, 2016, http://www.xinhuanet.com/politics/2016-06/26/c_1119111901.htm.

33. "China-ASEAN Cyberspace Forum closes, All Parties Agree to Build an Information Port," Xinhuanet, September 19, 2014, http://www.gx.xinhuanet.com/topic/2014dm/20140919/3031473_c.html.

up a platform for China-Arab business applications and a regional information hub.[34] China and the Arab countries will also continue technical cooperation in areas such as communication satellites.

(2) On the business level

The Chinese government also encourages Internet companies to take responsibility for network development and governance. President Xi Jinping mentioned in a speech that companies should work on their mission and responsibility as Internet enterprises, and join the government in endorsing the sustainable and healthy development of the Internet. Chinese companies are also increasingly going international, providing technical support to developing countries on the Internet.

In July 2014, Brazil's largest Internet security company PSafe launched a new generation of Internet security protection products, the core technology of which was provided by China's Qihoo 360 Company. The provision of this core technology will be extended to the entire Latin American region in the hope of guiding its Internet development.[35] In November 2014, the "Cloud Data Centre" was launched in Recife, the capital of the Brazilian state of Pernambuco, with technical support from Huawei. This was a great help to Brazil in propelling its Internet development, scientific research, finance, manufacturing, education, and medical care.

In 2015, Alibaba signed a cooperation agreement with Meraas, a Dubai-based company, for the building of a data center in Dubai to provide users and government agencies in the Middle East and North Africa with system integration services supported by cloud computing. Africa's Internet development is relatively backward, and China has been a source of assistance. In June 2016, three state-owned and central enterprises in China signed a memorandum of strategic cooperation on "Investment and Cooperation in African Telecom," aiming to launch the "Joint Sino-African Information Superhighway Project" in Africa, as well as a new African telecom market. The total investment of the project is expected to exceed USD 10 billion.[36] The support and assistance provided by state-owned and private enterprises

---

34. "The China-Arab States Expo Online Silk Road," People.cn, September 11, 2015, http://nx.people.com.cn/n/2015/0911/c192493-26326184.html.

35. "'Chinese Technology' Leading Brazil's Internet Safety," Xinhuanet, July 30, 2014, http://www.xinhuanet.com/world/2014-07/30/c_1111862793.htm.

36. "'The Joint Sino-African Information Superhighway Project' in Africa Is Expected to Have a Total Investment of over USD 10 Billion," Xinhuanet, June 6, 2016, http://www.xinhuanet.com/info/2016-06/06/c_135415898.htm.

to the underdeveloped areas of the Internet will strongly support the development and improvement of the global Internet, and also contribute to its comprehensive governance.

China participates in the creation of a new Internet order through international platforms, and supports the improvement of the overall global Internet through the development of multilateral and bilateral relations. The increasing overlap of interests and their interconnection and interdependence have resulted in the formation of an increasingly close community with a shared future between countries, between societies, and between people. The establishment of a new order in cyberspace is just around the corner.

3 China's Involvement in Internet Governance: Strategic Demands and Policies

In 2014, in his speech at the first meeting of the Central Leading Group for Cybersecurity and Informatization, President Xi Jinping proposed the idea of building a "Powerful Country on the Internet," and advancing it alongside China's "Two Centenary Goals." China's participation in global network governance has its own strategic demands, and only through the endorsement of specific policies can it become a true cyber power and achieve its "Two Centenary Goals."

3.1 China's strategic needs for participating in global network governance

Reviewing the "National Cyberspace Security Strategy" implemented by the Cyberspace Administration of China in 2016[37] and the speeches of General Secretary Xi Jinping, it is clear that China has invested heavily in Internet development and governance in recent years for two reasons: to become a cyber power, and to establish a community with a shared future in cyberspace. To be even more specific, China has the following strategic needs for participating in global network governance.

The first is to defend cyberspace sovereignty and safeguard national security. The Internet has no national borders, but cyberspace has sovereignty. President Xi

---

37. The main ideals of the "National Cyberspace Security Strategy" are to defend cyberspace sovereignty, safeguard national security, protect critical information infrastructure, reinforce the creation of a cyber culture, combat cyber terrorism and crime, improve the cyber governance system, and consolidate the cyber security foundation, to improve cyberspace protection capabilities and reinforce international cooperation in cyberspace. Refer to the "National Cyberspace Security Strategy," Cyberspace Administration of China, December 27, 2016, http://www.cac.gov.cn/2016-12/27/c_1120195926.htm.

Jinping has stated that countries need to respect each other's cyber sovereignty, and must be assertive when it comes to safeguarding it.[38] This means that the state has jurisdiction over domestic network infrastructure and information activities, and has the autonomy to formulate network rules and communication regulations. This is China's basic position and requirement for global network governance.

The second strategic need is to maintain network security. With the rapid expansion of Internet coverage, network security is a common threat to countries, societies, and individuals, and is a top priority for global network governance. Maintaining network security requires stable and reliable infrastructure, fast and effective ways to trace crimes and respond to intrusions, and a sound governance system. In addition to preventing the damage caused by criminals to the global network environment, countries should also avoid the use of cyber threats to deter each other.

The third strategic need is to endorse economic development and social governance on the Internet. The Internet has changed the way the world operates, and the information revolution has brought another qualitative leap in productivity. Economic development and social governance need to adapt to this change. China's proposed "Internet +" action plan and Big Data strategy are effective new models. The cooperation between China and other countries in the Internet field is also aimed at endorsing the development of the global Internet economy for a win-win situation. At the same time, the Internet has brought new ideas to social governance. Government work has become more transparent and open, channels of public opinion have increased, and the international community has become more closely connected.

The fourth strategic need is to improve the global network governance system and build a new order in global cyberspace. The perilous network environment requires governance, and establishing an institution is an effective way. However, there is still a long way to go for global network governance, and China is willing to make concerted efforts for it. The so-called "new order" aims to consistently improve existing systems and arrangements within the framework of the United Nations. The ultimate goal is to unite all countries in the world to jointly manage the network environment and solve the looming network security problems.

The fifth strategic need is to build a community with a shared future in cyberspace. China's participation in global network governance is not only out of consideration for its own interests, but also for every member of the community with a shared

---

38. Xi Jinping, "Accelerating the Innovation of Information Technology and Working towards the Goal of a Strong Network Country," *People's Daily*, October 10, 2016, 1.

future in cyberspace, ranging from countries to individuals. By defending network sovereignty, every country can have equal opportunities to participate in network governance; safeguarding network security means that national interests, social interests, and personal interests can be prioritized; by improving the global network governance system and ensuring that it keeps pace with the times, the Internet can truly benefit the world. All of this relies on joint global efforts. When the community with a shared future in cyberspace becomes unanimous, efforts will be consolidated, and the problems can be tackled and solved together.

3.2 China's policy direction in global network governance

To become a major cyber power and establish a community with a shared future as quickly as possible, China needs to work on its strategic needs through the following areas.

The first area is to improve its core technologies. President Xi Jinping said at the Internet Informatization Work Forum that "core technologies are vital to China, and it would be our biggest threat if these technologies were controlled by others."[39] The three core technologies are basic and general technology, asymmetric "killer" technology, and cutting-edge and disruptive technology. Currently, most of the global Internet infrastructure and key resources are in the hands of a few developed countries. China would first need to enhance the autonomy of basic and general technologies, such as core chips and basic processing software. On this basis, "killer" technology is the key to victory. At the same time, it is also necessary to endorse cutting-edge technologies for network development such as high-performance computing, mobile communication, and quantum communication. If China wants to take the initiative to develop its Internet, and ensure Internet security and national security, it must improve its core technology and strive to overtake developed countries in certain fields and aspects.[40]

In order to achieve this goal, President Xi Jinping proposed four specific measures:

(1) to manage the relationship between openness and independence; to encourage domestic enterprises to innovate independently while going abroad to reinforce international exchanges; to welcome excellent foreign Internet companies to enter China.

---

39. Xi Jinping, "Speech at the Internet Informatization Work Forum," *People's Daily*, April 26, 2016, 2.
40. Ibid.

(2) to focus on its investment for scientific research to boost technological innovation.

(3) to put core technological achievements into practice to allow these results to adapt to the market.

(4) to endorse the forging of strong alliances, and to encourage Internet companies to learn from and complement each other.[41]

The second area is to support enterprises and respect talent. Global network governance is led by the government, and enterprises are encouraged to participate more and take more responsibilities. According to Xi, "China's Internet companies have grown in size and strength, and have played an important role in stabilizing growth, supporting employment, and benefiting livelihoods."[42] The development of Internet companies also relies on government support and the participation of the public and society, and this is a mutually reinforcing process. Hence, in order to develop the Internet economy more effectively, Internet companies must be closely connected with the needs of the country, society, and people. They must participate in network governance, and create a suitable environment for their own development while benefiting the people. The state needs to enforce equal support and regulation, ensuring that both policy guidance and regulations are in place. It must also place equal importance on economic and social benefits.[43] At the same time, China must respect its talent, i.e., its entrepreneurs, technicians, experts, and scholars. The Internet is a technology-intensive industry, and it is only when employees are enthusiastic about work, take the initiative, and are creative that significant development can be achieved. It is important to increase investment in education, focus on cultivating talent in cyberspace, and provide more opportunities to young people. Personnel exchanges are also essential, and attention must be paid to attracting outstanding talent from all over the world to contribute to the development and governance of the Internet.

The third area is to enhance China's discourse and rule-making power over cyberspace on the international arena. The right to speak and rule-making are related to China's position in global cyberspace governance, and are crucial "soft power" tools and a supporting force for a cyber power. To enhance its right to a voice, China first needs to have the courage to speak out on the international platform

---

41. Xi Jinping, "Speech at the Internet Informatization Work Forum," *People's Daily*, April 26, 2016, 2.
42. Ibid.
43. Ibid.

and clarify its views and positions. Then, it needs to play a more important role in formulating solutions to Internet-related issues. To do this, it needs to participate in meetings on formulating solutions, paying attention to the input at these meetings and understanding the organizational structures. It also needs to approach network governance from a broader perspective, focusing on solving global problems rather than China problems, so as to win understanding and support around the world. Finally, China needs to mobilize all of its social units, especially enterprises, organizations, and individuals outside the government, to intensify exchanges and mutual understanding with the international community and broaden the scope of global governance of cyberspace.

The fourth area is to endorse extensive international cooperation and build a global cyberspace community with a shared future. President Xi Jinping has repeatedly stated that the Internet has turned the world into a global village, and the international community is gradually moving towards a community with a shared future. This is the same in the Internet field, where the world faces common problems and challenges, and nations depend on each other. We are stronger together and weaker apart. Global network governance depends on the cooperation of all countries. China advocates for close international cooperation and exchanges. Through infrastructure, core technologies, international conferences, negotiations, and dialogues, China has established connections with the world in various Internet fields at global, multilateral, and bilateral levels, and international cooperation will continue to be intensified. China firmly opposes cyber hegemony, and believes that global issues should be handled mutually through consultation. Only in this way can global cyber security and true cyber freedom be maintained.

China is making concerted efforts to secure a sound global cyberspace environment and a sound cyber governance mechanism, contributing its strength and knowledge. This is not only in its own interests, but also in the interests of people all over the world. China is willing to work with all countries to overcome difficulties, deal with global Internet problems, endorse network development, and create an attractive "fifth space" and a community with a shared future in cyberspace.

Postscript

SINCE THE 18ᵀᴴ NATIONAL CONGRESS, one of the highlights of China's diplomacy is the community with a shared future for humanity – an assessment by China's leaders of the current and future international environment. It is also an important mission within China's diplomatic transformation in the new era. China has advocated for the community with a shared future for humanity on various occasions, and also walks the talk at bilateral, sub-regional, regional, and global levels, building a community with a shared future with neighboring countries, with the ASEAN, and with Latin America. The community with a shared future for humanity needs to start either bilaterally or multilaterally, growing from specific fields such as economic and security.

Since the 18th National Congress, China's diplomacy has seen a series of new concepts, measures, and mechanisms. The concept of a community with a shared future for humanity integrates these factors and forms China's foreign strategy in the new era. The essence of this Chinese-style major-power diplomacy is to build a community with a shared future for humanity, through proposing new concepts such justice and interests, a new Asian security concept, and a new type of major-country relationship, and through implementing new measures such as the BRI and the AIIB. The consistent innovation and the creation of a community with a shared future for the environment and the Internet can be encompassed the community with a shared future for humanity. This forms the strategic approach and specific goals for a community with a shared future. Hence, it is highly appropriate to summarise major-power diplomacy after the 18th National Congress by using a community with a shared future for humanity as the core.

This book has discussed the ideological origins, main implications, and wider significance of the community with a shared future for humanity. It has also made an in-depth analysis of the practice of the community with a shared future for humanity in various regions and specific problem areas. However, due to constant changes in the Chinese and overseas environments, it is still difficult to accurately grasp the concept of a community with a shared future for humanity. In addition, the author's knowledge may be limited. Although there have been several drafts before publication, there are inevitably some flaws in the book. We urge readers to comment and correct these mistakes.

The structure of the book was suggested by Professor Wang Fan, Deputy Dean of the China Foreign Affairs University. The specific division of work is as follows:

- Preface: Wang Fan (Vice Dean and Professor of China Foreign Affairs University);
- Chapters 1, 2 and 3: Lu Jing (Professor of the Institute of International Relations at the China Foreign Affairs University);
- Chapters 4 and 5: Ning Tuanhui (Research Intern at the China Institute of International Studies);
- Chapters 6, 7, and 8: Ling Shengli (Associate Professor, Institute of International Relations at the China Foreign Affairs University);
- Chapter 9: Ge Hongliang (Associate Researcher, College of ASEAN Studies, Guangxi Minzhu University);
- Chapter 10: Chen Changshan (PhD candidate, Institute of International Relations at the China Foreign Affairs University);
- Chapter 11: He Shuangrong (Researcher, Institute of Latin American Studies, Chinese Academy of Social Sciences), and Wang Yuxin (Graduate Student, Institute of Latin American Studies, Chinese Academy of Social Sciences;
- Chapter 12: Wang Ruiping (Postdoctoral fellow at the Institute of International Relations at the China Foreign Affairs University), and Ling Shengli;
- Chapter 13: Wang Ruiping;
- Chapter 14: Jin Xin (Lecturer, Center for International Studies, Xi'an Jiaotong University);
- Chapter 15: Liu Chang (PhD candidate, Institute of International Relations at the China Foreign Affairs University);
- Chapter 16: Liang Xuanling (Graduate student, Institute of International Relations at the China Foreign Affairs University), and Ling Shengli.

Hunan People's Publishing House has worked hard on the publication of this book, and selected it as one of the key publications of the Publicity Department of the CPC and the State Administration of the Press, Publishing, Radio, Film, and Television in 2017. Special thanks go to editor Wu Xianghong for her hard work.

Wang Fan & Ling Shengli
August 5, 2017

ABOUT THE AUTHORS

WANG FAN, Vice President of China Foreign Affairs University, is a professor with a PhD in law. His major publications include *Great Power Diplomacy*, *International Relations Theory: Ideas, Paradigms and Propositions*, *East Asian Regional Cooperation and Sino-US Relations*, and *US Asia-Pacific Alliance*. His main research interests include Asia-Pacific security cooperation, Sino-US relations, US-Taiwan military relations, China's foreign strategy, and alliance issues.

LING SHENGLI is a PhD and associate professor at Institute International Relations, China Foreign Affairs University. His main research interests include international security and great power strategy, international relations in the Asia-Pacific region, and contemporary Chinese foreign policy. He is the author of books such as *Divided but Victorious: A Study of US Wedge Strategy in the Cold War Era*.